CONNECTING AFTER CHAOS

Connecting After Chaos

Social Media and the Extended Aftermath of Disaster

Stephen F. Ostertag

NEW YORK UNIVERSITY PRESS
New York

NEW YORK UNIVERSITY PRESS
New York
www.nyupress.org

© 2023 by New York University
All rights reserved

Please contact the Library of Congress for Cataloging-in-Publication data.

ISBN: 9781479815302 (hardback)
ISBN: 9781479815319 (paperback)
ISBN: 9781479815333 (library ebook)
ISBN: 9781479815326 (consumer ebook)

New York University Press books are printed on acid-free paper, and their binding materials are chosen for strength and durability. We strive to use environmentally responsible suppliers and materials to the greatest extent possible in publishing our books.

Manufactured in the United States of America

10 9 8 7 6 5 4 3 2 1

Also available as an ebook

To Gaye:

For seeing the potential in me and years of mentorship, honesty, and patience

To my parents:

For unwavering support through many settling times

To my family—Ivy, Marley, Bryce, and Teia:

For devotion, encouragement, laughter, and love

CONTENTS

Preface	ix
Introduction: Desperation and Strength in the Wake of Disaster	1
1. Settling Times: Hurricane Katrina, New Orleans, and the Destruction of a City	11
2. From Personal Disaster and Collective Trauma: The Turn to Blogs	31
3. Collective Trauma with Blogs: The Growth of a Local Blogosphere	44
4. Communicating Trauma: The Making and Sharing of Culture across Blogs	63
5. The Creation of a Collective Discourse: Forging a New Cultural Resource	82
6. Blogging and Collective Actions: Mobilizing over the Settling Period	107
7. As the City Settles: Predictability, Routine, and Fatigue	136
8. Communicating Culture: Ritual, Drama, and Blogs	152
Conclusion: Rethinking Culture and Action	163
Acknowledgments	177
Methodological and Theoretical Appendix	179
Notes	203
References	209
Index	221
About the Author	225

PREFACE

This book has been long in the making. The ideas behind it started a decade ago. I was completing a project on news and culture. It was an inductive study on what people thought about the news, what they "did" with it, and why that mattered. Epistemologically, I wanted to mimic public opinion surveys, but in a more open, exploratory way. I reasoned that this would be insightful in understanding how people use their news ecosystem in ways that speak to their social realities and senses of self. It was basically a study on how people use the news as cultural resources in justifying and sustaining their political realities. I interviewed fifty-six people and published a number of articles from this research. One discussed how people construct notions of trust around news sources and the lay theories they draw on to justify those notions. A second examined how people balance nonprofit news outlets (like PBS and NPR) with commercial news, using the nonprofits as news "safety nets," to catch that which escapes the more porous commercial news nets. Both were ultimately about how people use culture to construct and justify notions of truth and reality. A third took a slightly different turn. Instead of examining how people engage and use the news directly, it examined how people discuss and engage other people around the topic of news. While the other articles focused on how people use news, this one was about how we use news as a topic on which we construct senses of ourselves and others. I found that vague "generalized others" become important cultural resources that people construct and use to create their own sense of social belonging and their own civil purity.

While I did not have the vocabulary yet to formulate them, some new questions were arising. I became more curious about motives. What was motivating people to use culture as they were, whether it be their news or notion of others? This was a question about action, but not about action in how people use their cultural resources (which was the focus of my project) but on what collectively motivates action, the cultural structures that constitute motivated action and the system of meanings and feelings that make it so. Here, culture is seen as a causal force, a source of power, in and of itself, that manifests itself in collective actions. I did not have the vocabulary or scholarly insight yet, but this was what I wanted to investigate more thoroughly; and I was finding the existing literature on culture and action (i.e., culture in action) unsatisfactory. None of it seemed useful for understanding motivated action, and much of it seemed to somehow maneuver around or shift the focus in a kind of sleight of hand away from the actual action of acting. This was starting to bother me, especially because I saw so much motivated action in my own life and in the lives of everyone I knew. It just could not be true that sociologists could talk about action without actually addressing the issues of effort, intention, wants, and such. While I did see this topic sneak into some areas of scholarship, such as the role of grievances in motivating social movements, sociology of action literature nonetheless largely bait-and-switched me. This frustration did not disappear.

When I moved to New Orleans in 2009, and as I was finishing those articles, I started a new research project. I was becoming more fascinated with digital media, and in discussion with my mentor—Gaye Tuchman—I became particularly interested in blogs. During my first summer at Tulane (2010), an undergraduate sociology major, Barbara Selley, kindly offered her time to help any faculty member in the Sociology Department on their research. She contacted a colleague (Yuki Kato), who forwarded her request to other junior faculty, including me (I was a professor of practice at the time and fortunate to be included in these conversations). I responded to Barbara and asked her to search online for local bloggers and start compiling a list. My new project was going to be about blogging and news, largely as citizen news work. After a short time, she found the website for a local conference called Rising Tide that was organized by local bloggers and was to take place in late August, about three months away. Fortunately, I had already been moving on IRB approval and was about to construct some fliers to recruit blog users to interview. I reserved a booth at the conference to set up shop, made recruitment fliers with a brief description of the project, and went. This was the fifth Rising Tide conference. It was held in a music venue, and there were well over two hundred people in attendance. It was a daylong event, with panels, keynote speakers, and workshops, with time for a lunch break. The superintendent of the New Orleans Police Department was on a panel, and there were local newspaper reporters, heads of educational organizations, and others. I was amazed. What had these bloggers created? What had Barbara found?

Around this time, I applied for and won the 2010 International Communication Association's annual James W. Carey Award. The award provided $1,000 to support scholarship in the spirit of Carey. I was able to use this funding to start recruiting bloggers to take part in my study.

While I was recruiting participants at Rising Tide 5, I was stationed near a table for a newly created news organization called The Lens. I found that it was started by a blogger, apparently a rather well-known and influential blogger (which I did not know at the time). I also found this amazing—a news organization that started from a blogger! I eventually interviewed almost all of the journalists and news managers at the organization. This resulted in the 2012 publication "When Innovation Meets Legacy . . ." with Gaye Tuchman.

What I was seeing were a couple of new social organizations created by bloggers in part through the reputations, social capital, and networks they created through their blogging. I wanted to know more about the social processes that led to these formations, as well as the other less organized or lasting collective actions they created or took part in. How was culture implicated in these actions? Clearly blogs are cultural tools, as are the narratives they communicate, and they are used in various ways and according to various capacities. But why? Why are they used as they are? For that matter, why are they used at all? Surely their use was not mandatory or required, and yet here were a number of people using them and having done so for several years. And look what they were doing! I was impressed and wanted to know more about why. What is motivating these uses and the actions they contribute to? How is culture a motivating force here? A source of collective power? A cultural structure?

In researching the processes that these bloggers took part in and some of their manifestations, I discovered a complex process that took years to make. Lots of things were going on and had to happen to get to this point.

In 2010, I interviewed several bloggers and a few people who just read blogs. As I was finishing, I started developing some ideas and drafts of papers. The junior sociology faculty at Tulane University had organized a junior faculty workshop. Each week someone would provide an unfinished paper for us to read, and we would offer constructive criticism. One week I circulated a very rough draft of some paper that my colleague David G. Ortiz found interesting. He is a social movement scholar. As we talked after the workshop, he offered some ways I might address the social movement literature and suggested we work together on a paper. Over the next few years, we worked together. I conducted a second round of interviews. He offered social movement theory to this project and applied for funding from Tulane to support collecting blog-post data. We wrote four articles together, each contributing equally, and I benefited immensely from his intellectual contributions.

From 2011 to 2014, David and I won three internal grants from Tulane University, two from CELT (Center for Engaged Learning and Teaching), and a Monroe Fellowship from the New Orleans Center for the Gulf South. With this, we assembled a large amount of data about blog content. As my reading on news progressed, I began engaging more of not only the work in sociology and communication but also the research in anthropology, folklore, and moral psychology. Conceptual frames in my mind began merging: archetypes and moral foundations, ritual and rumor. We began coding for moral foundations and Jungian archetypes.

Yet something was missing. Moral foundations and archetypes, and the moral psychology, anthropology, and folklore traditions they represent, reflect ways we are similar. They are boundary crossing in their use. I needed a way of making the widespread and enduring more culturally and historically specific. This is where civil sphere theory (CST) became useful in my developing project. CST offered a more historically localized system of meaning, one that is more relevant to democratic societies and that I found quite conducive to the work in media anthropology, folklore, and moral psychology. It offered a notion of democratic societies organized and normatively constructed around three key themes: the motives of actors, the social relations they may form from these motives, and the social institutions they may create from these relations. A series of oppositional cultural codes are built around these themes, constructing cultural referents in civil or anticivil ways. This was how I could link the widespread and eternal moral foundations and archetypes with the culturally and historically specific codes and referents, and I could do so both in my analysis of blog content and in my the interviews with bloggers.

At the same time, I was becoming more interested in emotions, and my work speaking with bloggers, reading their posts, and attending their gatherings made it clear how important they were. I could not ignore them. They were fundamental to the bloggers' expressions, connections with each other, and different actions. We added a list of emotions to our coding scheme.

As we were collecting these data, I was attending subsequent Rising Tide conferences. I continued recruiting the following year at Rising Tide 6 (2011), and David accompanied me as an attendee at Rising Tide 7 (2012). I also attended a few other events that these blog users organized, including a book launch party, or that they took part in, such as panelists or speakers at public events. Over the following years, David and I would write about cultural trauma and repair, the meaning of blog discourse, the building of social ties and relations, and the taking part in collective actions. I also wrote a couple of single-authored book chapters focusing on the relationship among the cultural codes and referents of civil sphere theory, the platforms of moral foundation theory, and the emotional expressions of bloggers. This would become a key theme in my later work and one of the key contributions of this book: How do we understand the emotionality and interpretation of a complex, meaningfully layered discourse and the relationship between those layers of meaning? How did they come into existence? And (returning to my first project) what do people do with them? That is, how do we understand the motivated action that constructs a discursive cultural resource and how it is used? How did cultural power manifest itself out of thin air and make these different but related actions possible?

The setting of my study offered a context that was most conducive to this question, as it revealed an opening in the scholarship on action that I could explore. Hurricane Katrina destroyed much of New Orleans and the larger Gulf Coast. Moving to New Orleans in 2009, four years after the storm, I naively thought things were back to normal. I was very much wrong. Hurricane Katrina completely destabilized the region, scattering much of an entire city population and destroying the infrastructure. In the literature on culture and action, this would be characterized as an unsettled time. This is a condition in which sociologists recognize that the sharing of ideas and goals organizes and motivates collective action. Culture has causal power here. In settled times, on the other hand, people are more inclined to use culture as a tool, to justify action and social reality. What I was noticing over the course of my research was that states of society are not unsettled or settled. This binary is too ridged. Hurricane Katrina ushered in a state of unsettlement (to say it nicely), but it took years for any sense of settlement among residents to set in. Some would say that New Orleans is still not settled. This period in between is vitally important. I call it the *settling period*—the period of time from when a population seeks to recover from a catastrophic unsettling event until it may be said to be relatively settled. If culture is seen as a causal force in unsettled times, what does it look like shortly after, as a group of people seek settlement? That is, how does culture work, as a motivating, causal source of power, in the extended period of settling?

My second contribution, as I just hinted at, is to develop a theory of culturally motivated and oriented action. I call this *cultural work*. It is a form of cultural power that reflects an internally consistent system of complex meaning and emotionality that motivates and orients action. If culture informs action in unsettling times, what does it do in the settling period? How does it help us understand and explain the different collective actions that many of these bloggers took part in?

As I explored these questions more and more, I began to see something important. Action in sociology is so often rooted in pragmatic questions or normative social rewards. I was beginning to see that these are intimately related, as social rewards might derive from helping others answer pressing questions. The pragmatic and normative were coming together in a notion of action, one that was relational, symbiotic, and self-sustaining. I jokingly called this conceptual relationship the *flux capacitor* of action, as, taking from the movie *Back to the Future*, it is what makes action possible.[1] I began thinking about how this relationship might underlie the cultural work of my bloggers in the settling period of post–Hurricane Katrina New Orleans—how morals, archetypes, cultural codes and referents, emotions, and such might be brought together around the pragmatic and normative to explain the energy and meaning of action. The context of settling provides the social conditions in which such questions of action are most appropriate and suitable, and the collective use of blogs provides a form of cultural work that we may investigate more closely under these conditions.

Introduction

Desperation and Strength in the Wake of Disaster

This is a book about desperation and strength, the social conditions in which they take shape, and the collective actions they produce.

Regarding desperation, this book is about what happens when everything you hold dear and all that is familiar and comfortable is destroyed; when the future is in doubt and everything you do to try to create some semblance of stability and normality is under constant assault; when you are desperate for accurate information and news, for trustworthy and competent leaders, and for human connection with others who will listen and can share in your fears, angers, and every once in a while, your joys; when it is not just for days and weeks but for months and years, and it is not just you but your friends, family, and everyone around you.

Regarding strength, this book is about the strength that comes from desperation, when, despite constant threats, challenges, headaches, and heartaches, you nonetheless continue to fight for what is right and for what needs to be done; when the tasks ahead of you are so extensive that they seem impossible to complete; when you do not know where to start or how to move forward but you nonetheless muster the courage to get up and act. Day after day, you seek out and share news, do your best to hold elected leaders accountable, and support one another despite your own needs, to rebuild your piece of the city, one life and one house at a time.

This is the desperation and strength found among countless New Orleanians after Hurricane Katrina struck the city in late August 2005.

Hurricane Katrina and the flood that followed destroyed a beloved US city—a city rich with tradition and swelling with culture, a city where places and events are intimately and deeply tied into collective histories and identities. It threw into utter disarray the lives of everyone who lived there, destroying and making unrecognizable the signs and symbols that give life meaning and purpose, and it did so day after day, week after week, month after month, and year after year. As the flood waters receded, rescue operations ended, relief organizations packed up and left, and researchers finished collecting their data, the recovery and rebuilding work took shape. This introduced a whole new set of questions and problems that residents had to tackle. They had to deal with federal and local government agencies, private contractors, insurance companies, sensationalized media attention, and a nation that questioned whether or not the city should even be rebuilt. Anxious, angry, and desperate for news, validation, support, and some semblance of stability, residents found it within themselves to seek out and produce news on their own, reach out to each other, confront judgmental outsiders, and organize their involvement in the city's rebuilding work. In the process, they discovered blogs as useful tools with which they could channel their collective needs and efforts.

Hurricane Katrina struck New Orleans and the larger Gulf Coast during the early years of social media.[1] Facebook was in its infancy and only available to college students, and neither Twitter nor the iPhone existed. However, personal blogs did exist, and they were rising in popularity across the US. The number of local bloggers in New Orleans expanded rapidly in the months and years after Hurricane Katrina and at rates considerably greater than in other cities across the nation. A quick glance would probably lead us to see this rise as due rather directly to the hurricane and flood. But this would be premature. Most blogging in New Orleans did not take shape until a few months after the hurricane, and blogging rose continuously for the next couple of years, long after the waters receded and people were back in the city. It was not the hurricane per se that was the impetus for this growth. It was something that happened later. What was it about the aftermath that helps explain this movement to blog? How might we understand this collective movement to blog months and years after the hurricane struck New Orleans, floodwaters receded, and the nation's attention shifted elsewhere? And what impact did these bloggers have, on each other and on the city?

Most work on disaster centers on the disaster event itself. There are some good exceptions (Erikson 1976; Gotham and Greenberg 2014; Kroll-Smith, Baxter, and Jenkins 2015; Vanlandingham 2017), but overall as national interests wane, so does the research. While understanding the event itself is important, especially for emergency preparedness, things do not end there. As a disaster event turns into an extended crisis, the region recovers and rebuilds, as weeks turn into months, and months into years. With this, a host of new questions, problems, goals, and such arise. There is a lot to learn in this social condition, especially up close and from the perspective of residents forced to brave it out. *Connecting After Chaos: Social Media and the Extended Aftermath of Disaster* is a book about this condition and how a group of people responded to and confronted it using blogs. It is revealing for what it tells us both practically, in how people respond to a disaster over time and how they use social media in this process, and for what it suggests theoretically, about communication, culture, and action.

What Happened

Hurricane Katrina hit New Orleans and the surrounding Gulf Coast on Monday, August 29, 2005, as a category 4 "super storm." Its powerful winds and rains proved too much for the city's aging flood-protection system to handle, resulting in a systemic failure and the flooding of the city. Everybody was affected in some way. The storm, and flood that followed, destroyed not only the city's physical infrastructure but also its social and cultural infrastructure. Familiar places, routines, practices, and symbols were shattered or rendered unrecognizable. The almost complete physical and social destruction of the city meant that once-relied-on cultural frameworks and resources for predicting, understanding, and interpreting everyday "normal" life were no longer useful. This was just the beginning, as a host of new problems, questions, and concerns would unfold, shift, evolve, and dissipate in the following months and years (it may take a decade for a region to "recover"). This period of extended disaster recovery is riddled with controversy and uncertainty, as powerful interests jostle for control over recovery and rebuilding projects as part of what Kevin Gotham and Mariam Greenberg refer to as "crisis driven urbanization" (2014, 2) This extended aftermath, what I call the *settling period*, is seldom studied by disaster researchers, urban planners, sociologists, or communication scholars. But it is essential for understanding how residents, decision-makers, authority figures, organizations, and agencies all battle over the definition of the event, why it happened, where to place blame, and how to respond and rebuild. These questions extend over the months and years that follow a disaster, and they introduce ongoing, but shifting, problems that residents inevitably confront as they seek to rebuild their homes, neighborhoods, city, and collective lives.

This extended social condition, one we would not wish on anyone, is nonetheless revealing for what it suggests about culture and action. Almost by default, cultural sociology focuses overwhelmingly on what might be called "settled times."[2] These are social conditions of relative stability. Whether it be studies of cultural organizations, fandom, representations, industries, or resources, often taken for granted is the relative stability of broader social life. When this is the case, familiar cultural scripts, codes, resources, repertoires, and such are all accessible, useful, and capable of being drawn on as people negotiate their lives in relation to the problems they confront. While important, this heavy focus on settled times comes with epistemological blinders. It automatically precludes what it is about culture that draws scholarly attention and what it is about culture that goes unnoticed. This means that it also automatically limits what is theorized and therefore determines what goes untheorized.

Through an examination of how people come together in the wake of a disaster, over the settling period, and through their collective blogging, the unseen aspects of culture become more visible, revealing its potential to *cause* action rather than being solely a tool used *in* action. This quality of culture comes to light in the most desperate of times, and it shows itself in the collective strength of people forced to confront and engage their social conditions. A study of post–Hurricane Katrina settling, when residents must tackle not only the damage brought forth by the flood but then also the insurance companies, contractors, media, and authorities, draws attention to this kind of cultural power. As the landscape of targets shape-shifts and nothing is certain or stable, people work hard to fight for their needs and interests and to create that support and stability in their lives. In a backdrop of constantly unfolding uncertainty, across all realms of life and where the familiar and predictable are no more, how we use culture changes as well. People can no longer rely on their regular cultural schemas and the automatic thinking and acting that characterizes stable lives, as these are no longer useful for making sense of their world and acting accordingly. What they need now is to be more active, more direct, more intentional, and under these conditions, a different aspect of culture emerges. This is *cultural work*, collectively compelled action rooted in shared emotions and meanings. It becomes most clearly identifiable in settling times as people struggle to make sense of what happened and what is happening, as shared traumas emerge, shift, and evolve, and as the need for social stability, predictability, routine, and camaraderie demands our collective attention and motivates our collective action. This book explores these aspects of culture: culture as power, as collective will, as causal force involved in the collective need to learn, vent, help, and connect with each other as the disaster of Hurricane Katrina evolved into an ongoing crisis with no end in sight.

Cultural work needs an outlet. In 2005, post–Hurricane Katrina New Orleans, blogs became that outlet for a number of city residents, and it remained so for the next several years. When the essential needs of food, shelter, and water that follow immediately from a disaster are temporarily satisfied, people are faced with and start to think about new kinds of questions. What happened? What is happening? What is going to happen—with my life, my home, my neighborhood, and my city? How are our homes going to be repaired? When will the grocery stores reopen? When will schools start back up? What is happening with my job? Where are my neighbors? What beloved landmarks are gone forever, and what will replace them? Blogs were discovered as useful communication outlets as people tried to create stable lives on quicksand. People needed to air their grievances, vent their frustrations, search for information, ask questions, and inform others, all associated with the unfolding settling period. As time went on, blogs also became useful tools for finding support and validation, for connecting with each other and bonding, for developing relationships and trusting one another, and even for coordinating civic actions and new social organizations, all possible because of people's cultural work and the connections they made through their blogs.

This book speaks to several audiences, as it touches on a number important areas. With its focus on the urban environment after a disaster, this includes urban sociologists and planners, geographers, and disaster researchers. With its analysis of social media use, it includes communication scholars, media anthropologists, and media sociologists. Given its spotlight on shared meanings and feelings, where they come from and what they create, it includes cultural sociologists and sociologists of action. For urban sociologists, planners, geographers, and disaster researchers, I show the importance of settling times as a distinct social condition in need of sustained study. For communication scholars, media anthropologists, and media sociologists, I show why and how people may use social media in the extended wake of a disaster, what they collectively say, why they may stop, and some implications of this collective use. For cultural sociologists and sociologist of action, I show how we may reenter questions of culture and causality with my notion of *cultural work*—building on the paths that strong practice theorists, cognitive culturalists, and sociologists of emotion have already cleared, while avoiding the problems of structural functionalism that led scholars to abandon such questions over half a century ago.

While I offer more detail in the methodological and theoretical appendix, the evidence I put forth comes from several sources. From 2010 to around 2015, I interviewed twenty-seven "place bloggers" (Pignetti 2010), attended several conferences they organized, participated in one of their conferences as a panelist, studied formal organizations they created, blogged alongside them, and analyzed the blog posts of some of the most active participants, as well as a number of edited books they published. Because many of these blog posts were still available as I was collecting data and because such is the nature of retrospective methodologies, I was able to extend my analysis back to August 2005, just before the storm hit the city. This is important, as it provides valuable insight on topics of discussion and the formation of this local blogosphere. The reader will also see that I left all the typos and grammatical errors and all the other red, squiggly, underlined words and phrases that Microsoft Word noted. I did this so as to better capture the sentiment of the moments when people were posting. When you are trying to get your thoughts out, does it really matter if you put the apostrophe in "I've" or capitalize the "I"? To clean them up would seem insincere, not to mention that sometimes the best word to capture one's thoughts is not technically a word, such as "uglying up," "wooley," and "bastardo," which you will encounter later.

Together, these sources of data allowed me to cover a period of roughly ten years, gaining insight into the reasons people started blogging years earlier, what they blogged on and how these themes changed, how they met each other and what they did together, both on- and offline, as they sought to make sense of, confront, and act toward the unfolding and unpredictable settling period.

Meet the Bloggers

Who were these bloggers? The bloggers I met were mostly white, with two Black men, two Black women, and one woman who moved to New Orleans from Kuwait decades ago. Most were middle class and educated, with about a third growing up in the city and the rest having moved to the city years earlier. It was about half men and half women, with people who were lawyers, teachers, working for nonprofits, and in the private sector. Most were middle aged, ranging from their forties to sixties, and many lived in what is largely considered the Uptown area of New Orleans, though some lived in Midcity, Broadmoor, New Orleans East, the Sixth and Ninth Wards, and elsewhere throughout the city.[3]

These were the bloggers who made time to speak with me, a white outsider, male, and in my late thirties (at the time), who moved to New Orleans only a few years earlier. Some I met in my office, others in their homes, and others in coffeeshops and bars. As a white male who did not grow up in New Orleans, let alone the southeastern US, I had to reflect on my intersecting statuses and work at maintaining an interaction atmosphere that was nonthreatening, welcoming, and empathetic. This is why I asked the bloggers to suggest a place they would be most comfortable speaking and maintained a clear understanding that any questions or topics that were too uncomfortable or rooted in my own ignorance would be reframed, ignored, or corrected. My mixture of statuses and power over framing the study and questions had to remain flexible and open to adaptation. Fortunately, the bloggers in my sample did not shy away from clarifying faulty framings, conclusions, or questions. Indeed, that is why many blogged, to do just that, and being only several years removed from the flood and in the midst of the rebuilding work, the scars were still raw. The interview setting served as another outlet for them, even if they sometimes relived tragedies as they told their stories to me. Additionally, and if I may generalize for a moment, New Orleanians are a proud people, both natives and those who adopted the city years ago. They enjoy and take pride in sharing their knowledge of and experience with the city to those of us less in the know. To some degree, our meetings were opportunities to school me about their storied city and to showcase their intimate knowledge and experience. There is capital in such knowledge and experience, especially in a city as unique as New Orleans and that is inundated with post–Hurricane Katrina transplants.

Yet my sample does not reflect the overall demographics of New Orleans. The city is predominantly Black, with many families living here for generations. What neighborhood you are from, where you went to high school, and where your people are from are all powerful sources of identity and pride. Yet this book is not meant to be a representative study of New Orleans (a considerable challenge for a qualitative project). Nor is it a study of Mardi Gras rituals, cultural scenes, or the city's unique and fascinating history. There are great books on that already out there (Gotham 2007a; Campanella 2008; Powell 2012; Sakakeeny 2013; Thomas 2014). Rather, this is a book about some white and Black natives of the city and some mostly white transplants to the city, who tend to frequent, enjoy, and celebrate certain aspects of New Orleans. One native blogger I spoke with called many of these bloggers "New Orleans chic," referring to a group of people who moved to the city twenty years earlier, who did not go to elementary or high school in the city, and who consume a particular version of New Orleans, namely, the festivals, Mardi Gras, costuming, and such. This is accurate but not completely, as I did speak with a number of homegrown natives who do not quite fit that description.

Nonetheless, this book is less about distinctions, tastes, and consumption habits and more about what we can learn from focusing on what people have in common when confronting similar circumstances. It looks behind the constructs of race, class, gender, sexuality, and similar damaging systems and ideologies, not as a challenge but as an exercise in commensuration (Espeland and Stevens 1998; Lamont 2012). Most people's homes were damaged, everyone had to deal with rotting garbage collecting on the streets, the stench of putrid food in moldy refrigerators, streetlights that did not work, people driving like crazy, problems of rebuilding their homes, questions about jobs and schools, and city institutions in complete disarray, not to mention the criticisms and anger from outsiders. While the particulars differ, and that is important, there is something sociologically fascinating about their similarities and what they suggest about shared culture and collective action. They all dearly missed the things they loved about the city and were fearful that those things would not return. They all had to deal with the same agencies and institutions as they sought to rebuild their homes and lives. They all were left largely in the dark about what was happening in city hall and how the city would rebuild. They all supported each other when they could because they all knew what this felt like. And some started using blogs to various degrees as they tackled these problems. They shared in their desperation and in their strength, and blogs were one key outlet in which these processes and practices manifested themselves. Differences in perspective and particulars of experience matter for the form of their cultural work but less so for their cultural work per se, and the cultural work per se is where I want to draw attention with this book.

Looking Ahead

To capture the movement in and out of settling and the associated cultural work of blogging, I organize this book largely chronically. Chapter 1 provides information on Hurricane Katrina's impact on the largely settled city of New Orleans, creating a period of unsettlement and the conditions in which the city and its residents began the multiyear settling process. It uses these conditions to introduce my theory of cultural work as collective action. Chapter 2 focuses on trauma as the city shifted into the settling period, how personal problems and traumas became collective and the search for news and information emerged as a collective coping practice. It uses this context of collective problems, trauma, and coping to elaborate on my theory of cultural work. Chapter 3 highlights the growth of a local blogosphere and people's motives to read and write blogs as early indicators of cultural work.

Chapters 4 and 5 focus, at two levels, on the collective discourse expressed and shared across the emerging blogosphere. Chapter 4 highlights the collective traumas expressed across blogs and their areas of focus. It shows how these traumas shifted with the settling period, drawing on analyses of the collective blog discourse to illustrate these trends and then on interview data with bloggers for additional evidence.

Chapter 5 delves deeper into this collective blog content, offering a thicker description that reveals an emotionally laden moral discourse of archetypes, cultural codes, and referents. In so doing, it highlights a layered meaning system wrought with emotionality that is both culturally specific and also more enduring and widespread, noting how this collective discourse became a useful resource for people to create connections with each other and to stage offline collective actions.

Chapter 6 draws attention to the variety of offline collective actions that these bloggers helped organize or took part in, all made possible because of the connections they made with each other through their blogging. Chapter 7 highlights the dissipation of their cultural work of blogging, as the city and residents' lives became more settled. It notes the challenges to maintaining active blogs, the dwindling need to blog, and rewards for blogging that sustained it during the settling period. Chapter 8 asks what is it about blogs that made them such useful outlets for cultural work, drawing attention to the mechanical and cultural affordances of the blog platform and the cultural communication it enables (Carey 1989). Finally, chapter 9 asks us to consider the "everydayness" of cultural work, rather than just seeing it as something that emerges in settling times. It also elaborates on what a study of postdisaster settling, social media, and cultural work offers scholars, relief workers, and others, as we confront the fundamental problems of today, such as climate change and the threat to coastal communities due to rising sea levels.

The methodological and theoretical appendix follows and elaborates on the data and ideas I develop in this book. It is a useful section for those who want to understand the nuts and bolts of this study and the theory of cultural work.

1

Settling Times

Hurricane Katrina, New Orleans, and the Destruction of a City

> It's hard to put into words the thoughts that are going through my mind at this minute. Two weeks ago the only thing on my mind was my tailgate party for the Saint's first game. Today I am at square one in life having lost every possession I own in hurricane Katrina. . . . My entire family and most of my friends lost everything. I never thought we would all be starting over together at the same time. . . . Call me foolish but I have always waited for the day when things would turn around. I guess that day is near because it can't get much worse than it is now. I don't know what the future holds for me or the Big Easy.
> —Cliff, "Where Do I Begin?," *Cliff's Crib* (blog), September 11, 2005

Hurricane Katrina struck New Orleans and the surrounding Gulf Coast on August 29, 2005, thirteen days before Cliff's first and only post that September. The storm grew from a category 1 hurricane, as it passed over Florida, into a category 4 "super storm" a few days later, as it moved into the Gulf of Mexico and made landfall in southeastern Louisiana, Mississippi, and Alabama. In New Orleans, the call to evacuate went out a day before the hurricane hit. Many residents heeded the warning and left (approximately 70 percent of the 452,000 residents; Fussell 2015), sitting in traffic for hours along the few routes out of the city. Many others stayed. A few hurricanes had already hit the region early in the season, with most tending to have more bark than bite. Evacuating is laborious and expensive; some people took their chances this time. Others, especially the elderly, disabled, and the poor, had neither the opportunities nor the resources to leave. When Hurricane Katrina hit New Orleans, it was gusting winds of one hundred miles per hour with a storm surge of thirty feet (Frailing and Harper 2015). The Mississippi River Gulf Outlet canal (MR-GO), a controversial and expensive man-made canal built in the 1960s to serve as a direct route for ships to enter the city, provided a straight shot for Gulf waters to swell into Lake Pontchartrain, the 630-square-mile brackish lake that sits just north of the city. This, coupled with the heavy rains from the hurricane, swelled the lake, putting added pressure on the outlet canals that carried lake water across the city to the Mississippi River. But because of the heavy winds and rain, the outlet canals could not drain into the river and therefore were not capable of carrying away the added water in Lake Pontchartrain. This increased the pressure on the flood walls of the outlet canals across the city.

The canals were built and maintained by the Army Corp of Engineers and were controversial in their design. The storm surge led to fifty-three levee/floodwall breaches, and the MR-GO canal breached in twenty places, leading to a systemic failure of the city's flood protection. Over the next twenty-four hours, roughly 80 percent of the city flooded. In some neighborhoods, like the Ninth Ward, Broadmoor, Lake View, and New Orleans East (where a sizeable number of the city's Black, middle-class population resided), flood waters reached depths of nine to ten feet. People escaped to the attics of their one-story homes, where they found themselves trapped as the water continued to rise. Others were "fortunate" to escape onto their rooftops or found their way to elevated highways, where they waited in the hot sun, without food or water, for days hoping to be rescued.[1] As the hurricane moved north and the water stopped rising, it became clear that the storm devastated the city and its residents in almost every way imaginable. The exact number will never be known, but it is believed that approximately 1,577 Louisiana residents died as a result of the hurricane and what many locals would term the "federal flood" that followed (Bullard and Wright 2009; Eyerman 2015).[2]

Unfortunately, this was only the beginning, as the disaster caused by the hurricane and subsequent flood turned into a long-term crisis over the following months and years (Gotham and Greenberg 2014, 6). It took weeks for the flood waters to recede and months before residents who evacuated could return and assess the damage.[3] Many returned to discover that their physical belongings and irreplaceable sentimental possessions were gone forever. Homes were covered in black mold, food in refrigerators had spoiled, vehicles were washed out, and bloated, dead bodies lay in the streets. Couches, beds, and tables were strewn all over. Those who were fortunate enough to live on higher ground experienced "survivor's remorse," thankful in that they did not suffer the worst but guilty in that their friends, loved ones, and others lost everything. Those who were able to evacuate returned to a city, neighborhoods, and homes that were unrecognizable and eerily quiet, as if the apocalypse had come.[4]

In the meantime, the Federal Emergency Management Agency (FEMA) assumed rescue efforts. Led by an inexperienced political appointee in Michael "Brownie" Brown, FEMA bumbled through its relief efforts. With one of its primary projects being the housing of residents who lost their homes, FEMA provided trailers that were later found to be contaminated with formaldehyde, making many of those who were housed in them sick (Bullard and Wright 2009). The National Guard was put in charge of security, monitoring for violence, and controlling the entryways into the city. Some residents knew how to circumvent them, using backroads to get past checkpoints and see their devastated homes and neighborhoods. Residents' view of military personnel was mixed. At first, they felt as if they were living in a third-world country that was being occupied by outside forces. The military carried weapons and used threats and force to control both evacuees and those who stayed. Later, General Russel L. Honoré took charge of the response efforts. He became a local hero, as he quickly adopted a more sympathetic, inclusive attitude in how the military interacted and treated suffering residents (Lee 2006).

At the same time, the state of Louisiana seemed at a loss for what to do. Governor Kathleen Blanco declared a state of emergency on August 26, 2005, as the storm moved over Florida and into the Gulf but refused a proposal from the White House to put Louisiana National Guard troops under the control of the federal government. It was believed that this would help in coordinating rescue efforts by simplifying the command structure, but it also made it difficult to then enforce state law. Later on, the state of Louisiana and Governor Blanco were largely quiet, allowing FEMA and the city of New Orleans to dictate and organize much of the response and recovery periods.

The city of New Orleans was in such disarray that the mayor and other key decision-makers lacked much of the personnel, competence, and infrastructure to be effective in the immediate aftermath. Buses that could have been used to evacuate residents lay flooded in parking lots. An offer to use Amtrak to help evacuate residents was rejected. Residents without access to some form of mobility were moved into the Superdome, the sixty-five-thousand-seat downtown arena where the city's National Football League (NFL) team, the New Orleans Saints, played football. Others were brought to the Ernest Morial Convention Center, also in the downtown area. Local hotels also housed people, as did hospitals, nursing homes, and residents who stayed and were fortunate not to flood. Clean drinking water, food, and human-waste disposal quickly became major concerns as people scrambled to take care of everyone in need. Some residents sought to cross the Mississippi River and head into Algiers Point, a small piece of land on the Westbank that is part of Orleans Parish, only to be greeted by white armed militias that turned them away.

Meanwhile, the national news and other media outlets from around the world were flocking to the city to cover the unfolding chaos and devastation. Yet, it soon became clear that their coverage was for viewers in other parts of the country (Pignetti 2010). Residents and evacuees desperate for news and information found little that was useful in the national media. Staying close to the French Quarter and convention center, these national outlets seldom strayed into other parts of the city and focused their attention mostly on the scintillating stories of deviance, transgressions, and other shock entertainment found downtown, turning this event into a national spectacle (Gotham 2007b). Exploiting the pain and suffering of residents for the entertainment of outsiders infuriated many residents, while others found it easier to simply dismiss them, as there were plenty of other things that needed attention.

Over the following weeks and months, and as the national media settled in, the city began taking over more of the recovery and rebuilding work. Over this same period, residents, having taken in the social and personal devastation, began to try to rebuild their lives, homes, and everything else they lost. In the process, many had to deal with insurance companies and private contractors, as well as disorganized, corrupt, unresponsive, and incompetent city agencies and agents, exacerbating the frustration and hopelessness many experienced directly from the flood. Insurance companies relied on technicalities to deny claims, and when they did pay out, they did so in amounts far from sufficient to repair the damage. Federal community block grants, designed to help in the rebuilding processes, allocated funds on the basis of property assessments, which were often too little to repair the damage or rebuild, and tended to understate the value of the property (Gotham 2015). Some of this was the fault of insurance companies and grantors, but another part was due to the assessment values of the homes. The city's assessor, an elected position, commonly undervalued homes in the interest of residents so that they could save on their yearly home owner's taxes. Together, the result was that many people who wanted to return were not able to due to the costly repairs (Chamlee-Wright and Storr 2009). Others decided to keep their insurance money and live elsewhere. Houston and Atlanta were popular destinations. Former city residents could purchase larger homes on larger plots of land and be somewhat removed from the violence, poor schools, political cronyism, and other social problems that characterized the "city that care forgot" (Chamlee-Wright and Storr 2009).

At the same time, private contractors from all over the country arrived to line their pockets with the influx of federal monies allocated to help in the rebuilding period. Many made promises to do repairs that they never did or completed, taking the money and leaving homes unfinished and unlivable. Many others used cheap materials, some of which made people sick and would need to be replaced. The widespread use of what was termed "Chinese drywall" became a major problem during this rebuilding period, as the inexpensive material manufactured in China would emit carbon disulfide, carbon sulfide, and hydrogen sulfide, releasing a sulfuric odor and causing problems for copper pipes, electrical wiring, and air-conditioning coils. It exacerbated breathing difficulties, caused chronic headaches, fatigue, nausea, eye and throat irritation, and sinus problems, which worsened with increased heat and humidity. Approximately fifty-two million pounds of "Chinese drywall" made its way into New Orleans in the months following the flood, much of it needing to be replaced as home owners later discovered its presence in their rebuilt homes.

Moreover, much of the rebuilding was completed by immigrant labor, rather than the skilled Black labor force that had built so much of the city in the first place (Bullard and Wright 2009). As a result, much of the federal monies allocated for rebuilding went to outside contractors and newly arrived immigrant labor, preventing the city's skilled Black labor population from both earning the paychecks they needed to start over and contributing to a legacy of skilled Black craftsmanship that built many of the homes that were destroyed. In other cities, where previous generations of immigrants enjoyed intergenerational social mobility and the privileges of becoming white, this would simply be a continuation of previous practices. However, in New Orleans, one of the few cities with a sizeable Black middle class, construction was a core means of creating and maintaining a Black middle-class standing despite a historical context of white supremacy. The same is true for the city's public schoolteachers, many of whom also lost their jobs, as the city's education system shifted to a charter-school model and as new "transplants" (i.e., white people from elsewhere) took up teaching jobs that had previously been held by Black New Orleanians with historical connections to the city (Buerger and Harris 2015; Chanin 2021).

These issues having to do with the response, recovery, and rebuilding periods illuminate the ongoing and all-encompassing sources of stress, anxiety, frustration, and trauma that continued long after the flood waters receded, as the disaster of Hurricane Katrina turned into a long-term crisis (Gotham and Greenberg 2014). Now, almost two decades later, much of the city has been rebuilt, but far from all. The city has implemented a massive and controversial social experiment regarding its education system, installing a citywide charter-school system. It has built a new and highly contentious jail. It settled court cases involving the police killings on the Danziger Bridge (and elsewhere) days after the flood. It closed its primary trauma hospital (Charity Hospital) and demolished over one thousand homes in a historic part of the city just north of downtown to build a massive medical center (University Medical Center and the Veterans Administration Medical Center). It vamped up investment in tourism as a primary economic industry (Gotham 2007a; Thomas 2014) and implemented numerous new public-private partnerships. The historically Black neighborhoods of Bywater, Treme (mostly referred to as the Sixth Ward until David Simon's show *Treme* appeared on HBO in 2010), and Freret Street have experienced massive population change through gentrification, displacing former residents and businesses with artisan shops that cater to hipsters and their dogs and people with more disposable incomes.

But many residents did not return. Some decided to take the settlement money (which was seldom enough to cover repairs) and leave the city, relocating to Houston, Atlanta, and elsewhere. Others were priced out, as rents and housing values skyrocketed to accommodate the massive influx of new residents and social justice warriors moving to the city to take part in the rebuilding. New Orleans East, once home to a sizeable Black middle-class population, remains largely abandoned, with scattered vacant homes in varying stages of decay and little commercial development (there are only two grocery stores and one hospital for the roughly seventy thousand residents at the time of this writing). The problem of neglect has become so significant that a movement to secede from New Orleans has developed.[5]

There has been an extensive amount of change occurring since Hurricane Katrina hit the Gulf Coast and flooded New Orleans. Despite controversies and conflict, the city has moved forward, rebuilding local institutions, investing in different economic goals (e.g., tourism), and forming various public-private partnerships (Tierney 2015). While we may debate at what point a city might be considered settled, and the existence of conflicts and power struggles in this process, it is safe to say that in the decade and a half since the flood, New Orleans has returned to a state of "relative settlement." Wrought with ongoing controversy, inequality, and unfairness, the city and its residents nonetheless have sought to reestablish local social institutions (as they were before or in a new light) and foment newly familiar routines and practices as they have transitioned from a period of unsettlement due to the flood's immediate and complete destruction toward a period of settlement. This extended transitional period is a period of *settling*, an important but often ignored or overlooked period in the research on disaster, culture, and civil society.

Trauma, Coping, and Cultural Work in the Settling Period

A disaster is a "potentially traumatic event that is collectively experienced, has an acute onset, and is time-delimited" (McFarlane and Norris 2006, 4). Disasters may be natural, such as an earthquake or volcano; technological, such as an oil spill; or human, such as terrorism. While these may be contested and not mutually exclusive categories, disasters nonetheless often produce "physical, social, psychosocial, sociodemographic, socioeconomic, and political consequences" (Houston, Pfefferbaum, and Rosenholtz 2012, 607). Normally disasters are conceptualized in phases and can be understood as including a pre-event, event, and post-event phase (Houston, Pfefferbaum, and Rosenholtz 2012; Houston et al. 2014). R. W. Kates and colleagues (2006, 14655) identify four periods of disasters and postdisasters common across cases: (1) the *emergency period* of search and rescue efforts, emergency sheltering, accessing food and water, establishing social order, and clearing transportation lanes and other obstructions; (2) the *restoration period*, when the essential needs of life are patched and temporarily repaired; (3) the *first reconstruction period* of replacement addressing infrastructure, housing, and jobs; and (4) the *second reconstruction period* of commemoration and betterment, when improvements and upgrades to predisaster institutions and systems are planned and sought. Each period tends to last considerably longer than previous periods, which is why full recovery often takes over a decade.

Importantly, this decade-long process of recovery from disaster involves shifting problematics and therefore shifting questions, for local political figures, formal organizations and institutions, and residents (Luft 2009; Tierney 2015). As initial questions about food and shelter associated with the *emergency* and *restoration* periods are addressed, they become less relevant, and new questions and problematics arise, ones associated with the later stages of disaster recovery, the *first* and *second reconstruction* periods. Here, city agencies, decision-makers, institutions, and residents face new questions about infrastructure, housing, jobs, schools, and how to improve on what was, hoping to avoid the mistakes of the past.

A study of settling times will capture these shifting concerns and how people adapt to, engage with, and otherwise act in relation to them. Settling is a collective process, requiring that we have first collectively experienced unsettlement. Unsettled times are characterized by a period of collective mass disruption, physically with the damage to homes and infrastructure, social psychologically in the disruption of individual relationships and destruction of meaningful places, and psychologically in the form of ontological insecurity, anxiety, and fear associated with the uncertainty and risk that such conditions produce. In the extended period of settling that follows, collective needs and concerns arise around these related issues. Social order may be restored, basic needs of survival and living may be satisfied, but the long-term problems of replacing infrastructure, housing, jobs, schools, familiar places, and such remain. Further, attention shifts from the strictly immediate personal needs of survival and living to collective questions about what happened and how. Where do we place blame? How do we protect ourselves from similar disasters in the future? How do we rebuild? These are the questions of reconstruction.

How these questions arise, are debated and acted on, and get answered, established, and institutionalized are all characteristics of settling times, as they represent our movement toward settlement. Here, settlement, in its ideal-typical form, is a state of society that is socially integrated, in which things are predictable and in relative working order. Settled times offer an image we collectively work toward in different variances and in accordance with different collective identities. With this conception, settlement is never fully complete; it is impossible, an ideal-type. But it is nonetheless a collective goal that we work toward, as it provides security, a sense of belonging, and stability (Chamlee-Wright and Storr 2009). As such, settling times are those in which new ideas are institutionalized and established, infrastructure and institutions are rebuilt and restored, and routines and practices become predictable and familiar. Disasters destroy this relative stability to its core, ushering in a period of unsettlement and producing the conditions in which long-term settling occurs.

Unsettlement is a period of collective destabilization, a period of shared physical and social shock and destruction; social and personal networks are severed, and basic understandings and assumptions about society, prediction, and safety are thrown into disarray. The survival of self and loved ones is of paramount concern. People do not naturally want to be in this state. It is a state of fear, dread, and anxiety. During periods of unsettlement, people are concerned with the well-being of themselves and their loved ones; attention is focused almost exclusively on personal needs (food, water, shelter, etc.). Yet these do not all occur at once, right away. As different problematics and questions arise and disappear, the mechanisms of unsettlement and then of the settling process shift. Over time, individual frustrations become collective problems, just as individual interpretations become shared understandings and individual acts become collective actions.

The settling process is a social process. It is the coming together after the disruption, like a school of sardines after a hungry fish swims through it and scatters them about. Individual, personal concerns merge with those of others around new, social questions, problematics, and concerns. Collective ways of thinking and acting emerge. People form new groups and identities around their shared experiences and interpretation of them (Hoffman 1999; Al-Ani, Mark and Semaan 2010). These emerge as power shifts among decision-makers and authority figures, different institutions and agents come and go, and people find time to devote attention to shared questions about what happened, why, and what is going to happen. The settling process is also a time of extended trauma and therefore extended coping. We experience and seek answers to collective problems and questions. We might experience these problems personally, but by communicating with others, we come to recognize them and act collectively. Common areas of attention include finding a source, or sources, to blame as the cause of the problem. Was it an act of God? Were there existing controversies that came to fruition? How should we respond? What are our elected officials and other decision-makers doing? Are they fixing the problem? Are they repeating the mistakes of the past? Is the process open and fair, or is it plagued by secrecy and nepotism? These discussions reflect the collective coping processes that are so much a part of the settling period—the period of coming together and bonding over shared experiences, shared interpretations and understandings, shared meaning systems and feelings of anger, fear, humiliation, and at times, compassion, rooted in the disaster event but cultivated in the weeks, months, and years that follow. During settling times, both individually and collectively we seek to reorganize life, make familiar routines, and improve on what once was as we collectively reconstruct our social scaffolding (Al-Ani, Mark, and Semaan 2010). This was the case in New Orleans in the weeks, months, and years after Hurricane Katrina and the "federal flood" that devastated the city.

In the process of settling after a disaster, we are confronted with shifting problems and questions as we experience shifting forms of trauma.

As new problems and questions emerge, our coping strategies shift, as do the meanings and motives of our actions. This means, how we use culture, the reasons we use it, and its implications all shift. Cultural tools that were once used for other purposes or newly created are (re)formulated, becoming essential resources for dealing with these shifting questions and coping with the unfolding trauma. Cultural codes and referents that were once expressed in very different contexts coalesce in light of new references, informing new meaning systems. Collectives that were previously nonexistent, lay dormant, or were engaged in different purposes find new energy and power in light of new goals and interests. The extended period of settling traverses the often too ridged binary between settled and unsettled times and the assumptions about how culture "works" in these times. In the context of extended postdisaster recovery and rebuilding, the versatility of culture becomes manifest; resources, codes, and goals merge to motivate, direct, and impact collective action. People work together to create new resources in light of extended, multiplying, and shifting needs, and they put these resources to different uses and toward different goals, over time.

Hurricane Katrina, New Orleans, and Settling Times

Hurricane Katrina and its aftermath were transitional periods for the city of New Orleans, its infrastructure and residents. We might see the period before the flood as largely reflecting a *settled time*. This is not to adhere to some idealistic, utopian vision of social harmony but to point out that people's routines were largely familiar, normalized, and predictable, rooted to a sense of place that provided security, belonging, and stability (Hay 1998; cf. Chamlee-Wright and Storr 2009, 617). Much of residents' day was on autopilot. They were walking their dogs, watching the Saints play, sitting on their front porches greeting neighbors, enjoying picnics and family reunions in City Park, and eating shrimp or crawfish and drinking daiquiris and sweet tea. They went to work, picked up their kids from school, did the laundry, made groceries, took out the garbage, and went to church on Saturdays and Sundays. As Cliff notes in the epigraph to this chapter, "Two weeks ago [i.e., just before the hurricane] the only thing on my mind was my tailgate party for the Saint's first game." Residents' attention and actions were largely focused around the everyday predictable routines of a collectively settled life,—autopilot, cruise control. On August 29, 2005, this all changed.

We might see the storm and subsequent flooding of the city as ushering in a period of *unsettlement*—a massive disruption that forced taken-for-granted routines, ways of being, and attention onto other, immediate, emergency concerns of survival and safety. This is the *emergency* period (Kates et al. 2006), when essential needs of food, shelter, water, and human waste disposal are pushed to the forefront. In New Orleans, this period lasted several weeks, from when the storm hit the city until the flood waters receded and people began coming back to assess the damage and figure out where to go from there. This was followed by the *restoration* period, as trash and obstructions littered across the city were removed, transportation lanes cleared, and work toward restoring electricity, water, and sewage began.

A longer-term approach, however, would focus on the reconstruction stages of replacement and commemoration/betterment, the months and years of recovery and rebuilding that follow a disaster (Pignetti 2010)—the *settling* period. Here, people start to understand their situation and acknowledge and accept what has happened. They begin to take steps toward reestablishing their lives and thinking about the future. The initial shock of what happened and assessment of the damages are over. People know what happened to the city, their neighborhoods, their homes, and other familiar places. They know what happened to their friends and family and to their own personal lives. Now, they are accepting the reality of what happened and what is and taking steps toward what might seem like the insurmountable tasks of moving forward. They may start this journey as scattered individuals taking baby steps but complete it as collectives taking larger strides. They are seeking to return to normal, clearing out and rebuilding their homes, getting their kids back in school, returning to work, reconnecting with neighbors and loved ones. They are looking for familiarity and predictability, finding joy and peace in the cicadas' call, stop lights that work, air conditioning and working refrigerators, their favorite snowball shop and watering hole reopening, and the numerous other mundane and previously taken-for-granted things of daily life. In the meantime, they are also learning more details about what happened, figuring out who is to blame for the damage, what needs to be done to prevent future risks, and how they should collectively rebuild in both familiar and new, presumably better, ways. They are seeking to have some say in the framing of the disaster and themselves and in their collective futures. They are getting involved in citywide discussions and decisions. This is the prolonged period of settling, a process of accepting, grounding in the present, and thinking ahead, finding familiarity and predictability as people begin to collectively work toward more settled, stable lives.

The periods of unsettlement and settling in New Orleans are largely parallel with what local rescue workers and authority figures have termed the response, recovery, and rebuilding periods. These periods correspond with what disaster scholars have termed the Emergency, Restoration, Reconstruction I (replacement), and Reconstruction II (commemoration and betterment) periods (Kates et al. 2006), with each period lasting ten times longer than the previous (Fussell 2015) and with considerable overlap among periods. In New Orleans, the settling period was a prolonged period of recovery and rebuilding: the recovery from the physical devastation and social disruption, the rebuilding of social institutions, personal and social lives, and social order. This is what took place over the extended period of time between the disaster event and return to relative stability, over a decade later. This period of settling might offer cultural sociologists new insights on culture and action, such as how culture operates as a collective causal agent, embodying the power to motivate and orient collective action around shared meanings, feelings, and anticipated futures—that is, *cultural work*.

Disaster, Settling, and Cultural Action

Sociologists tend to note different roles of culture and action for settled versus unsettled times. They claim that during unsettled times, culture is more important in its ability to identify interests and goals toward which people act. Here, culture is more clearly a motivational, future-oriented, causal agent, identifying goals and directing action like Max Weber's switchman (Swidler 1986, 2001a; Weber [1922] 1978). However, sociologists argue that during settled times, culture is more commonly used as a set of resources people draw on to interpret and justify action. Yet times are often treated as distinct and in isolation, as either settled or unsettled, and therefore so is culture, as a tool for either justifying action or identifying goals and directing action.⁶ What we see in the context of disaster and its long-term aftermath is that the distinction between settled and unsettled, and therefore the different conceptions of culture and action, is not so clear-cut. Unsettled times turn into settled times, and they do so through the prolonged, transitional period of *settling*. Culture plays a dynamic role in this process; it is both public and private, providing external resources we use collectively and informing meanings, feelings, and motives we collectively act toward. These are not mutually exclusive (Vaisey 2009).

Looking at culture and communication in settling times provides some insight into how culture works. By "works," I do not mean the "influences [that] particular symbols have on what people think and how they act," as Michael Schudson once noted (1989, 153). In that sense, work is something culture does to people; that is, culture is understood as external, publicly available symbols that work on or "influence" us. Instead, by "work," I mean something more in line with what we would see in physics. Work involves the transference of potential energy into kinetic action. Work is force. It is strength. It is courage. It is power. Work is something people do, not something done to people. It comes from within and manifests itself in action, as this is the only way to alleviate built-up energy.

To capture the notion of cultural work that I develop here, we need a sufficient understanding of culture, one that allows us to think about the transference of energy into action, where it comes from and what shape it takes. Orlando Patterson's conception is useful, as it captures the sources of this energy, their "layeredness" and resonance with basic social and ontological needs. For Patterson, culture is

> the conjugated product of two interconnected, componential processes. The *first* is a dynamically stable process of collectively made, reproduced, and unevenly shared knowledge about the world that is both informational and meaningful.... Its basic processes are shared schemata that are internally embodied and externally represented. They provide predictability and regularity, coordination equilibria, continuity, and meaning in human actions and interaction and meet certain core motives such as belonging and self-enhancement.... The *second* is a pragmatic component of culture that grounds the first, and it has its own rules of usage and

a pragmatically derived structure of practical knowledge and provides routine ways of interactionally using the constituted cultural structures. (2014, 5–7)

What is useful about this conception is that it provides a way to think about culture and action in which action is normatively meaningful and guided (e.g., toward belonging and self-enhancement) but pragmatically rooted in and informed by shared problems associated with routine and practical knowledge. These are the "two interconnected, componential processes" from which culture emerges in the form of rule-based, meaningfully motivated action. This is where stimuli register in ways that create energy and transfer that energy into meaningful, emotionally motivated action. Further, Patterson's conception of culture allows us to capture both the normative and pragmatic qualities of culture and motivated action simultaneously, so we can understand the duality of action—actions of problem-solving and actions of social rewards coexisting and being related.

Building on this conception of culture, cultural work is emotionally motivated and meaningfully oriented collective agency. It involves the transference of emotionally motivated energy into meaningfully oriented action related to an anticipated future. By engaging questions about how culture works in settling times, this book offers a model of cultural power in which shared meanings and feelings are systematically interconnected in internally consistent and dynamic ways that both motivate and direct collective action (Alexander 2013; Jasper 2018). As I will show, this cultural work has roots in both pragmatism and normativity, as it emerged in the need to address ongoing shared problems and then the social rewards that people earned in helping address those problems.

What did this cultural work look like? It took shape in the collective movement toward blogs for news and information, the making of a much-needed cultural resource, and then the movement into physical-world collective actions directed toward the recovery and rebuilding work of a settling New Orleans. While it is true that many of these outcomes were not necessarily planned long before they happened, shared meanings and feelings informed the baby steps that led up to them and then the larger strides that constituted them. These are important sociological phenomena that are often discounted or overlooked in studies of culture and action. Yet they are fundamentally important for what develops in the form of cultural resources and collective actions and therefore are in need of sociological attention.

The context of disaster is important for understanding cultural work. Disasters are unsettling events, by definition, and during unsettled times and the extended settling period that follows, cultural work becomes clearer, as cultural powers emerge from their slumber to take shape in more deliberate and intentional ways. Yet most research on disasters fails to examine the settling period, instead relying on short-term approaches, focusing on a period of weeks or months for collecting data and publishing reports, and usually focusing on relief organizations like the Red Cross. Long-term recovery and reconstruction periods as well as the perspectives of everyday people with strong connections to place often go unstudied (Chamlee-Wright and Storr 2009; Frailing and Harper 2015) and therefore untheorized. Over time, as people respond, recover, and rebuild from a disaster, they face different problems and therefore different social goals and rewards. These have important implications for why and how they act collectively and the different characteristics of their actions (Kroll-Smith, Baxter, and Jenkins 2015).

People have different needs in times of crisis, and their needs shift over time as conditions change. They have personal needs associated with survival, risk, and well-being and social needs associated with recovering and rebuilding social institutions, connecting with friends and neighbors, and working toward shared goals based on shared understandings of what needs to be done to help each other return to stability. Over this extended settling period, problems and questions shift; once-important questions are replaced by newly discovered problems. Key decision-makers and institutions change. After one area of social life is settled, attention turns immediately to other unsolved problems and unsettled social realms. Stability is rare and tenuous. Uncertainty, especially ongoing uncertainty, motivates information-seeking and problem-solving actions. Information will provide some answers, helping people know that they are not alone and that others are experiencing the tragedy with them (Spence, Lachlan, and Burke 2007, 658). Interactions form around these shared problems, as do trusting social ties and relationships. Collectives may emerge—groups of like-minded people working together in varying degrees to solve their problems and exert some control over the reconstruction and rebuilding processes (Hoffman 1999). Normative meanings and reward systems emerge in response to the problems posed by the disaster (Houston et al. 2014), as do senses of pride, social belonging, and self-enhancement for the help and support people may offer others in need.

Communication and Coping

Addressing common questions about causes, blame, and how to react and respond that arise as a city and its residents settle is part of the extended, collective coping process, but so too is the reward system that arises in relation to these questions. "Coping" refers to "the thoughts and behaviors people use to manage the demands of stressful transactions." They are reactions to "conditions of psychological stress, which requires mobilization and excludes automatized behaviors and thoughts that do not require effort" (Lazarus and Folkman 1984, 142; Spence, Lachlan, and Burke 2007, 656–657). Communication technologies are essential coping tools under such conditions. They provide avenues for people who experience the disaster to ask questions, seek answers, connect with others, and reward those who provide these services (Al-Ani, Mark, and Semaan 2010).

However, disasters may destroy the infrastructure of a particular place. Commonly relied on communication avenues may be ruined, leading to reduced availability and decreased flow of information (Shklovski et al. 2010). The diminished communication capacity occurs at a time when uncertainty and threat are great, producing a high demand for information (Houston et al. 2014, 1) but a lack of access to it. Under such conditions, we may become creative and improvise (Shibutani 1966), using alternative means of communication to provide needed information and suggest solutions. In so doing, we earn the validation and senses of belonging and self-enhancement that derive from these services.

A significant amount of scholarship has been published over the past decade on the use of communication in times of disaster, especially with the diffusion and accessibility of digital social-networking media. Mike Thelwall and David Stuart (2007) note three needs that arise in times of crisis and that communication helps address. These are *general information needs*, *personal information needs*, and what they refer to as *information usage*. "General information needs" refer to the need for information about the actual event. "Personal information needs" refer to the need for information about loved ones, friends, personal belongings, and other more intimate affairs. "Information usage" refers to how people use information to raise questions, to attribute blame, to devise understandings of the event and solutions, and to point out the warning signs for others. With these needs, there is a clear time-order element. We satisfy our personal and general needs first and then, as we continue to learn more about the disaster, begin to engage in information usage. Building on this idea, David Ortiz and I introduced *resource mobilization usage* to refer to the use of media as both a resource in and of itself and a means of accumulating other resources in the context of disaster and the shifting collective traumas of long-term recovery (Ortiz and Ostertag 2014).

In the context of disaster, when the institutions and infrastructure of legacy media are destroyed or hindered in their production capacities and reach, digital, personalized social-networking media may be the only means of accessing and communicating news and other important information (e.g., "I'm safe." "Anyone heard what happened to my house?" "How's mom? Has anyone heard from her?" "What's Lakeview look like?" "Can I get to my neighborhood yet?"). These are the primary questions and problematics related to unsettlement. They are the questions people ask immediately after the disaster event. They are the core problematics associated with the *emergency period* of search and rescue efforts, emergency sheltering, accessing food and water, establishing social order, and clearing transportation lanes and other obstructions and the *restoration period*, when the essential needs of life are patched and temporarily repaired. They are voiced through personalized communication technologies because these are accessible and usable and there might be few other options.

Yet, as people address these very personal, immediate needs, they move into a prolonged period of settling, in which collective questions and needs arise and are confronted. This is the *first reconstruction period* of replacement, addressing infrastructure, housing, and jobs, and the *second reconstruction period* of commemoration and betterment, when improvements and upgrades to predisaster institutions and systems are planned and sought (Kates et al. 2006). In these periods, digital media use and social networking shift to address these shared, communal issues. People use them to communicate news, gossip, rumor, and other information that might be of use to others who share in their grievances and struggle to return to life as they knew it or to something forever different. As unsettlement morphs into settling, the questions and problematics shift; they become more collective, even when they are personal. Questions arise about the causes of the disaster, how to respond, and how to avoid similar disasters in the future. Questions about the status of favored landmarks, businesses, parks, and such emerge, as do discussions on where to place the blame, who to trust, and what rebuilding will and should look like. The movement from unsettled to settled—that is, the settling period—is revealing for questions about cultural work, as emotionally meaningful collective action becomes manifest in people creating new cultural resources or using existing ones differently, all as questions, problematics, and concerns shift.

In the wake of Hurricane Katrina in New Orleans, blogs became an important tool for addressing these questions and, by extension, for building a meaningful system of rewards around the social support and collective answers people were able to provide each other. Blogs were turned into essential coping tools, as collective traumas emerged, shifted, and reemerged for years after the city flooded. People used blogs to communicate and consume needed news and information, to analyze, editorialize, and offer opinions on what happened, why, and what needs to be done to prevent future disasters, to critique and inform others of what key decision-makers were doing in Washington, DC, city hall, and elsewhere, and to offer support and validation to those who were providing useful information, exposing their vulnerabilities, and trying to keep their sanity.

Under these conditions, we might consider the collective actions these bloggers took part in over the months and years of recovery and rebuilding as *cultural work*. Hurricane Katrina and the flood that followed were a massive disaster. This shock forced people to collectively confront new problems and questions of survival and safety, which shifted over the recovery and rebuilding periods. They used blogs to address these questions and, in so doing, constructed a normative meaning system of social rewards and goals that reflected the shifting collective traumas they confronted as the city settled. The meaning systems and emotional energies that constitute cultural work motivated and directed much of their collective action, including their use of blogs, the collective discourse they created across their blogs, and the social ties, relationships, sense of community, and collective actions they formed and took part in long after the flood waters receded. Their blogging eventually diminished as fatigue set in, their lives became more settled, and the emotional energies necessary to continue their work shifted elsewhere or fizzled out. This is the process of cultural work that I highlight in this book.

2

From Personal Disaster and Collective Trauma

The Turn to Blogs

There were a shitload of new blogs after Katrina.
—Loki, interview by the author

Hurricane Katrina, Unsettlement, and Trauma

Hurricane Katrina was a massive disaster that unsettled an entire region and its residents. It was physically, symbolically, emotionally, and psychologically traumatic (Picou and Marshall 2007; Spence, Lachlam, and Burke 2007). Approximately 80 percent of the city of New Orleans flooded, making it the largest residential disaster in US history. More than a million people in the Gulf Coast region were displaced. The city of New Orleans lost over half its population, and roughly 70 percent of all occupied housing units were damaged. Many of those who could not or did not evacuate found emergency shelter in the Superdome and Convention Center, as well as local hospitals and hotels. Yet this was only temporary, as many were then bused to different relief shelters located outside the state. Adding to the mass confusion was the fact that often these individuals did not know the destination to which they were being sent. Three-quarters of the individuals displaced found themselves within 250 miles of the city, but tens of thousands were more than 1,000 miles away from New Orleans. In fact, displaced individuals were registered in every US state (Nigg, Barnshaw, and Torres 2006). Those who stayed and whose homes did not flood were also traumatized. They had to witness the devastation of the city, the suffering of others, and the uncertainty about when the flood waters would stop rising and whether their homes would be destroyed.

Important, however, is the fact that the trauma people experienced did not end once the city stopped flooding and the water receded. Nor did it end once people found loved ones and returned home. For both those who stayed and those who evacuated (willingly or not), this was just the beginning (Pignetti 2010). Their trauma would continue and shape-shift over the next several years. As the disaster event turned into an extended crisis (Gotham and Greenberg 2014), residents would encounter incompetence, ignorance, greed, exploitation, and humiliation at the hands of the federal government, city officials, national media, judgmental outsiders, and private interests.

For those who were affected by Hurricane Katrina, the disaster and aftermath produced a torrent of emotions. Under these conditions, individuals often experience high levels of uncertainty that can produce what Karl Weick calls a "cosmology episode" (1993, 633), when individuals suddenly and deeply feel that their universe is no longer a rational, orderly system. This condition does not end when the disaster ends but can be extended over the long-term recovery (Hoffman and Oliver-Smith 1999). Both the disaster event and the settling process contributed to this feeling at an extended, collective level. The disaster produced the initial shock that caused uncertainty and fear, but the recovery and rebuilding periods extended those feelings over time and across a region. Instead of a cosmology episode, we might think of the weeks, months, and years of a settling New Orleans as creating a *collective cosmological series*.

The devastation and shock caused by Hurricane Katrina and the flood that followed initially forced people's attention to very personal issues of survival and safety: *Where are my loved ones? Are they safe? What happened to my house? Where am I going to live?* But, as these questions and problematics of unsettlement receded with the toxic flood waters, and residents learned the status of their loved ones and possessions, attention became more collective and shifted toward the social elements of settling. *When will garbage be collected? When will the schools be open? When will the grocery stores return? What is happening with Mardi Gras this year?* The period of settling did not bring about the end of the trauma. Instead, trauma shifted. *Personal trauma* associated with the loss of homes and loved ones was fused with newly emerging *collective traumas* associated with problems of infrastructure, social institutions, representations, and what "the city lost in terms of tradition, population and meaning of place" (Pignetti 2010, 50). This was a time of critical victim blaming from ignorant outsiders who could not understand why people stayed, as well as a time for the incompetent, greedy, and deceitful actions of authority figures, businesses, and private interests involved in the recovery and rebuilding. As the settling period progressed, the problems, questions, and concerns that people confronted shifted, and therefore so did the quality and character of their trauma and their related cultural work.[1]

The period between unsettled and settled, the settling period, corresponds with the response, recovery, and rebuilding periods of the long-term Katrina aftermath. The *response* period involves immediate needs (food, water, shelter, waste), using military, police, and medical resources to control populations, establish initial order, clear transportation lanes, and such. During this time, people are dealing primarily with personal needs. The response is the immediate reaction to the unsettling event. This is the initial source of uncertainty and the fear and anxiety that come with it. It typically lasts only a few weeks, as food, water, and shelter get figured out and people take stock and come to a general understanding and acceptance of what happened. Now, the cleanup work begins. The response period blends into the next phase, the recovery period.

The *recovery* period reflects a different set of goals. This is the period of removing debris and getting people back into the city in some organized fashion. Some order is emerging out of the chaos of the disaster event. Personal needs get figured out for the time being, and social needs start to emerge: getting garbage collected, electricity up and running, and streetlights and signals working. Some social institutions and organizations start operating, but in a limited capacity. This period can last for several months up to a couple of years. It overlaps with and is followed by the rebuilding period.

The *rebuilding* period involves reconstructing what was destroyed and looking ahead, the collective work toward setting up a stable future. Social organizations and institutions may be up and running, and decision-makers and people in power are planning for the future and implementing their plans. Education, housing, jobs, familiar places, and so on are all rebuilding, many with new visions of how to "improve" on the past.[2] This may start from roughly a year after the event through the following decade.

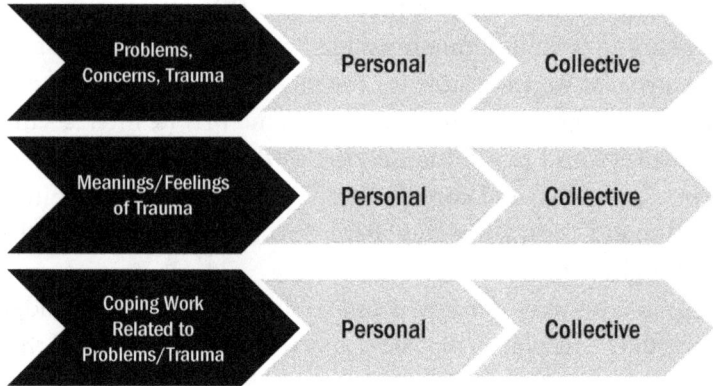

Figure 2.1. Process of emerging cultural work

The response, recovery, and rebuilding periods are heuristic tools to help us get a grasp of the long-term recovery from disaster and some sense of what "progress" is and should look like as a city seeks to return to settled times. They are fuzzy concepts that in reality are contentious, overlap, blend together, and are differentially reflected and experienced across the city. Nonetheless, they are useful guides for linking time and change after a disaster. In Katrina-ravaged New Orleans, the response, recovery, and rebuilding periods help capture one measurement of time and change that corresponds with the periods of unsettlement and settling. The crisis event causes unsettlement. It is the beginning of what becomes a massively traumatic collective cosmological series, wrought with uncertainty and the fear, worry, anxiety, and anger that comes with it. We can characterize the time from the event through the response period (a few weeks after the event) as a period of unsettlement. We can characterize the recovery and rebuilding periods (from a few months to several years) as the settling period. It is the long-term aftermath that often goes understudied in disaster research (Frailing and Harper 2015). By looking at the settling period, we can see how individual problems and concerns shift into social problems and concerns, as do the traumas people experience (from personal to collective), the meanings and feelings of these problems and sources of trauma (from personal to collective), and the kinds and quality of coping work that informs and motivates their action (from personal to collective). It is over the course of settling from disaster, and the collective cosmological series that characterizes people's experience with this period, that cultural work foments energizing and orienting collective actions in relation to these ongoing traumas (see figure 2.1).

Disaster, Crisis, and Communication Theory

In the context of massive disasters and the traumas associated with them, people need to communicate. Yet their needs and uses of communication technologies shift over time, as the traumas they encounter shift and as the disaster event evolves into the postdisaster crisis. Wendy Macias, Karen Hilyard, and Vicki Freimuth (2009) note two general trends in how people use communication technologies in such times. These include *informational needs/uses*, in which communication technologies are used to deal with the immediate needs of survival, safety, and security, and *social needs/uses*, in which communication technologies are used to deal with shared issues of solidarity and social inclusion. These do not typically emerge simultaneously but rather develop over time as the pressing issues shift and unsettlement merges into settling. Questions of survival are fundamental, powerful, and prioritized, until they become somewhat stabilized. As this happens, new, more social questions, concerns, and problematics arise (Curato 2017). These may be sources of new, different forms of trauma. As with informational needs, people will find ways to engage them, using communication technologies as key resources in doing so. Through whatever medium/media they can, they will communicate and consume rumor, gossip, and news as a way of addressing uncertainty and alleviating the fear and anxiety brought forth in a collective cosmological series.

Over the past decade and a half, digital and personalized social media have been turned into important cultural resources in the context of disaster. They are versatile communication tools people creatively use to answer pressing questions and address immediate problems, as well as those that emerge over time. Media System Dependency (MSD) theory provides a framework to explain the relationship between individuals and media in disaster situations. According to MSD theory, the importance of mass media in an individual's life varies according to the *social environment* and the *intensity of an individual's goals* (Ball-Rokeach 1985).

In disaster situations, be it natural or human made, the social environment suddenly becomes uncertain, as people experience a collective cosmological episode. In ambiguous situations like these, dependency on mass media increases because mass media outlets are likely to contain important and exclusive information that is not available from other sources (Ball-Rokeach 1998). Here, people use media to help understand themselves and their social environments, orient their action, and interact with others. This was the case after the attacks on New York and Washington, DC, on September 11, 2001, the 2011 earthquake in Japan, and the 2013 supertyphoon Haiyan in the Philippines (Ball-Rokeach 1985; J.-Y. Jung 2012; David, Ong, and Legara 2016).[3]

Communication Infrastructure Theory (CIT) builds on MSD by embracing various means of communication, including new media and local/ethnic media (Ball-Rokeach and Jung 2009), and focusing on the collective "storytelling network" that individuals and organizations create and maintain across media. These stories do not flow one-way, as MST theory assumes, but flow two or more ways and may be communicated and consumed by people with a range of perspectives, voices, and degrees of access to power (J.-Y. Jung 2012). Moreover, implied in CIT is an emphasis on time; a storytelling network and its development through mediated interaction takes time to develop. These features suggest that CIT is a suitable theory for understanding citizen media use over an extended collective cosmological series.

These theories help us understand what happened in New Orleans after Hurricane Katrina and how blogs were used. MSD acknowledges the interest in media and why; CIT introduces networking media, the flow of voices, and the stories told, as well as the numerous nondominant media that exist at the same time, contributing to these emergent collective stories. In New Orleans, while the "nation" was watching the spectacle of Katrina on their televisions or computers from afar (Gotham 2007b), most residents did not have access to power. And even if they did, the national media was not much help. Reporters did not know the city; they gave the wrong names for places, focused on the chaos and crime, and reported mostly on the French Quarter and Superdome (Pignetti 2010). Not only was this coverage useless for most locals, but much of it was downright infuriating in its ignorance and negativity. At the same time, there was little local news and information available.

Reporters could not get access to places, and the production and distribution of print news was greatly diminished due to the destruction of the city's infrastructure. Information needs were high, but output was low. As people have done in the past, they improvised (Shibutani 1966), and blogs became important resources in their improvisations.

Communication Needs and Uses in a Settling New Orleans (2005–2013)

With Hurricane Katrina, the flood, and the aftermath, New Orleanians experienced not so much a cosmology episode, as Weick describes it (1993), but an extended, collective cosmological series. For some, blogs became important tools for communicating about the uncertainty of survival, safety, and stability associated with the unsettled period, as well as the personal trauma that individuals experienced (Joyce 2015). Later, and for many others, blogs became important tools for communicating on personal *and* collective trauma, associated with social and cultural concerns, problematics, and questions of the settling period (Ostertag and Ortiz 2013; Ortiz and Ostertag 2014).

In times of crisis, people commonly have two general needs, those that are personal and those that are more general and social (Thelwal and Stuart 2007). These correspond with the different kinds of trauma they experience and how these traumas shape-shift in relation to the material and symbolic conditions of unsettled and settling periods. While the scholarship on needs and people's use of communication technologies in relation to these needs is insightful, this work tends not to differentiate among media technologies or among different voices, as CIT would argue is necessary. Different communication technologies tend to afford different narrative characteristics, connectivity, and interactions, suggesting that they are used to address some needs better or worse than they address others (Ostertag and Ortiz 2017; Khazraee and Novak 2018). Digital social-networking media, for example, tend to be more accessible to amateur and citizen users than are the tools of professional, legacy media (Earl and Kimport 2011). Digital social-networking media are versatile communication tools (Ortiz and Ostertag 2014; David, Ong, and Legara 2016). People use them for learning and expressing, for gathering resources, networking, and accumulating other forms of social capital, and as a field on which battles over meaning and understanding take place (Ostertag and Ortiz 2013; Ortiz and Ostertag 2014). Further, users shift from communicators to consumers frequently and fluidly, reading content and then sharing, adding, or commenting on it. People might be writing a blog post one minute, and the next, they are reading a post from another blog. Users frequently and seamlessly switch their hats from reader to writer and vice versa, over time and as their needs and priorities change.

In the immediacy of the flood, and shortly after, when *personal information needs* were front and center, blogs were, for the most part, not all that important or useful. Few people were blogging in New Orleans before and during the storm. People needed portable, battery-operated mobile communication, as they were standing on their rooftops, sitting in hot and crowded buses, or laid up in shelters somewhere. Cellphones were the preferred and most accessible communication technology and a particularly important means of communicating. People called loved ones to let them know they were okay or that they needed help or in some cases to let them know they might never talk to them again.[4] Many stood on their rooftops, with their hands held high, trying to send text messages on their status and seeking information on the status of loved ones.[5] People exchanged personal information through text messages and, if they were lucky, voice calls with their cellphones, until their batteries died or they got access to a computer or landline, often days or weeks later. This helped them address, to some degree, the personal information needs associated with the personal trauma of massive unsettlement.

As people found places to stay and immediate concerns over housing and the status of loved ones were temporarily relieved, they began communicating over computers, some personal, some public (e.g., in libraries and coffee shops). This opened up other possibilities for communication, in the form of emails, listservs, message boards, and eventually blogs and other webpages.[6] As people learned about their homes and loved ones, their friends and pets, as they found places to stay with family, friends, and kind strangers both near and far, they began using these technologies to address general information needs and the social issues associated with collective trauma. These technologies afforded people the time and space to communicate more elaborate messages, to speak to broader audiences, and to discover and address broader, social questions and problematics. As Communication Infrastructure Theory would predict, they allowed for the building of a storytelling network among amateur media users, designed to address the social needs and collective traumas of a collective cosmological series, as they unfolded over the months and years of a settling New Orleans.

A Growing Blogosphere

The utility and importance of blogs as a means of collective communication emerged in the settling period, when people had the time to start their own blogs and to search out and read others. They continued to be important communication tools for several years after. Their versatility manifested itself as the collective traumas and associated problems, questions, and concerns shifted with the settling period. They allowed for the building of a storytelling network among amateur media users. They became useful resources to share and consume news and information, interact with others, and create a network of social support and solidarity. Their openness afforded them the ability to cater to a variety of needs, simultaneously. People vented frustrations and shared their thoughts and feelings with others, posting stories, pictures, news, and commentary on a variety of things related to the recovery and rebuilding periods. In so doing, they helped each other and created a digital social support network that fomented a shared identity and sense of community. This network started online but over time took occasional forays offline, as users sought to exert some say over the recovery and rebuilding work.

As the floodwaters receded, people returned to take stock of the damage and start rebuilding their homes and lives. It was during this period of settling, the weeks, months, and even years after the flood, that people "discovered" and started using blogs. Blogs became useful outlets both for personal expression and in satisfying other, more collective needs. If we look at the years after the flood and count the number of new blogs created each year, we see a sizeable spike in blogging from one to three years after the flood (see figure 2.2). In total, 254 blogs were in use in New Orleans by 2011, roughly five and a quarter years after Hurricane Katrina.[7]

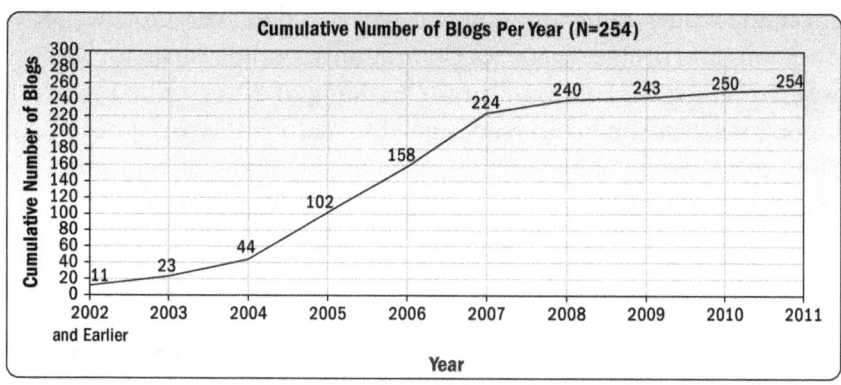

Figure 2.2. Cumulative number of blogs per year (*N* = 254)

In 2004, there were only forty-four blogs, indicating a sizeable spike in new blogs over these several years.[8] The fact that blog use rose in the early 2000s is not surprising, as this corresponds with national trends (Raine 2005), but the timing, context, and fivefold increase in new blogs points to Hurricane Katrina and the collective traumas that followed in the settling period as being the primary impetus for this local blogosphere.

Intuitively, this is not surprising. Nonetheless, empirical evidence can provide more clarity on this relationship. In 2004, twenty-one new blogs were created.[9] In 2005, this number increased to thirty-one before the storm (signifying a general trend more broadly), but fifty-eight new blogs were created in the *quarter of year after the flood*. Further, when we look during the later recovery and rebuilding periods of 2006 and 2007, we find that fifty-six new blogs were created in 2006 and sixty-six new blogs were created in 2007 (see figure 2.3). This is a sizeable spike from 2004 and at a greater rate than the Pew Research Center reported on blog growth in general. Further evidence of Hurricane Katrina serving as the impetus for people to start blogging can be found in some of the blog names. During this period of blog growth, we see a number of blogs referencing Hurricane Katrina or its collective traumas in their names. For example, *Tin Can Trailer Trash* (referencing the FEMA trailers), *Thank You Katrina* (a satirical show of appreciation), and *Fix the Pumps* (referencing part of the city's flood-protection system), while others refer to what might be lost due to the flood, such as *Last Magnolia* and *Squandered Heritage*.

It is not surprising that the flooding of New Orleans that followed Hurricane Katrina served as the impetus for growth in this local blogosphere. But what exactly about the flood motivated people to seek out and use blogs? We know *that* people turned to blogs in the wake of Katrina but little about *why* or *what* blogs meant to those who started using them, as writers and readers. Looking closer, what was actually motivating and directing this movement toward and use of blogs?

People's movement into blogging in the context of post–Hurricane Katrina recovery and rebuilding was motivated by both personal and collective reasons and validates what scholars have found in other contexts (Yao 2009; Kjellberg 2010; Chung and Kim 2008). They started to blog primarily so they could vent their frustrations and correct misconceptions, both related to their shifting traumas. Personally, they needed an outlet to vent, somewhere to express themselves about the insanity of the recovery and rebuilding periods. They needed to "get it out there." Socially, they needed to inform others of what was happening in New Orleans and with the recovery and rebuilding work, to correct the faulty and insulting content they were seeing in the national media, and to

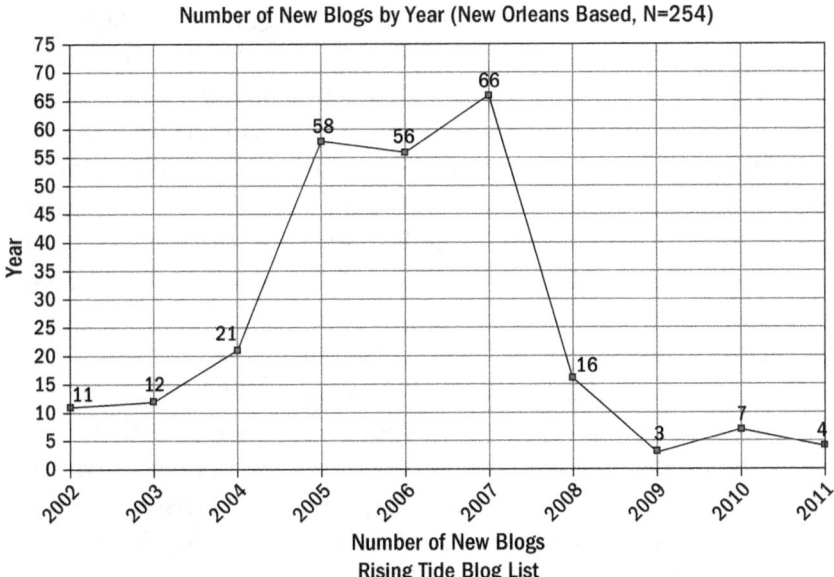

Figure 2.3. Number of newly created blogs by year of first post (2002–2011)

offer insight for those who were sharing in the collective trauma. Relatedly, people read blogs because they were desperate for information and local bloggers could provide intimate, knowledgeable news that helped readers address ongoing questions and concerns, commiserate over similar frustrations, and find validation and positive takes on city residents working together to recover and rebuild (Joyce 2015).

While people's turn to blogs largely occurred over the months and years after the flood, as they stabilized their lives, some digital pioneers had started before. Using blogs as personal diaries, to express their thoughts on a variety of things and to document certain aspects of life, these few people were prepared to use blogs to communicate about the flood in its immediacy. One local blogger in particular became well-known among evacuated residents who were able to access a computer and web connection, as well as among interested outsiders consuming the disaster from afar. The *GulfSails* blogger is a white man with blond hair and glasses. He looked to be in his midforties when I saw him speak in 2010. He lived in the Lakeview area of New Orleans, which is close to Lake Pontchartrain and at the edge of Orleans Parish. He stayed and live-blogged the storm and subsequent flood and was one of the first people to use a blog to describe and communicate information from the ground during a major disaster. He started blogging a few days before Katrina, initially because he wanted to track it but then to record the rising waters and devastation and then as an outlet to express himself as he processed what happened. The *GulfSails* blogger had no idea how popular his blog had become. He recalled in a 2010 panel called "Katrina 5.0," commemorating the fifth anniversary of the flood, that the news agency Reuters tracked him down several days after the hurricane to ask him about his blogging. This surprised him, as he did not know if anyone was paying attention to his blog. When he asked who was reading his blog, the reporter from Reuters replied, "the world."

Once people found temporary living arrangements, usually somewhere outside the city (such as Houston, Atlanta, or Mississippi), they sought out news and information. The national news was not helpful, and the infrastructure of local news was largely destroyed. Listservs, message boards, and other websites designed to help popped up from around the country. Blogs, however, provided an intimate and more nuanced look into the city, at a time when locals and others tied to the city were desperate for any useful news from a knowledgeable source. In this context of unsettlement turning into settling, blogs served very personal needs and then more social and collective needs, as people used them to communicate and consume news about their homes and loved ones, their neighborhoods and their city, how to prevent future disasters, and how to rebuild for a new but familiar future.

Having demonstrated and located the growth of this local blogosphere in the context of Hurricane Katrina and the settling period that followed, I next provide a "thicker" description of this process. In chapter 3, I draw on qualitative data to highlight the reasons people started reading and writing blogs and how this collective movement serves as an early manifestation of their cultural work. I then examine the storytelling network that emerged through their blog use and the collective stories they shared with each other, as these were to become important cultural resources that they would draw on for relief and support and to organize and stage offline mobilizations and collective actions as the settling period progressed.

3

Collective Trauma with Blogs

The Growth of a Local Blogosphere

All of these writers had things in common. A frantic need to know what was really happening to the city and its people. A passionate desire to make sure the world understood the scale of the tragedy, the impact on those who suffered, and the future implications for the rest of the country; why New Orleans mattered, and what was being lost. A furious rage as insults piled upon injuries. And deep down, an indescribable pain, a wide-eyed teeth-grinding emotional trauma. A scream out of every nerve ending. A psychic howl of pain and exhaustion and abandonment.
—Ray Shea, in *A Howling in the Wires* (Jasper and Folse 2010, xii–xiii)

Hurricane Katrina was a traumatic event, but trauma comes in different forms. While the devastation of the flood was traumatic, especially on a very personal level, the aftermath was also traumatic. This was a different form of trauma from the personal trauma of the event and the unsettled period. It was a longer, drawn-out, collective form of trauma (Smelser 2004). *Collective trauma* is an individually but also collectively experienced and negotiated form of trauma. It involves two distinct characteristics, one social and one cultural. *Social trauma* refers to the devastation of material, structural forces and institutions and how this disrupts life routines and introduces new and ongoing risks and problems (Erikson 1976). *Cultural trauma* refers to the threat and degradation of a shared cultural identity and how this demeans a collective sense of self- and social identity (Alexander 2004; Eyerman 2008; Ostertag and Ortiz 2013). These traumas reflect the problematics and questions that shift onto collective, social issues and concerns. In the settling period in New Orleans after Katrina, people found blogs useful resources to learn about, express, construct, and commiserate around collective trauma. It is around these traumas of the settling period that the cultural work of bloggers coalesced and around which they formed online social networks of storytelling and support, as well as the collectives and mobilizations that followed. For many, this journey was rooted in very personal needs, concerns, and areas of focus, but it evolved into collective ones as they discovered each other and what they shared with regard to problems, questions, concerns, and needs.

Recall that one of the qualities of digital social-networking media like blogs is that readers and writers may be one and the same. Indeed, this is one of the key points of Communication Infrastructure Theory. Blog writers might post a personal story about their experience dealing with insurance companies or the city's Road Home program or about the city's plan to close a hospital and then read another blog to learn about the city's plan to fire teachers and implement a citywide charter-school system. Then, they might return to their blog, post an editorial piece on what they just read, link to the original blog post, and maybe add some more information to it. These are different practices of reading and writing that can be separated out for analytic purposes but that, in actuality, coexist almost simultaneously in an ongoing flow of practices around communication technologies and content.

Reading Blogs

In the context of Hurricane Katrina, people read blogs for a variety of reasons. Dealing with an extended collective cosmological series and the collective trauma associated with the settling period was one of the most important of these reasons. People needed to learn about things happening in the city and how these things might impact their lives. They also wanted information that was more positive in how it framed residents and their decisions. They were experiencing an extended collective cosmological series and suffering from collective trauma. They were uncertain about the status of their lives, their futures, their city, and everything they held dear. They became news omnivores (Massanari and Howard 2011), devouring local print media (to the extent they could), television news, listservs, message boards, and citizen bloggers who were reporting on their own research, analysis, and insights. In this context, local bloggers became trusted sources for news and information, even if they editorialized and did not necessarily follow all the conventions of professional journalism. They knew the city well, could focus on a certain area or phenomenon, offer proper context, and show the civility of residents working to rebuild. They became a form of quasi-crowdsourced accountability for city officials who were taking over the recovery and rebuilding work (Joyce 2015). In a time of heightened and prolonged uncertainty of the extended settling period, blogs became useful resources for news, information, analysis, and thoughtful commentary and eventually a source of social support and solidarity. Among other things, they helped people address uncertainty and alleviate the fear and anxiety brought forth with a prolonged cosmological series and the collective traumas of a settling New Orleans.

B.rox (pronounce the dot) was originally from Indiana and moved to New Orleans about twenty years before we met. He is white and tall, was in his forties when we met, and worked as a tech guy for a local university. He consulted local blogs because they helped him get a sense of what was going on in the city.

> So, ah, before Katrina, I was vaguely aware of some local blogs. I wasn't particularly interested in reading any local blogs. If I was looking for a blog to read, it would be on a topic, you know, topical blogs of some sort, but I really wasn't reading a whole lot of blogs anyway. . . . After Katrina, that all changed, and I was like reading, ah, those blogs [local blogs] exclusively and at a very high volume. They were popping up like a new one everyday, at that time, and I would add them to my feed reader, and I would spend it seemed like half my day [reading them]. I mean, it was so chaotic and so weird. . . . I would spend half my day either reading blogs or writing about [the recovery] and trying to develop a sense of what's going on in the city.

Karen, the *Squandered Heritage* blogger, is also a transplant. She is a white woman and was in her fifties when we talked. She is originally from the Northeast and was raising a school-age daughter in the city. She consulted local blogs while she was recovering from cancer and before she started her own blog. "When I finally ended up in Austin and had a lot of time—it was fucking hot, unbelievably hot—and so when I was sick, . . . and I found specifically this one woman's blog [Maitri's *VatulBlog*], . . . and she's since left, but she was doing a day-by-day chronicle. . . . She was in Houston, but she would come back [to New Orleans], and she'd take pictures and write about it and sort of compile news. And so that was one of the first blogs I really, really got engaged with."

Dangerblond, a middle-aged white woman from Mississippi with a law degree and good sense of humor, discussed how she first sought news online, found a message board about law school, and then searched out local bloggers for more news and information.

> When the hurricane came, and we had to evacuate, um, everything was down. You know, the cellphones were down, um, no TV coming out of New Orleans, um, you know, communication was just down, and I start—I was in law school at the time, and we just had our first week of classes, and I was in my second year in law school, and I evacuated to my son's house in Lafayette. He had a computer, and his cellphone wasn't working—that was just out. There was no way that you could make a phone call and find out anything. So I started searching online for people, and the first place I found was the Nola.com forums,[1] and people on there were saying, "Go here if you want to find out information about this, and go here if you want to find out information about that," and somebody put, "Go to this blog if you want to find out information about Loyola Law School." So I went to the blog, and it was a guy in North Carolina who was friends with one of the law librarians at Loyola Law School. And this friend of his set up a blog in North Carolina and sent out emails and posted on everything that had to do with New Orleans that he could find. . . . And then I started thinking, "I wonder if there's any other people blogging about New Orleans." So I started looking all over the internet, and I found different people who were blogging and saying what was going on in New Orleans and you know, "I've been back to my house and here's what I found."

Again, in the context of an unsettled and settling postdisaster New Orleans, people were desperate for news and information. The national media was not helpful and in many ways made things worse. Local media was in disarray, with distribution and access heavily impeded by the breakdown of the city's infrastructure. People sought news elsewheres (Ostertag 2009), finding local blogs to be useful resources in their extended time of need. As they continued to consume, senses of trust and camaraderie developed among writers and readers, and many decided to start their own blogs. There were lots of things going on in the city. People needed an outlet to express themselves, and they wanted to help others who were in similar positions of uncertainty as themselves. People started blogging for both personal and collective reasons. Personal reasons were more common in the immediate aftermath of the flood, when personal information needs were front and center, but collective reasons emerged over time. Personal needs remained, but blogging came to serve collective needs as well.

Writing Blogs: Personal

People blogged because they simply needed an outlet to express themselves. It was a personal diary, a therapeutic tool to get thoughts out. For B.rox, his blogging is an extension of a much longer history of personal journaling and documenting. He has been journaling for years, as a way to document things he finds interesting and, now, as a way to record family growth. In the context of flooded New Orleans, B.rox's blogging remained focused on personal life but shifted to issues related to the devastation. G Bitch, an author, English professor, native New Orleanian, and Black woman in her lower forties, was not blogging before the flood but turned to it because she needed an outlet to express herself, and doing so at home was taking its toll on family life. Blogging provided her a place to express herself and "get it out." Likewise, Patrap, an older white man who is also a veteran, started blogging while laid up in a hospital bed for a few days. He needed something to do, and blogging provided an outlet for what his Veterans Administration doctors later diagnosed as reoccurring posttraumatic stress disorder (PTSD). Later on, when he started hearing things about how outsiders were talking about the city and its residents (e.g., Barbara Bush's statement about evacuees staying in Houston was particularly maddening for Patrap and others [*New York Times* 2005]), "it was on!" as he said. He had to step up his blogging because people were developing false conceptions of what was going on in New Orleans and of the residents who evacuated. They were not all "criminals," nor were people in the city sitting around waiting for handouts from others. This infuriated Patrap, as well as others, and they used blogs to address it.

A white woman in her fifties, a bit on the "wild" side, and a source of friendship and aid for the down-and-out living in and around the French Quarter, Sam Jasper, the *NOLA Slate* blogger, turned to blogging for a variety of reasons in the context of the storm, but one was very personal.[2] Blogging provided an outlet for self-expression at a time when she needed it and her previous outlets were destroyed. As she recalled,

> I used to paint, but Katrina ate all my supplies and all that, and I just haven't had the energy to go back to painting. It ate twenty-five years of negatives, all of my journals. In my view, in a way [Katrina] annihilated my personality, who I am. It annihilated every form of expression that I had ever chosen. And I struggled hard with that. And I know most people won't understand that, but you put everything out, all the words, images, and shots you ever took, and when all of that is gone, including all of your family heirlooms, all of your family photographs, all of your daughter's graduation pictures, the last picture of your dad—that kind of stuff—it's like your identity has been wiped out. . . . So I guess what keeps me going [blogging] is that when I painted, anything that hurt or bothered me would wind up—it was easier to put it on that canvas and get it out of here so I didn't have to lug it around, and now I don't have that canvas anymore. So I put it there [on the blog], I guess. . . . And if it connects with somebody, that's cool.

Cliff of *Cliff's Crib* is a native New Orleanian. A Black man in about his midforties and with young children at the time, Cliff grew up in the Ninth Ward but had moved to New Orleans East. We met at his house one evening, and sitting at his kitchen table, he explained that he evacuated to a friend's house, where he spent the first six months of the flood sleeping on an inflatable mattress. He lost everything. Blogging helped him cope. When he moved back home, he found himself writing constantly. He started a series of posts documenting his return to the city in late January 2006, called "Day 1," "Day 2," and so on. Later, in October 2007, he started a series of posts called "Sitting on my Porch,

Day X." These were general musing on what he was seeing and experiencing upon his return to his home and then regarding the city more generally—ways of processing what was inexplicable. Blogs helped him cope.

> And then once I came home, I was staying with my best friend at his house on an air mattress for about six months, and that was a real, ahh, kind of depressing time. But writing-wise, that was like some of the best writing I did. It was like 2006 and 2007, like the post-Katrina, when I was still working everything out. I don't know why I did so much writing then, but probably because it was easier to write it than it was to talk to people about it. So, for some strange reason, I felt compelled to put it out there for the whole world to read. . . . Those were really heavy years, writing-wise.

Part of addressing personal trauma for people after Katrina was to vent their frustrations by telling their stories, and they used blogs to do so. People communicated their personal experiences. Many consumers could relate, and those who could not at least could empathize. Blogging helped them cope with their personal needs. As with Patrap, G Bitch, Sam of *NOLA Slate*, Cliff, and others, their reasons for blogging shifted over time, as they began interacting with other, new bloggers and as the material and symbolic aspects of the settling period evolved. As the social environment changed, so did people's relationship with media, the meanings of communication technologies like blogs, and how they were used as tools in their cultural work.

Writing Blogs: Collective

In the context of settling, residents dealt with newly emergent questions: questions about getting their utilities up and running, the garbage collected, stoplights fixed, getting back to work, and their kids in school. These were questions about the city's basic infrastructure. They were shared issues that were individually experienced. Here, we see more collective needs and the personalization of those needs. This is when people started talking about what the event means, who or what is to blame, what to do in the short and long term, how to improve on the mistakes of the past and move forward. Reconstruction periods 1 and 2 (Kates et al. 2006) are the time of *collective trauma*. Collective traumas are the material and symbolic aspects of trauma that a group of people share, where the focus of attention in on meso- or macro-level "social things." They are composed of both social and cultural elements. *Social trauma* arises from the destruction of infrastructure and social institutions. Civil and political society breaks down. Transportation and communication avenues are disabled. Schools and jobs are thrown into question. People in power seem incompetent, corrupt, or reckless in their handling of the recovery and in the rebuilding periods. People's lives are at continuous risk. Uncertainty, fear, and anxiety abound. *Cultural trauma* refers to the trauma experienced in the framing or constructing of a cultural identity. Who "we" are is threatened and attacked to its core (Eyerman 2015). It needs defending and positive counterconstructions. Cultural trauma is the trauma brought forth when a shared cultural identity is collectively humiliated, insulted, or in any other way publicly degraded or threatened (Alexander 2004; Lo and Fan 2022). For many people after Katrina, collective trauma was their reason to start blogging. And for those who were already blogging, collective trauma led them to shift their writing over the settling period. For both, collective trauma was their reason for continuing to blog months and years after the initial damage caused by the flood. It was the fundamental stimulus in how personal work turned into cultural work.

Karen started *Squandered Heritage* shortly after the flood, as the city was clearing property to make way for the rebuilding stages. She used her blog as a tool to engage issues of memory, loss, and remembrance with the city's architectural landscape and the meanings of places. As the city started implementing plans to demolish homes and other properties on a massive scale, she photographed them. Later on, her writing shifted somewhat, and she became a well-known blogger who photographed homes slated for demolition as part of the city's recovery and rebuilding plans. She got hold of the list of homes slated for demolition and took pictures of them. Some looked far from imminent danger. She even contacted home owners about the status of their homes. Many were away and not aware that the city had planned on demolishing their homes (Gadbois 2007).

Likewise, the blogger Liprap of *Liprap's Lament* started blogging in the settling period. Liprap was a glassblower and named her blog after a particular glassblowing technique called "lip wrap." She is a white woman who moved to New Orleans years earlier. She is a mother, and blogging was a form of therapy, to "preserve [her] sanity," much like for her blogging friends. Blogging helped her deal with the problems of schooling for her children, medical care in the city, a broken postal system, and other issues of the city's infrastructure that she confronted as she moved back to New Orleans after evacuating.

The examples of Karen and Liprap both indicate the role of social trauma in people's reasons to blog. Karen, Liprap, and others started blogging because they needed an outlet to cope with the infrastructural damage and frustrations that followed in the settling period. Blogging served as a means to preserve their sanity, as Liprap noted. G Bitch also emphasized the role of social trauma in her starting and continuing to blog. She started to blog for two reasons. One was related to the social trauma. The other was, as a woman of color born and raised in New Orleans, she felt that the predominantly white and nonnative bloggers had some important blind spots that needed correcting. Regarding why she started and continues (at the time of our interview) to blog, she said,

> Outrage [*laughs a bit*]. Sheer outrage, sheer outrage. Um, you know, I would say that, well, I'll put it this way: New Orleans before the storm was a kind of broken place. We had our issues, we had a lot of things that weren't working right. But then post-Katrina, there's been a kind of effort to—and I'm speaking a lot about education.... There was this "Oh! It's a new day. We're going to start all over." All that stuff. "We're going to start all over. Throw all that away. We'll start all over." You know. My outreach kind of centers on the logic, the stupidity of politicians, the callousness of the so-called school reforms, and the kind of lack of information and kind of almost secretive nature of information, say, about the schools.... Like, I try to negotiate the Department of Education's website, RSD's [Recovery School District's] website, it's like I can't find anything here.

Patrap started blogging in April 2006. He lost his home due to the flood and had to stay in a FEMA trailer. For a short while, he was in the hospital, where he would first write up his posts on physical paper and in long form and then would go to the library and use the computer to post the entry. The following quote illustrates the role of cultural trauma in his starting to blog and continuing to blog. His narrative also shows how he used blogging as a coping mechanism to deal with the trauma he experienced.

> I been through a long road since the storm [Hurricane Katrina]. I've been a member of the Wunderground community [a blogging community that focuses on weather]online, but I never knew what a blog was literally until after the hurricane.... So we got the FEMA trailer in December of 2005, and it was about April of 2006 when I developed diverticulitis real bad. So I'd been reading Jeff Maris's blog entries, and I seen that there was a whole list and that you can do your own blog. So literally I jumped in there, in my FEMA trailer, in my little Dell and my keyboard, and I just started really projecting what the doctors at the VA—my PTSD doctors figured I started projecting my experiences, because there was a lot of online misconceptions about what happened during the storm. And so I just jumped in there, and now I've had over 250 entries and over 85,000 comments on all of the blogs. So it's been like a labor of love, and it's been like a purging almost. But as far as the blogging goes, I mean, I got—I literally got mad when people would call us "them people" and stuff like that. I just jumped in, and I never knew I was a writer until I was becoming a writer [*laughs*]. And then what I did, is just, ah, I've been doing it ever since, literally.

Patrap was frustrated with how outsiders were framing New Orleanians, those who evacuated and those who stayed. This was a threat to his cultural identity with the city and thus a form of cultural trauma. He noted how the national news was reporting about the alleged nonstop violence in the city but how that was not his experience. He was also particularly hurt and angered by former First Lady Barbara Bush's words about evacuees who were being housed in the Astrodome in Houston, referring to how fortunate they were to be staying in the Astrodome because so many of them were "underprivileged anyway." These were examples of cultural trauma that Patrap offered. They accumulated over time and became reasons for his blogging once he had the time and know-how to blog.

Sam of *NOLA Slate* initially started with an email listserv that she titled *Katrina Refrigerator* (in reference to the spoiled food and rancid smell of thousands of refrigerators in the wake of the flood). Her first email was on September 12, 2005, roughly three weeks after the city flooded. She used email to contact people to let them know what she was seeing as she returned to the city. Her emails were forwarded to others, who then requested to be included in future emails, so that in a short time, she was emailing well over 250 people (with a dialup modem!). In March 2006, she shifted her focus to blogging, as this was a more manageable format, and created *NOLA Slate*. Cultural trauma was one of the key reasons she started the email listserv and then why she started *NOLA Slate*. It was also a focus in some of her later writing and her writing in other outlets. As she said, "Then we started watching what was on the news, in Alabama, when we finally got to Alabama, and we were so appalled by what we were seeing—the endless looping of the same footage with no actual information—that we said, 'Screw it. We're going home.' And everybody thought that we were out of our mind, and we said, 'Too bad,' and we came. And so it was about a week, ten days later that I started writing those emails."

In the process of using blogs to deal with social and cultural trauma, it was also a way to reconnect with similar others and with the city in general. The *American Zombie* blogger, whom I discuss in more detail in chapter 6, noted this as one of the reasons he blogged.

> To me, blogging, even in 2006, was like a whole new thing to me, you know, and also I was displaced. Just emotionally, I felt like it was a way for me to reconnect too. I mean, when I look back on it, I think it was a way for me to reconnect. I don't think that I thought that when I was doing it. But, um, you know, my family was displaced for eighteen months after the storm. My house got flooded, and I was going through a pretty emotional time during that period, really wrestling with the concept of, Why bring your family back into a city that might not be here in one hundred years? . . . The blog helped me connect, I think, also reconnect with the city.

For many of the bloggers I spoke with, blogging served as both a way to vent their frustrations and an attempt to correct misconceptions and clarify information for outsiders. It also became a way of providing knowledgeable and insightful information for locals, especially as this local blogosphere expanded, and of reconnecting with the city. Loki, a [former] chain-smoking, trench-coat-wearing, white native of New Orleans whose ancestry with the city goes back generations, started the blog *Humid City* as an alternative music/culture blog before Hurricane Katrina but turned it into a tool for providing needed information on the response and recovery periods and for documenting an oral history of the flood and aftermath. This was a conscious decision, one he expressed clearly in a September 29, 2005, post titled "Site Mission—A Post Katrina Reconfiguration":

> *Humid City* started out as an entertainment and events site for the local New Orleans area, since the advent of Katrina it has evolved into a networking point for refugees to share resources, discuss our future, and mobilize as activists to ensure that the government malfeasance on all levels during this disaster does not escape accountability.... Please continue to post resources for both survival and activism, but also please post your personal tales and thoughts.... Keep posting resources and political info, but also help us to create a window into these times for those who will come after us!

People's reasons for blogging are associated with the social and cultural traumas they were experiencing in the settling period. Importantly, blogging served both very personal needs and also social needs. People's needs and their reasons for blogging were not mutually exclusive. In the context of disaster and the settling period that followed, people were confronted with a host of problems, questions, and concerns that demanded attention, and blogging served as a useful tool for addressing those compounding issues. They may have started blogging as individuals, due to their own, idiosyncratic reasons, but they were all tied to the broader collective traumas. This is how personal work turns into cultural work. As the city started to settle and shared problems and questions about the city's future and its image in the national eye emerged, the personal became collective, and the personal work of individual blogging turned into the cultural work of collective blogging.

But how do we explain this movement to blogs as collective action? What, theoretically, happened? Action does not arise automatically from collective trauma. As Kai Erikson (1976) noted, many of those who were traumatized by the Buffalo Creek flood were also apathetic and depressed, suffering from a collective internal numbness because they grieved for so long. They had no more energy to give. While many people in New Orleans may be characterized similarly in the wake of Katrina, my attention is on those who did act. Collective trauma and coping are useful for understanding their collective action, but they are not enough by themselves. How might we better understand the collective action of blogging as the city settled from Hurricane Katrina?

Collective Trauma, Coping, and the Cultural Work of Blogging

Sam of *NOLA Slate* related something that happened in a bar in the French Quarter days after Hurricane Katrina:

> Over in the left was this little old man. He was a psychiatrist, and he didn't say a word for the longest time. And we're all drinking and getting rowdy, and he sat there calmly listening to all of us, and finally he says, "Yes, we lost people, lives, houses, entire neighborhoods, but the thing that we will grieve the most is the belief that we have a stake, that we have a social contract with our government. And I don't know if we'll ever get over that." And he's right. In fact, I contributed to a book, *Where We Know*, and I had submitted a piece about that, about breach of contract. And that one wound up in the book and wound up on NPR because there is a sense of—and certainly then and still, we maintain a sense of not being a part of regular America. . . . I don't know that we'll ever get over that.

In the context of Hurricane Katrina and the collective cosmological series associated with the settling period that followed, blogs became valuable and versatile coping tools. They helped people cope with the varieties of trauma they experienced as these shifted over time, serving as outlets to vent their fears and worries, pent-up frustrations, and anger, to offer insights and corrections for outsiders, and to learn about and share what was happening in the city. Personal trauma explains the rise in blogging in the weeks and months after the flood. Collective trauma explains the rise in, and continuation of, blogging over the following months and years, as people found the time and space to focus on bigger issues. It explains why previously existing bloggers continued to write and how bloggers' narratives shifted over the settling period. As more personal and pressing needs were somewhat addressed and as residents' lives became somewhat stable, their attention shifted to broader questions and concerns about the flood, to social needs. Why did it happen? How are things getting fixed for the immediate needs of city residents? How are things being addressed for the future? What is happening with Mardi Gras? At the same time, recovery and rebuilding work was taking place. Authority figures were making decisions on how to rebuild the city, while insurance companies were handling claims and contractors were coming to the city to profit off the rebuilding work. These were sources of social trauma. This kind of trauma disrupts and threatens social life. It involves the breakdown of familiar, predictable routines and introduces significant challenges to organizing and stabilizing social life.

Overlapping significantly with social traumas was the fact that many residents were also beginning to see themselves as "others" in the national eye. Indeed Sam's sense that New Orleanians were no longer treated as Americans was not uncommon, given the sloppy federal response and the national discourse. What was once a national discourse of compassion in the weeks after the flood quickly shifted to a national discourse of contempt, victim-blaming and abandonment. As compassion fatigue set in, people started asking why New Orleans should be rebuilt and noted the supposedly widespread though largely unsubstantiated looting, rapes, and murders occurring in the city (Pignetti 2010). This helped cultivate another form of trauma, cultural trauma, a threat to a shared collective cultural identity, a threat to the core of who people are and the places they are from. People used blogs to read and write about this cultural trauma as well.

At one level, collective trauma and the need to cope with it helps explain the rise of blogging in post–Hurricane Katrina New Orleans and the cultural work behind it, but by itself, this is not enough. After all, responses to collective trauma may vary; people may respond with action or inaction. In order to understand how and why collective trauma fomented action, we must delve a bit deeper. Recall from chapter 2 that the weeks, months, and years after a disaster may be understood as a collective cosmological series, an extended period when a collectivity deeply feels that the universe and all that it involves is no longer a rational and orderly system. The rules and logics on which social order once stood no longer seem in place or applicable. This is a thoroughly destabilizing social condition, one that collective traumas may activate and sustain. But what exactly does this social condition do to us that gets us moving? Here we must turn to a different literature, the literature on cognition, the neurosciences, and the biosocial. Most importantly for my argument is the literature on *embodied autopoiesis*, as this is the fundamental factor that explains action. It is the heartbeat of cultural work.

Embodied Autopoiesis

Psychologists and biologists refer to the continued production of oneself as a process of *autopoiesis*. It involves concerned interaction with the environment and is the basis for teleology and sense-making (Weber and Varela 2002). The creation of meaning involves the interaction between a living system and its environment. It is adaptive, reacting to the immediate environment, the past, and to some degree an anticipated future. Autopoiesis involves *embodied cognition*, with action emerging in real-time interaction between a larger nervous system in a body with particular capabilities and an environment that offers stimuli, opportunities for behavior, and information about those opportunities. The brain and body exist together in a relationship of embodied cognition rooted in autopoiesis that is called *embodied autopoiesis*. It serves as the core bodily mechanism that energizes and orients behavior at a fundamental human level. My theory of cultural work is based on embodied autopoiesis, as it is on this grounding that motives emerge, energizing and orienting collective action within particular cultural contexts.

Embodied autopoiesis involves cognition, the "extraction of significance from the noisy informational barrage that the world generates" (Norton 2020, 51). Most of the time, cognition is routine, and therefore so is much of our action—practical consciousness, automatic cognition, minimal mental effort required or exerted to process stimuli, navigate our environments, and act in relation to familiar and predictable experiences and anticipations. This is cognition on autopilot, embodied autopoiesis on cruise control. The making of significance from our environment and the process of re-creating ourselves is fairly predictable, routine, and familiar. Here, we are very much "meaning-maintainers," as Orlando Patterson (2014) has aptly noted, using cultural tools to reproduce our social worlds according to familiar scripts, schema, and practices. This informs the action of settled times, the role of culture *in* action. Actors rely on externalized, stable cultural scaffolding to guide behavior, taking advantage of cheap, cognitively optimal, and efficient action operating at the level of discursive consciousness (Lizardo and Strand 2010). Existing schemata effectively help us process our environments in predictable and familiar ways. Little in the form of motivation or intention is needed to act. Rather, meaningful action in these settled times largely involves justification (Swidler 1986, 2001a), with intentionality and motive as outliers, arising "when conduct is 'frustrated' in some way" (Campbell 1996, 107). This is action in settled times.

But what about unsettled times, or the "gaps" and "crevices" of settled times, where the cultural scaffolding that provides continuity, routine, and stability is disrupted, when our trusted and taken-for-granted schemata fail (DiMaggio 1997; Lizardo and Strand 2010)? In these conditions, what was once novel and regular is now problematic and must be reexamined (Hitlin and Johnson 2015; Cerulo 2010, 118). Embodied autopoiesis is no longer on autopilot. Cognition requires more attention in order to restore it. These are "problem situations," with the "potential to lay bare causal connections that often go unnoticed in the inertia of everyday life" (Edelmann 2018, 335). Military veterans returning to civilian life (Edelmann 2018), adolescents in the tenuous life stages between childhood and adulthood (Fine 2004), and other transitions over the life course in general (Hitlin and Johnson 2015) represent common "transitional moments" (Edelmann 2018), when we traverse the gaps and crevices between familiar institutions that usually provide continuity, routine, and predictability (Lizardo and Strand 2010). When the ontological and existential status of the world and ourselves is thrown into question (Giddens 1991), when we encounter an ongoing, collective cosmological series, when we do not know what the future holds for us or where we live (as Cliff noted in the epigraph to chapter 1) and the collective traumas we face are constantly shifting and evolving, we must be more deliberate, intentional, and conscious of our action.

Disruptions in embodied autopoiesis and cognition provide a baseline for action rooted in changes to familiar, routine, and predictable environmental stimuli. How we respond to and act toward these environments will be based on a combination of our emotional and mental interpretations. Our emotions speak to changes in our bodily chemical states that drain or energize action as a response to these stimuli. Our mentality speaks to how we understand these stimuli and what they mean to us. The motives to use blogs were related to the chronic collective traumas noted in this chapter, but deeper down, they were related to threats in collective embodied autopoiesis that the unfolding collective traumas symbolized in both feelings and meanings and the need to cope with these.

This is how the personal coping work of individuals and their idiosyncratic problems and needs turned into the cultural work of collective coping. In the wake of Hurricane Katrina, personal trauma shifted into collective trauma, personal coping shifted into collective coping, and the personal work of reading and writing news and information shifted into the cultural work of collective blogging. Shared meanings and feelings associated with collective trauma and the need to cope motivated and gave direction to people's blog use. *This is the causal power of culture, coping with collective embodied autopoiesis in the context of a collective cosmological series over the settling period*: "A frantic need to know what was really happening to the city and its people, . . . a psychic howl of pain and exhaustion and abandonment" (Ray Shea). "It was so chaotic and so weird. . . . [I] would spend half my day either reading blogs or writing about [the recovery] and trying to develop a sense of what's going on in the city" (B.rox). "It's like your identity has been wiped out" (Sam of *NOLA Slate*). "My PTSD doctors figured I started projecting my experiences, because there was a lot of online misconceptions about what happened during the storm" (Patrap). "The stupidity of politicians, the callousness of the so-called school reforms. And the kind of lack of information, and kind of almost secretive nature of information" (G Bitch). "It was like 2006 and 2007, like the post-Katrina when I was still working everything out. . . . I felt compelled to put it out there for the whole world to read" (Cliff). "A sense of not being a part of regular America" (Sam of *NOLA Slate*). What was familiar, routine, and predictable, about both self and society, was destroyed with the flood and remained unstable over the settling period. The cultural scaffolding that sustained reality and the schematic structures that constituted social order had fallen apart, compounded by judgmental outsiders and authority figures who could not be trusted to put the safety and security of city residents before all else. Residents needed accurate and useful news on the recovery and rebuilding work, yet they struggled to find this information, all while key decisions were being made behind closed doors. They needed others to know that the city and its residents were not accurately reflected in the chaos, violence, and laziness depicted on the national news. As the national media abandoned the city, to return during Katrina anniversaries and Mardi Gras, they needed to remind the nation that things were not all right. They were helping each other out, actively working on repairing their homes and rebuilding the city. Despite countless "Katrina specials" in the national media (as noted on the blog *NOitsjustme*), the city was still in disarray and in need of national support. People's ability to use their external environment to create and reproduce familiar, predicable meanings of self and society had fallen apart, as there was no stable external environment in which to do so. They needed a way to communicate these things, but the tools they would typically rely on were not available or sufficient (local news) or, even worse, were part of the problem (national news). Doing nothing was not an option.

It was under these conditions of great personal and collective need that people discovered and turned to blogs. Blogs were versatile tools put to use in the context of an extended cosmological series and the collective traumas of a settling New Orleans. Blogs helped people to access news and information about Hurricane Katrina and the aftermath and to express themselves. Their uses reflected the specific concerns and tastes of amateur media users as these shifted given the social environment and as individual concerns became collective goals.

Cultural work rooted in embodied autopoiesis, a collective cosmological series, and collective trauma helps explain the collective attention to blogs, but this was not the end of their cultural work. The cultural work that energized and directed G Bitch, Cliff, Sam of *NOLA Slate*, and others to blog also informed a richly dynamic collective discourse. It was this discourse that ultimately was the tool to help alleviate uncertainty, vent frustrations, and develop social support networks to cope with the collective traumas of a settling New Orleans. Their collective discourse was a coping resource they built with their cultural work. With this, they created camaraderie and a social support network with each other and then used it to organize and take part in different offline collective actions having to do with the city's recovery and rebuilding process. This is the topic of chapter 4. It illustrates how the reasons for using blogs (writing and reading, personal and collective trauma) were manifest in the blog content and how it shifted in focus over the settling period.

4

Communicating Trauma

The Making and Sharing of Culture across Blogs

The settling period in New Orleans was one of great uncertainty, an extended cosmological series that threatened collective embodied autopoiesis. People were both desperate for information and needed outlets to share what they knew and express themselves. Blogs became useful coping tools to deal with these traumas, a resource to read and write about the response, recovery, and rebuilding periods in a time of extended need. Yet, if blogs were used as tools to cope with collective trauma, then how so? What made blogs effective resources that people put to use to help them cope? If blogging is a medium for communicating and consuming news, commentary, and other information, what exactly was being communicated and consumed? What was the information people used to help them cope? In constructing a collective discourse, these bloggers constructed their own resource to help them cope. A cultural object emerged from their cultural work. What kind of resource did they build? In this chapter and chapter 5, I analyze and discuss the collective discourse that found expression across this local blogosphere.

As people turned to blogs to read and write about the flood and its associated collective traumas, they cultivated a storytelling network that spanned this local blogosphere. This chapter offers a closer investigation into this collective discourse in the context of a settling New Orleans. It offers data on collective trauma blog posts, linking this form of expression to the collective traumas that motivated and gave reason to blogging, as I noted in chapter 3. It shows how, over a twenty-eight month period (from August 2005 to December 2007), the collective blog posts shifted to reflect the locus of power over decisions associated with the recovery and rebuilding periods. At first, bloggers' reading and writing focused on the national level, as FEMA, George W. Bush, and others in Washington,

DC, controlled the decision-making process. As the settling period progressed and decision-making powers shifted to the city, the collective blog discourse shifted onto local authority figures and institutions. Throughout, a narrative on private interests, associated with (national) media, insurance companies, and contractors, remained a consistent underlying theme, as did a focus on regional-level political issues.

This collective blog discourse is a multifaceted cultural phenomenon, simultaneously linking to the past and extending toward the future. It is a product of cultural work in that it is the result of collective action rooted in similar meanings and feelings associated with shared material and symbolic experiences of the immediate past. Here, it is a tool for needed expression and for addressing the uncertainty of the recovery and rebuilding periods. It is an outgrowth of the collective cosmological series and collective trauma of a post–Hurricane Katrina, settling New Orleans. At the same time, it extends to the future, as a mobilizing tool, used to construct understandings and interpretations of the past and present in ways that motivated these bloggers to organize and take part in collective, offline actions oriented toward the city's future rebuilding work. In both cases, it reflects a system of internally related cultural codes, referents, moralities, and archetypes. The fact that this collective discourse exists and the way it was used were due to the "relatively autonomous" causal power of cultural work.

Collective trauma was an important impetus for people to use blogs in the aftermath of Katrina, as a tool both to express themselves and correct misconceptions and to consult for needed information. Collective trauma is composed of social and cultural elements. The social and cultural elements of collective trauma are experienced both materially and symbolically. The material, social trauma appeared to be the first and most significant force, while the symbolic, cultural trauma became an important subtheme that emerged in people's blogging. If we examine the discourse of blogs over a twenty-eight-month period, we can see how these traumas were negotiated and communicated, their shifting qualities, and their relationship with changes occurring over the settling period. This evolving discourse was the material communicated and consumed in the turn to blogging identified in chapter 3. It is an outcome of bloggers' cultural work, a resource people used to cope and, later, to organize and mobilize offline.

Social Trauma in Blog Discourse

On the basis of my interview data, social trauma was a primary impetus for people to start blogging and a common theme in blog posts. Figure 4.1 presents data on the percentage of total posts that touch on social trauma over the twenty-eight-month period that I examined. Looking at these data over time allows us to see how these posts resonate with the changing context of recovery and rebuilding. First, we can see how the incidences of social trauma posts as a percentage of total posts shifted over time, reaching a high point in November 2005 through January 2006 of around 37 percent of total posts. From here, there was a gradual decline in social trauma posts as a percentage of the total, so that at the end of the twenty-eight-month period, in December 2007, social trauma posts represented slightly fewer than 20 percent of total posts. I discuss this decline in chapter 7.

By looking more closely at this content, we can generate some idea of the various sources of this trauma. Figure 4.2 reflects the disaggregated indices of social trauma by focus over this same twenty-eight-month period, taking into consideration national-level, regional-level, local-level, and private interests. From these data, we can see that trauma with national-level referents were the most commonly referenced sources of social trauma for the first seven months after the flood. Here, we see criticisms of President George W. Bush and Vice President Dick Cheney, of Speaker of the House Dennis Hastert and Congress, and of FEMA and its director, Michael Brown. However, over time, and as the recovery and rebuilding periods progressed and local authorities took over more of the decision-making powers, we see a rise in the number of local-level referents. First, for about a year, from March 2006 to June 2007, both national and local social trauma referents appeared at roughly the same rates in the blog-post data, representing on average about 35 percent of posts. However, starting in July 2007 and for the remaining four months, we see social trauma at the local level becoming the most significantly referenced source. These findings are consistent with the movement of control over to local authorities. Over the course of the settling period, local authorities took over the recovery and rebuilding work. At that time, there were more posts about the city's crime problem, criticisms of Mayor C. Ray Nagin and other authority figures of the city, and calls for

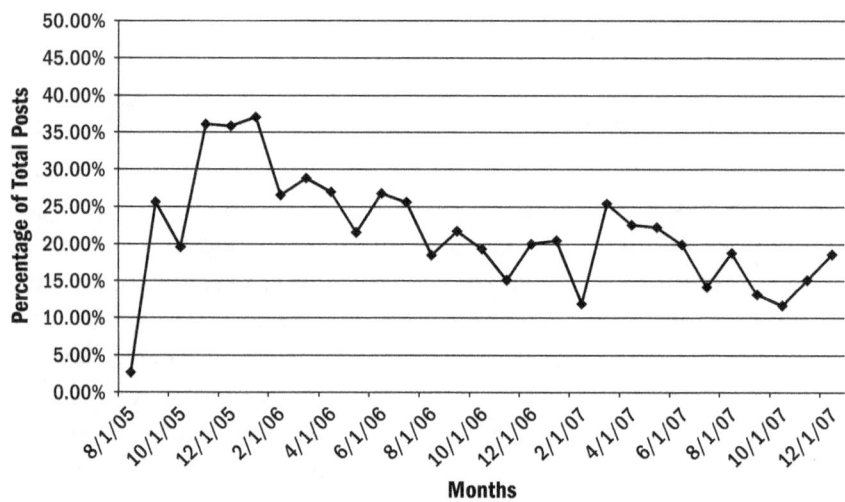

Figure 4.1. Social trauma posts as a percentage of total posts

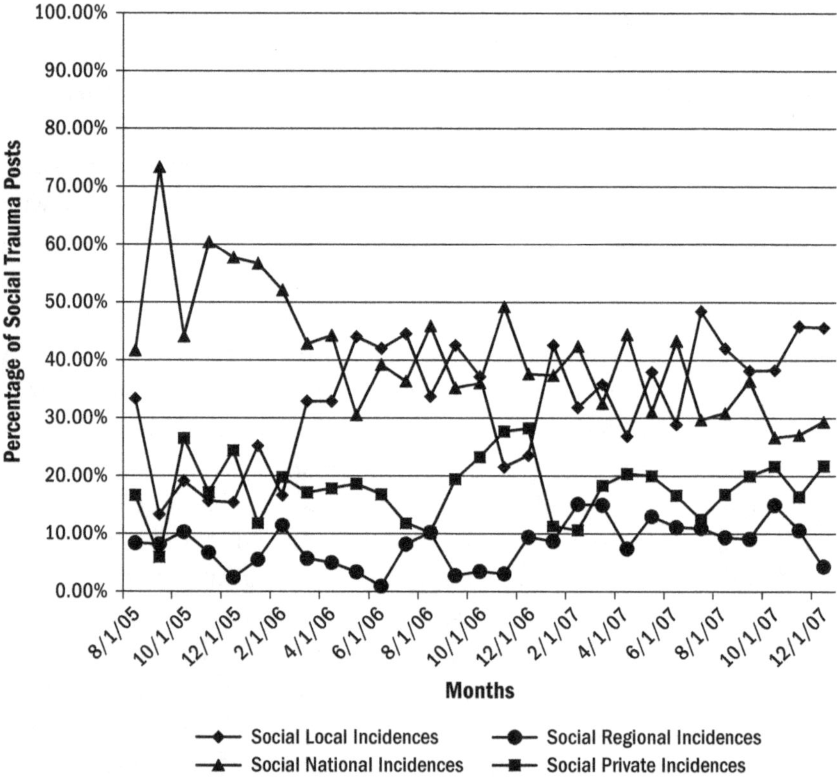

Figure 4.2. Disaggregated social trauma posts: local, regional, national, and private sources

then–District Attorney Eddie Jordan to resign amid signs of incompetence. Figure 4.3 captures this transition in social trauma discourse, as it shifted from national level referents to local referents.

What did this shift look like in actual posts? The blog *Ray in Exile* provides a good example of social trauma directed at national-level referents. In a September 2, 2005, post, Ray told his readers to stick with the local news outlets (nola.com, wwl.com, and wwltv.com) for more trustworthy and accurate coverage of the flood. His focus on Washington referred to the federal government's work on building and maintaining the city's flood-protection system, something that had been controversial for years: "Stick to nola.com and wwl.com and wwltv.com for the real story. Call your elected representatives and demand accountability for those in Washington who committed this act of mass negligent homicide. And donate to the Red Cross."

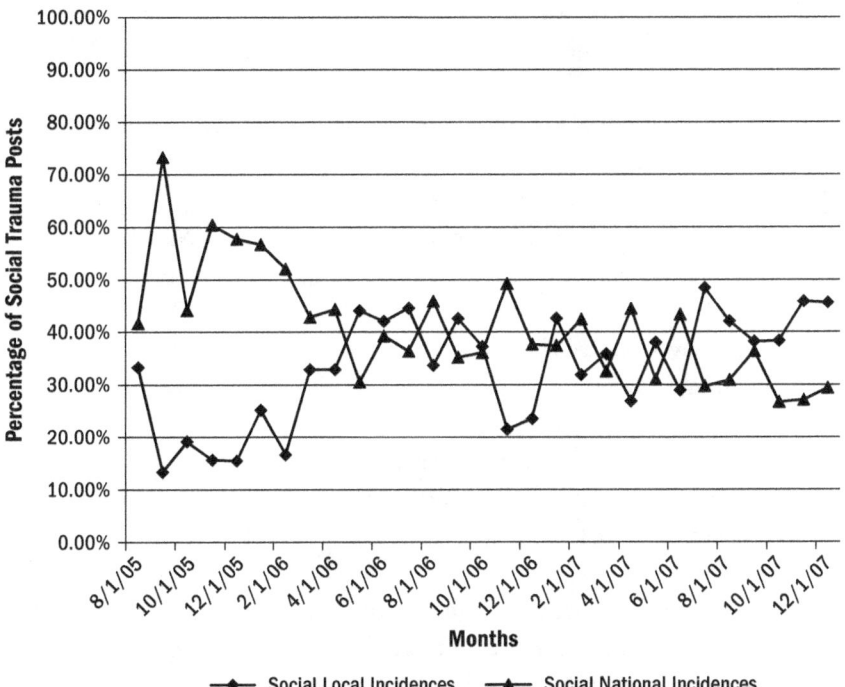

Figure 4.3. Percentage of social trauma posts with national- and local-level referents, by month

Sometimes posts were longer and more complex, touching on multiple sources of social trauma. Here, in a September 23, 2005, post, Library Chronicles, one of the most active bloggers, criticizes both the national government and the city:

> Yesterday I watched two of the most disturbing press conferences yet. The first one featured Bush bristling at reporters whining about how hard it would be to figure out how much hurricane relief would cost the feds. Meanwhile two Senators already had a pretty good idea as to that. Bush, in fact, seemed to be saying that the feds were working (its hard work) to figure out exactly what was the bare minimum they were legally required to spend. And then there was this. Gets weirder every day.
>
> Later in the day, we were treated to a similarly bizarre performance by Mayor Nagin. (So much later in the day, in fact, that reporters on the scene were wondering out loud if they were being kept waiting out of malice.) When the Q & A finally began, the mayor bristled angrily at reporters at one point wondering out loud, "Will you believe me?" before answering the first question. Then came this exchange:
>
> Q: Mr. Mayor, what can you tell us about the leak in the levees at the industrial canal?
> A: I haven't heard anything about that.
> Q: Mr. Mayor, we've got some pictures we can show you. We talked to FEMA crews earlier who said they're pulling people out of the Ninth Ward . . .
> A: Well I haven't heard about that yet. The Corps hasn't told me anything.
>
> This morning, the levee patch has completely failed and flood waters are rushing back into the Ninth Ward. The Corps is calling it an "overtopping." I don't believe that.

As figure 4.3 illustrates, though, the frequency of social trauma posts with national-level referents diminished over the settling period, while the frequency of social trauma posts with local-level referents increased. Library Chronicles' post on the debates over changing the city's school system from later in the recovery period (June 23, 2007, almost two years after the hurricane) is illustrative of this shift:

1) Read this article on the City Council's approval of the adopted Unified New Orleans Plan. Explain in detail how a $14 billion haphazardly brainstormed wishlist citywide rebuilding plan will be funded by a questionable reworking of a $260 million bond issue combined with $117 million in grant money that LRA may withhold anyway in order to fund the Road Home program. What, in your opinion, is the difference between "capital improvements" and "citywide rebuilding" expressed in monetary terms? . . .

2) Consider this quote from Karran Harper Royal that appeared at the end of Thursday's story about corruption on the Orleans Parish School Board. Although some public school critics might use the Brooks-Simms episode to argue against any return of city schools to local control, Royal thinks the balkanization of the system could lead to bigger problems down the road.

"The School Board is just one board with seven members," she said. "Now, with the push to chartering, you've got many, many boards, and many, many members, and there's no infrastructure in place for proper oversight and accountability for things like this. You can't tell me that (U.S. Attorney Jim) Letten will be able to be on top of all these boards like he was on top of this issue. I think an atmosphere has been created for much more corruption."

Do you believe the bizarre experimental "reforms" which have fragmented the New Orleans public school system will lead to more or less incompetence and corruption in the future? Does this incident of employee abuse and corporal punishment of students at one New Orleans charter school affect your answer? Keep in mind that "It can't possibly get any worse" is not an acceptable response as things most certainly can always get worse.

3) Bonus points will be awarded to anyone who can relate their answers to the above questions to a brief discussion of how potentially damaging "reforms" have exacerbated rather than eased the difficulties of rebuilding a post-flood New Orleans due to a "Myth of the Blank Slate" mentality prevalent among its daydreaming residents.

While national- and local-level sources of social trauma were the most commonly referenced in posts, another consistent, underlying source was also due to private interests involved in the rebuilding period. Common private sources of social trauma included insurance companies and contractors, both heavily involved in people rebuilding their homes. In the wake of the flood, construction workers and contractors swarmed to New Orleans for work and to take advantage of the massive influx of federal money directed to rebuilding the city. Many residents felt cheated in the work that was completed and the cost of that work. Homes were partially rebuilt, construction projects were rushed, and shoddy materials were used. Adding to this problem were the insurance companies. Insurance payouts were seldom enough to rebuild people's homes. Insurance payouts distinguished between damage from the rising water and damage from the hurricane-force winds. Residents who had hurricane insurance but not flood insurance were out of luck. Maybe they could rebuild their roofs, but they could not address the water damage that came from the ground and ruined their walls, furniture, and other personal belongings. Residents who had flood insurance but not hurricane insurance might be able to repair their walls but not their roofs or blown-in windows, nor could they replace the "Chinese drywall," which was often discovered months after repair work was completed and paid for. In both cases, insurance payments often covered only a fraction of the work needed to rebuild people's homes. Two of the primary sources people relied on to rebuild their homes and therefore their lives (insurance agencies and contractors) were unreliable, untrustworthy, and incompetent. They cheated people out of their money by finding technicalities to limit coverage and failed to complete needed repair work, adding insult to the deep injury residents already sustained, contributing to their ongoing trauma.

Figure 4.4 presents data on the total percentage of social trauma posts that focused on private interests. Here we see a steady stream of posts on private interests as sources of social trauma, ranging between 10 percent and almost 30 percent in late 2006, as the rebuilding work was well under way. The drop in incidences in early 2007 corresponds with a sharp decline in national-level social trauma posts as well, but with an increase in local social trauma posts. The blogger Dambala, with the blog *American Zombie*, provides one example of social trauma with

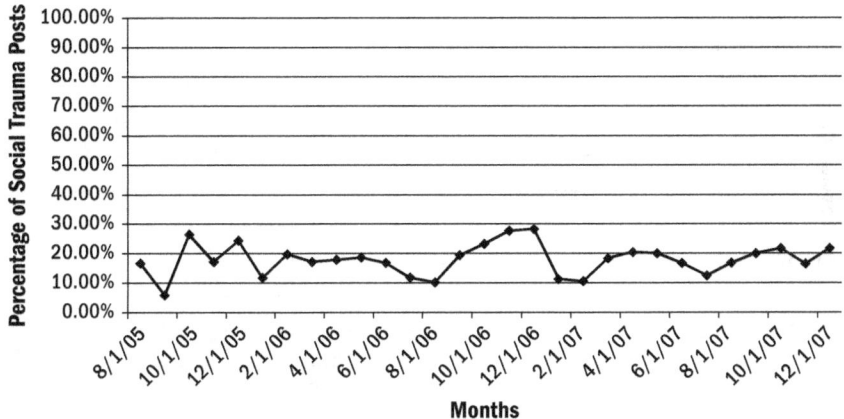

Figure 4.4. Percentage of social trauma posts focusing on private interests

private referents. Writing in late August 2006, just as posts on insurance companies and contractors are spiking, he wrote, "I am still paying a mortgage on a house I can't live in, I can't tear down, I can't sell, and I can't fix. I am suing my insurance company. I can't get Road Home money to fix my house because I had insurance, but the insurance company has screwed me, so I am essentially penalized for having had insurance. I'm still in the same hole I've been in for the whole year."

Finally, figure 4.5 focuses on regional levels of social trauma in blog content. Regional levels mostly referred to the state of Louisiana and then-Governor Kathleen Blanco, as well as sometimes federal authorities, such as the Army Corp of Engineers—the agency responsible for maintaining the city's flood-protection system and controlling the massive water system that surrounds the city—if they were clearly linked to a regional figure. One area of controversy was the Mississippi River Gulf Outlet (MR-GO) canal. In late 2006, early 2007, then-Senator David Vitter of Louisiana was actively seeking congressional approval to direct the Army Corp of Engineers to close it. The MR-GO canal was a 1960s project that involved creating a new, seventy-six-mile-long, artificial canal linking the Gulf of Mexico to the Port of New Orleans. The idea was that this would make it easier for ships carrying cargo to enter the city, but it damaged much of the natural resources that protected the city and surrounding areas from flooding (e.g., seventy-six hundred acres of wetlands, lagoon habitat, and cypress forests). During Hurricane Katrina,

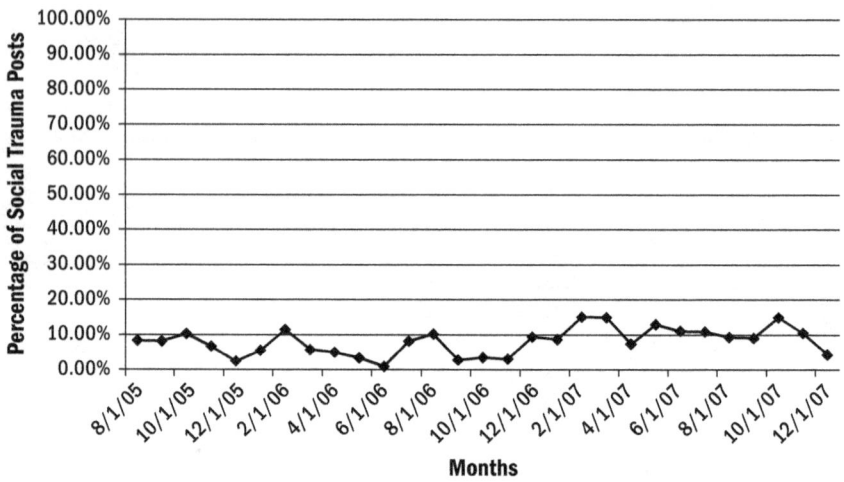

Figure 4.5. Percentage of social trauma posts focusing on regional interests

the canal exasperated problems by allowing Gulf waters to further flood the city. While the canal was a subject of controversy since its inception, it became a larger focus in the wake of Katrina and in debates over its role in the city's flooding. Discussions over the MR-GO canal and its effects on the city's flooding found their way into the local press and among local bloggers, helping explain the small spike in regional-level social trauma posts that occurred in late 2006 and early 2007.

Cliff of *Cliff's Crib* provides one example of a regional social trauma referent. While his focus at first might appear vague, it nonetheless rests on those who built the levees protecting the city and surrounding area, the Army Corps of Engineers. Upon one of his visits back into the city, Cliff took note of the state of the predominantly African American neighborhoods that he and his "people" are from. After his temporary visit back, Cliff said,

> I went to New Orleans yesterday and I have to ask the question. Does anyone care about the neighborhoods where my people lived? The researchers have already proved that the levees failed because the assholes built them wrong. I just posted the article. The least they could do for the citizens of the city now is spend as much money as possible to make our lives as normal as possible and to compensate the families that lost loved

ones. It won't bring anyone back to life but it's the right thing to do. Hurricane Katrina did more to kill my patriotism, state and civil pride[1] in one than any other stupid thing over 31 years. (Day One, January 26, 2006)

Blog posts often focused on several things at once. The sources of collective trauma were not monolithic but multiple, intersecting people's lives in various ways. Blog posts often captured these various sources of trauma and anger in single expressions. For example, the *GulfSails* blogger captures this dynamic in his November 11, 2005, post titled "Secret Government?," a post he wrote at a time when he was working to rebuild what he lost: "We are struggling to rebuild, but while we try and rebuild our homes and businesses, the government dallies over red tape, insurance agencies will not answer phone calls, and other cities strip-mine us of our businesses."

As we can see in these data, social trauma was a significant theme in people's blog posts during the settling period. Disaggregating social trauma by national, regional, local, and private referents offers further insight into this more general trend. National and local levels were the most common sources of social trauma, with private interests and to some degree regional interests being less common over the twenty-eight-month period. Importantly, as power shifted from the national government to the city in the recovery and rebuilding periods of 2006–2007, there corresponded a similar shift in blog content. National referents were dominant sources of social trauma in the beginning months. Then, for the next several months, they diminished. while local referents of social trauma increased somewhat. In the final months of 2007, local referents surpassed national referents as the primary source of social trauma. This transition in blog content tracks pretty closely with the federal government's involvement in the recovery and rebuilding periods, the transition of power to local authority figures, and then the withdrawal of the federal government in the rebuilding periods.

Cultural Trauma

I now turn to a discussion of cultural trauma in the blog content. This was about collective humiliation, especially in the national eye. While cultural traumas were much less a topic in blog posts over the

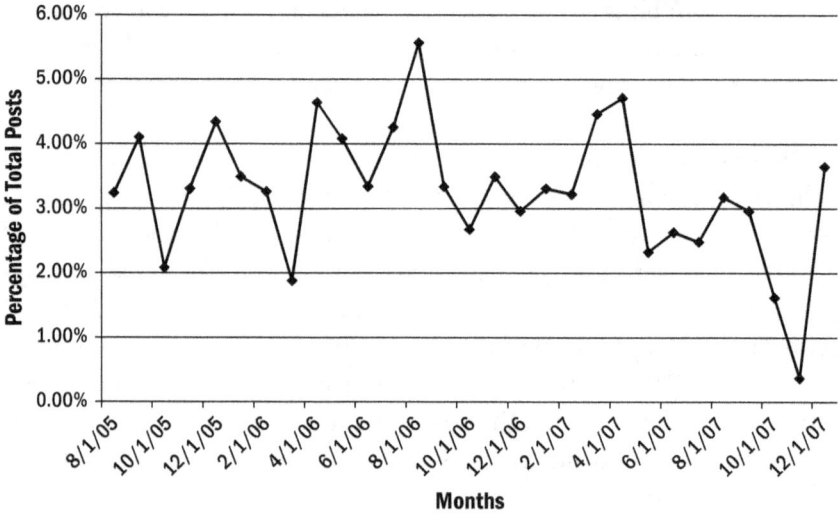

Figure 4.6. Cultural trauma posts as a percentage of total posts

twenty-eight months of the examination period, they nonetheless emerged as an important theme in the collective discourse and in my discussions with bloggers while at various events and during interviews. Cultural trauma is an assault on a social or collective identity. As residents were coping with the social traumas of the recovery and rebuilding periods, some were also forced to contend with what they saw as negative and harmful images of the city and its residents from media outlets and judgmental outsiders. This is a form of collective humiliation, and it added further insult to the material injury of the flood and its subsequent social traumas. Figure 4.6 illustrates the percentage of cultural traumas reflected in the total blogs posts.

There were 335 incidences of cultural trauma noted in the blog posts, constituting a small percentage of total posts. Nonetheless, cultural trauma appeared to be a common theme in my interviews with bloggers regarding why they started and continued to blog. This leads me to believe that while cultural trauma was not very common in the blog content, it nonetheless carried a disproportionate amount of weight as a factor in people's blog use. That is, the significance of cultural trauma in people's narratives was less likely to translate into actual expressions in blog content. In any case, of the cultural trauma posts that did exist, almost half were directed at national-levels referents. Figure 4.7 disaggregates the focus of cultural trauma blog posts by national, regional, local, and private referents.

When looked at by month, national and private interests emerged as initial sources of cultural trauma. National sources of cultural trauma would have referred to national figures, while private interests would have referred to the media or vague, unspecified others (e.g., Fox News or "people," referring to those not from or living in New Orleans). However, as with the social trauma referents, toward the end of the sample period, local sources of cultural trauma emerged as an

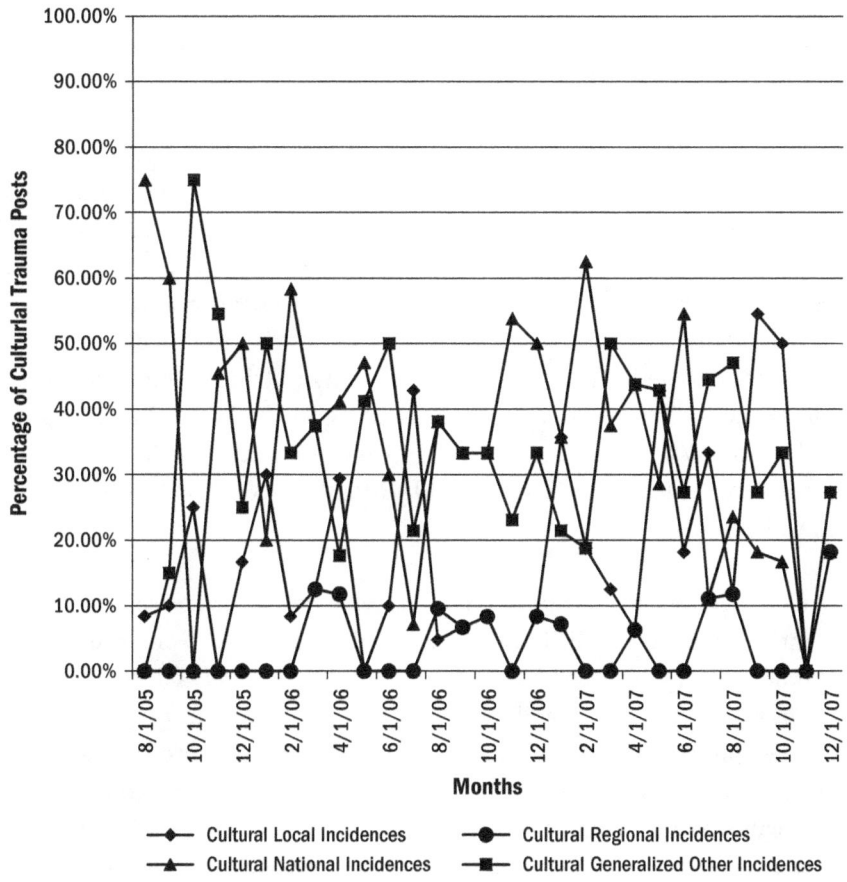

Figure 4.7. Disaggregated cultural trauma posts: local, regional, national, and general sources

important theme, though only temporarily replacing the frequency of incidents referencing national sources. This probably has to do with the national media leaving the city as the flood and its aftermath were no longer sources of continued interest. While national media interest in the day-to-day diminished months after the flood, it returned periodically to check on progress and update the nation. This usually occurred during yearly "Katrina anniversaries" or during Mardi Gras. The return of the national media often reignited frustrations and anger in part because it was shallow reporting and tended to ignore the agency and hard work of the city's residents who were making things happen. Some of the national reporting was also critical of Mardi Gras, asking why the city would host the important holiday celebration given the devastation, another sign of the national media's ignorance of what is vital to this city and the power of street culture to bring people together. Later, stories would focus on resilience and how the city was "coming back," even though many residents were still struggling to get their insurance money and much of the federal help remained elusive, thus giving the impression that the rebuilding was complete. We can see this dynamic in the spikes in national and generalized sources of cultural trauma around August 2006 and August 2007, as these were following "Katrina anniversaries." It is also evident in February 2006 and 2007, as residents enjoyed Mardi Gras, a topic many outsiders were critical of and saw as a distraction from the rebuilding work. Ashley Morris's post on his attending a work meeting (he was employed outside Louisiana) accurately captures this sentiment. In March 2006, shortly after Mardi Gras, he wrote,

> I had a University Benefits committee meeting this week, and some asked me if I went to Mardi Gras. I looked at them as if they were from another country (oh yeah . . . they don't live in NOLA), and said yeah, sure. They asked how it was, and I told them how wonderful the people were, how humorous the floats were, and how pleasant the entire experience was. Then someone said "Well, I know there was some controversy about whether or not to hold it this year." I instantly responded with "Yeah, we decided to celebrate Christmas this year, too." He looked at me for a second, and then got it. Sinn Fein, baby.

Another example may further clarify the role of cultural trauma as a topic among bloggers. Tim of *Tims Nameless Blog* wrote about his experience engaging a blogger who found fault with the city's residents for the slow recovery. Tim replied to this blogger and wrote about his exchange on his own blog. In a February 23, 2007, post, he wrote,

> I stumbled upon a blog that had some fairly callous things to say about Louisiana and our slow recovery from the injuries of Hurricane Katrina. The blog advertised itself as a "right wing" blog, so I should have surfed away.
> But I didn't.
> The blog and its commenters put 100% of the blame for the before, during and after Katrina problems completely on Louisiana and New Orleans. Their view was that President Bush and the federal government had done everything they could and should, and that nothing more remained but for the locals to finish the job. In their view, people here are stupid, lazy and corrupt, and all our elected officials are eligible for a cameo on The Sopranos.
> I thought if they heard more of the facts, they'd understand. I thought if they heard our side of the story, they'd empathize. I thought if they actually interacted with a living human being, they could drop their cruel stereotypes and grasp what their fellow Americans are going through.
> You probably see where this is headed. When I went on that right-wing blog to criticize the federal response to Katrina, they jumped all over me.

Sometimes people posted about their personal experiences with judgmental others but situated their posts within a larger story of cultural trauma. Many of those who evacuated had to deal with outsiders passing judgment on their actions. Cliff of *Cliff's Crib* provides one example from his time while evacuated and staying at a friend's house in Memphis. In a post titled "Words from a Friend" on January 26, 2006, he wrote the following:

> Sometimes . . . i wonder . . . would it just have been better to stay and drown in my home than to have to deal with living in a cruel world.

One of my neighbors this morning ... made a comment to me, that rubbed me the wrong way. Well, she's been doing this for some time now, but i've managed to ignore her up until today. She has helped me with a few rides to places here (I ruined my car evacuating the city, so I have been carless in Memphis since i've been here up until yesterday), but while she's given me rides, she's taken that opportunity to question me about what benefits i may or may not be getting from agencies and whatever else she feels she needs to know about my business. She's made statements to me about not wearing a coat, ... that i am going to get sick and what is my problem for doing that and so on. I never really responded, just blew it off with a smile. ... Of course, this woman never thought to herself maybe this woman lost her coat in her house, ... but u know that was too much like right for her to think that. She sees all my kids have coats. ... Memphis hasnt been all that kind in assisting us here. ... The city is a greedy one, and I personally believe that it has taken alot of things that were for evacuees and kept it for themselves. ... So i bought my kids coats. I have no problem with that because i am supposed to provide for my kids whether the govt gives me coats or not. The mother i've always been, i always do for my kids first, i come after that. ... Whatever they need, they come first. ... I have always done without things for my kids to have what they need. ... I felt them having coats was more of a neccessity than me having one. ... So i didnt get me one ... until a few weeks ago when i could afford to get one for myself. ... I've dressed in layers to keep myself warm in the interim.

This lady saw me this morning with a coat, ... and yeah its a nice one. ... The one i lost was nice, so why shouldnt i have a nice coat. ... Was that the reason she had to say something? Is it jealousy? I would hope not. ... I dont desire envy, ... but I am also not going to short change myself for the sake of making others feel good for me to have less than what they have or what they expect for me to have. So ... anyway, the lady says hello and i say hey, ... and as she is getting into her car she says ... "Its about time u put on a coat" and gets in her car. ...

Folks, yeah, she pissed me off. ... I didnt get ignorant, ... but I felt I had to put her in her place, so i walked up to her car ... and tapped on her window as she was heating it up. ... And she rolled it down and i said ... "I want u to know that, the statement u made offended me. ... The reason i have not had a coat was because i lost mine in the flood water and i had to buy my kids coats first before i could get one for myself. . . . That's why i am just now wearing a coat because i am just now able to get one." . . . She says "oh Im sorry baby . . ." I smiled, and walked away.

If anyone is reading this that is not from New Orleans . . . i want u to understand something and I believe I speak for everyone on this. . . . I dont care what the govt gives us, or how many new things we aquire . . . even if those things are better than what we had. . . . There is something still missing in each and everyone of us. I guess we cannot expect for u to understand it . . . and understand why we continued to live in an economically difficient and crime ridden city. The culture of New Orleans is like no other. . . . The substance of it, is unexplainable. I miss sitting outside with my neighbors on the porch just talking, . . . shooting the sh*t. . . . I miss the children playing up and down the street, riding bikes, . . . and the ones that had bikes, knew the ones that didnt have them so they just let thier bikes sit . . . and said, well, what can we play that all of us can play . . . ? I miss those kids going inside and getting telephone cords to jump rope . . . and playing catch with each other. . . . And there was no happier moment for them . . . then just hanging . . . and that's just a little bit . . . of every dayum thing that we had as a whole that made us happy. It dont never have to make sense to anybody . . . but us. And if i could turn back the hands of time today . . . I'd take what i had over what i have now anyday . . . because i feel like my life was way more abundant than now (Im in tears as i write this).

So . . . please people . . . that arent directly affected by this . . . think before u speak . . . and understand, that life isnt as superficial as u think it is.

To mah Homies from the N.O. . . . Stay Up!

Finally, Varge at *The Chicory* provides another example of cultural trauma directed at national-level referents. He draws attention to CNN and Anderson Cooper in the wake of Mayor Nagin's "Chocolate City" comments during his January 2006 Martin Luther King Jr. Day speech. In his speech, Mayor Nagin talked about New Orleans as a "chocolate" city, meaning a Black city. His comments were widely discussed in the national media and among locals. Varge originally posted these comments on January 17, 2006, but reposted ten months later, on October 10, 2006:

Nagin's comment on MLK Day were troubling and insensitive. But watching CNN tonight just made me realize how out of touch mainstream media is about what is going on down here.

Why are the words "chocolate city" more of a talking point than words like "category-5 levees" or "coastal restoration?" I hate what Nagin said. I think it set us back. But to hear CNN try [and] attempt to grind their axe about Nagin canceling on them and postulating that somehow Nagin breaking away from Bring Back New Orleans to talk about a political gaffe he made the day before is even more insulting.

The show seemed to be a hatchet job. Very little positive was said about Nagin and there really wasn't much as far as well-rounded reporting. I'm not sticking up for Nagin, I just would rather him be meeting with Bring Back New Orleans than getting lambasted by Anderson Cooper.

In this chapter, I have noted the existence and frequency of both social and cultural trauma over a twenty-eight-month period, starting on August 2005 and ending on December 2007. What the collective blog content reveals is that social trauma was a common topic in the blog posts, and the sources of social trauma shifted from the national level to the city level as the recovery and rebuilding work shifted to city officials as well. Private interests were also common sources of social trauma but less so, occupying a steady underlying theme in blog content, especially during the last third of 2006. Regional sources of social trauma were the least common but nonetheless were a present theme, perking up once in a while depending on regional work on flood protection and other issues associated with the recovery and rebuilding period.

I have also discussed cultural trauma. Cultural trauma was a less commonly discussed theme in the blog content, though that is incommensurate with its significance in the interview data and its being an important component in people's narratives and in their organizing later on. While cultural trauma might have represented only a small percentage of blog posts, its significance appeared to be more substantial than that infrequency would suggest. Looking over the twenty-eight-month period, we were able to see how cultural trauma took on a more sizeable place in blog content at certain points in time, especially when national attention returned to the city. This was usually during each August–September for the hurricane anniversary and then in February or March for Mardi Gras. Adding to this were critical outsiders who felt the need to offer disparaging and judgmental comments, whether it be on blog posts, as was the case for Tim, or face to face, as in Cliff's example. I offered several excerpts from the blog content as examples of what these traumas looked like in practice.

While it is interesting to see how collective trauma resonates in the collective blog content over time, so far, I have presented only a thin description of this emergent blog discourse. We can see how the reasons people turned to blogs that I noted in chapter 3 resonate in the collective blog content but only at a surface level. While these data validate the interview data, they provide little insight into what exactly was useful about blogs as coping tools and then mobilizing resources. Nor do they illustrate in more detail how the cultural work of blogging informed the basic frames and themes of the blog posts. I now turn to a thick description of this discourse, where we see a rich, complex, and layered system of meanings and feelings manifesting itself across blog content.

5

The Creation of a Collective Discourse

Forging a New Cultural Resource

The almost complete breakdown of New Orleans's social institutions and infrastructure, as well as the ongoing threats to the shared cultural identities of many city residents, was traumatic. It was traumatic because it threw the world into disarray. What was once seen as predictable, orderly, and familiar was no more, and this was a threat to residents' sense of self and survival, as they could no longer make sense of their environment and their place in it. This was a collective experience that gave meaning and motivation to people's blog use, and it found expression in the blog content on collective trauma noted in chapter 4. But chapter 4 provided only a thin description of this content, the expressions of social and cultural trauma, their general areas of focus and frequencies, and some examples from blog posts.

Yet this discourse is much more. It is dynamic and layered, expressing not only collective traumas and information about them but simultaneously a system of meanings and feelings that resonates with much more enduring forms of communication as ritual. James Carey referred to this as "cultural communication," as communication not only about information but also about sharing and fellowship, a celebration of commonness, communion, community that operates "towards the maintenance of society in time" through the "representation of shared beliefs"; here, communication "draws people together in fellowship and commonality" (Carey 1989, 15). Thick description of the blog discourse reveals its qualities both as a source of necessary information and also as a tool for creating a sense of commonness that was lost with Hurricane Katrina and was much needed over the settling period. I call this an *emotionally laden, moral discourse of archetypes, cultural codes, and referents.* It is a manifestation of collective cultural work rooted in the ongoing and shape-shifting collective traumas and cosmological series of a post–Hurricane Katrina settling New Orleans and its evolving threats to collective embodied autopoiesis. In desperate need for news and information, material on which to establish some sense of reality, predictability, and routine, these "Katrina bloggers" created a new cultural resource, a richly meaningful and emotive discourse they could use to help cope with their trauma. While this discourse is a manifestation of their cultural work beforehand, it is also a resource they will use to inform and motivate their cultural work in the future (a topic I take up in chapter 6).

Let me briefly identify and explain each part of this discourse. First, it is the manifestation of a shared discourse that emerged over people's blogging. This is not about a post or a particular blogger but about the collective themes that emerged across the storytelling network of blogs. To be clear, not everyone contributed equally or necessarily at all to this discourse, but enough people did enough of the time, with some regularity and some more actively than others, that I could identify a collective discourse with distinct qualities. Second, this shared discourse is emotionally laden. It is constructed in a highly emotional context of the settling city and the shifting concerns, questions, and problems people constantly confronted. It is, therefore, packed with emotionality, mostly in the form of fear, anxiety, and anger generated from ongoing uncertainty and humiliation but occasionally in the form of pride and joy too. Third, it is morally meaningful. That is, it is rooted in and communicates broad, abstract moral intuitions about themes associated with fairness and cheating, care and harm, loyalty and betrayal, and other extensive moral foundations that have emerged from our shared experiences as human beings living on this planet for hundreds of thousands of years. They are common to people across the globe and are associated with the extended collective trauma people experienced after Hurricane Katrina. These moralities are performed through equally expansive *archetypes*, or common characters people use to tell enduring stories about right and wrong and that prime and guide interpretation (Campbell 1949; Jung 1969; Lule 2001). Fourth, it expresses particular cultural *codes and referents* that resonate with and are meaningful within particular cultural environments. These culturally and historically specific codes are rooted in shared notions of civility and anticivility as these matter in democratic civil societies (Alexander 2006). They represent more culturally specific manifestations of moral intuitions. Likewise, the cultural referents embodied with these codes and intuitions serve as culturally specific archetypes, common characters playing culturally specific roles relative to culturally specific contexts. Together, these elements constitute the emotionally laden, moral discourse of archetypes, cultural codes, and referents that arose through blogs in the recovery and rebuilding periods of the settling city.[1] This discourse both is a result of cultural work enacted through blogs and is a resource for cultural work enacted in subsequent, offline collective action.

As I noted in chapters 2 and 3 when discussing people's movement to use blogs, the emotionally laden moral discourse of archetypes, cultural codes, and referents I note here expresses both immediate and more enduring meaning systems. In a way similar to Isaac Ariail Reed's notion of deep culture (2015) and social semiotics (Barthes 1972), I organize these into first-order and second-order meanings, with second-order meanings assuming a "deeper" role. The specific discourse of the flood and references to the specific cultural codes and referents reflect the immediate cultural context within a broader democratic society. This is the discourse's first order of meaning. It is situated within a context of the flood, New Orleans, and civil society more broadly. It was the familiarity of this meaning system that was most threatened and shattered in the settling period of post–Hurricane Katrina New Orleans. The second order of meaning involves the moral platforms/foundation and archetypes. These speak to a deeper, more transcendent system of meaning. This is a system of meaning that spans societies and historical periods, grounding and informing the first order of meaning. It is linked to evolutionary developments of embodied autopoiesis that we share as human beings and how we have adapted together to similar questions and concerns associated with safety, survival, cooperation, and living together. This is the "deeper," second-order meaning.

While analytically distinct, these two orders of meaning do not exist independently. Rather, they are mutually codependent. Widespread moralities and archetypes are abstract but made specifically meaningful in how they take shape and resonate within distinct cultural and historical contexts. Likewise, cultural codes are made meaningful in how they express and resonate with more enduring and expansive moralities. Civil and anticivil cultural codes matter because of how they resonate with more fundamental moral platforms and the abstract concerns of safety, survival, and cooperation that underlie their evolution. Likewise, moral platforms are "populated" or made meaningful in how they resonate and manifest themselves in more specific contexts, where the abstract is made concrete. Meanings reflect the amalgamation of both, the widespread and enduring with the specific and current. This helps make it possible for people who may not share a cultural context and its system of signs, symbols, and meanings to nonetheless understand and empathize with those who do. I conceptualize this as a dynamic emotional meaning system. Emotions inform how we process stimuli so as to favor the interpretation of certain moralities and cultural codes, just as they develop out of and are constructed through certain moral interpretations and cultural codes.

In what follows, I present the empirical evidence of this discourse as it relates to each component of the dynamic emotional meaning system in the context of a settling New Orleans and the collective traumas people experienced over time. I begin with the first-order cultural codes and referents and then move to the second order of more enduring moral foundations and archetypes. I then discuss the emotionality of this discourse, completing the dynamic emotional meaning system of cultural codes/referents and moral platforms/archetypes.

First-Order Meaning System of Blog Content: Cultural Codes and Referents

Democratic societies are narratively structured (and constructed) through a system of shared civil and anticivil codes (Alexander and Smith 1993; Alexander 2006). These codes inform an expansive discourse focused on three related areas. These are the motives of actors, the relations they may form from their motives, and the social institutions they may create out of their relations (the specific codes are offered in the appendix). More recent scholarship has found evidence of this discourse in non- or undemocratic societies as well, suggesting both the spread of democratic ideas and values and that there is something more generalizable to the notion of civility and anticivility as it applies to collective understandings of actors' motives, relations, and institutions.

In the context of post–Hurricane Katrina New Orleans and its collective traumas, civil and anticivil cultural codes found expression in the blog content (Ostertag 2016). Here, we see the specific leaders, decision-makers, cultural critics, and institutions as the cultural referents, the objects of collective, civil-minded attention. They populate the cultural codes, bringing their abstract qualities to concrete life. In New Orleans, popular cultural referents were both local and national in scope and included George W. Bush, Michael Brown, Anderson Cooper, Fox News, Ray Nagin, the Army Corp of Engineers, city residents, authority figures, and other bloggers. These were the real-life, culturally meaningful referents and therefore the topics of social and cultural trauma noted in chapter 4.

What does this discourse look like as actual text? Liprap's post on insurance companies offers one example of anticivil codes: "My dad thought that the way the cancellations were done was idiotically priceless. Adjusters driving by, noting whether or not they thought the place being investigated was inhabited or not from behind their car doors, and then driving off to happily cancel policies isn't what most homeowners have in mind when they expect their homes to be 'in good hands'" (March 13, 2007). Here we see the actions of insurance adjusters as irrational and distorted, suspicious and greedy, and arbitrary and factious. These are anticivil codes directed toward private interests. Cliff from *Cliff's Crib* offers another example of anticivil codes: "President Bush was in New Orleans yesterday to let us know that we are not forgotten. Have you ever had a friend that owes you money who always mentions it whenever you two are together but can't seem to find the time to reach into his wallet and give it to you? That's what it feels like whenever we get a visit from the federal government" (March 2, 2007). This post focuses on the national level and discusses President George W. Bush's visit to the city in March 2007. It is anticivil in that it is suspicious as to whether President Bush, or the federal government in general, will follow up on his promise to help the city recover and rebuild.

Bloggers' writing was not all negative, however. In acts of civil repair (Ostertag and Ortiz 2013), they also highlighted progress, agency, and other things that reflected civil codes. Liprap provides one clear example: "It's not much of a secret that the bylines of many of the local news items I've picked on here have had the name of this guy on 'em. You gotta love a guy who bucks tradition right off and goes for the jugular with his column. This city wouldn't be what it is without Chris Rose, and in honor of his most recent honor, I suggest buying his book. You'll be contributing to a few NOLA charities in the bargain, since he donates a chunk of the proceeds from book sales to them" (January 7, 2007). Here we see a post about the local author and *New Orleans Times-Picayune* journalist Chris Rose. Rose is framed in civil ways, both overtly and by implication. By claiming that Rose is "buck[ing] tradition" and "going for the jugular," Liprap is drawing attention to Rose's solidarity with city residents and indicating that he can be trusted. By extension, she presents him as disdaining the same secretive and self-interested "powers that be" and that threaten the fairness and security of city residents in the settling period. Further, by referencing Rose's donations to charities in New Orleans, Liprap frames him as altruistic and honorable. He is someone to be trusted, appreciated, and celebrated for his civil purity among these bloggers.

A second example comes from *Cliff's Crib*. Cliff draws on a similar civil discourse to frame two nurses who created a medical clinic in an underserved section of the city:

> I would like to dedicate this blog to Sister Patricia Berryhill and Sister Alice Craft-Kerney for opening and running the Lower Ninth Ward Medical clinic at 5228 St. Claude St. Number one, it takes a lot of good to sacrifice your personal space for the benefit of the community. The clinic is in Ms. Berryhill's home. Number two, when everyone else was grieving, or having reservations about what to do, these sisters came home and made it happen. Number three, I grew up in the 5400 block of St. Claude St and we used to play football in the vacant lot right next to her house. I don't think she was living there when the church people used to call the police because we were burning ant piles out of the grass. You sisters need a medal from the president or an NAACP award or something. (March 15, 2007)

Here we see the blogger drawing attention to and advocating for the collective appreciation of two "sisters" for their altruism in opening a medical clinic out of their homes. He implies civil motives in these women's active and autonomous actions and their trusting, honorable, and altruistic civil relations with the city, neighborhood, and kids in need.

Another example, from Schroeder of the blog *People Get Ready*, commends the New Orleans Saints (the city's NFL team) and one resident who is rebuilding her home for their loyalty and dedication to the city:

> I salute the Saints for playing an extraordinarily successful season, for committing themselves to New Orleans, for being the vehicle of our hopes and prayers, and for keeping us in the consciousness of the nation when there is so much more do to.
>
> God knows, New Orleanians aren't strangers to adversity. I met a couple living just a football field's length from the new sheetpiling at the breach in the 17th Street Canal levee wall. They know that their decision to be the first ones on their blog to rebuild isn't a rational proposition, but they felt that's what they needed to do. They're making a stand. They are model Americans. They possess the finest of the American pioneering spirit, forging a course of action in a hostile environment—not so much the natural environment, because that can be restored and improved—but a hostile policy environment, or should I say a hostile anti-policy environment. (January 22, 2007)

This post is rich with civil codes. The Saints and the first couple to rebuild their home in their neighborhood (right next to where one of the levees burst) reflect honorable relations with the city and its residents. Further, the rebuilding couple also reflects active and autonomous motives, taking it upon themselves to spearhead their rebuilding despite the presumed passive, suspicious, and arbitrary anticivil codes linked to federal and local authorities that are assumed in the hostile "policy" or "anti-policy" environment.

Often blog posts communicate civil and anticivil codes simultaneously, sometimes overtly and sometimes by implication. Cliff of *Cliff's Crib* provides one example, highlighting an absent federal government, a mayor who could do more but is hindered by the negligent federal government, and residents who are doing what they can to contribute to the rebuilding:

> Mayor Nagin needs to ask the federal government to send him enough extra large trucks and manpower to make massive trash pickups. The little progress that has been made in the city is due to homeowners and

small business men that have come back to clean out and start working on their homes and establishments. How about picking up some of the debris to show them that the government is at least trying to meet them half way. I have to be real about it and say that other than a few crews picking up asbestos, I don't see ANYTHING going on that's related to the government. The locals are putting up a good fight and are trying to save their city but even with people coming back all the time and homeowners vowing to rebuild, the quality of life here will be low unless the local, state, and federal government all do something to make the things around better. (February 1, 2006)

Civil codes tended to have a local focus, noting specific or general city residents, including some people at city hall, other bloggers and critical journalists, or locals who were clearly going above and beyond in altruistic fashion. Anticivil codes were both local and national in focus. President George W. Bush, Mayor Ray Nagin, the Army Corp of Engineers, and other figures and institutions were all topics of anticivil constructions. Sometimes there was disagreement about the civility or anticivility of a specific referent among specific bloggers. For example, many bloggers saw Ray Nagin as largely incompetent or even criminal, but others saw him as doing his best given the situation and the lack of federal help. The presentation of cultural referents coded as civil was often juxtaposed with referents coded as anticivil. Likewise, the presentation of cultural referents as anticivil was often juxtaposed with referents coded as civil. This comparative context allowed authors to better illustrate and justify their points.

Cultural codes of civility and anticivility and their referents represent the first-order meaning system of the blogging discourse. However, it cannot be fully appreciated until it is linked with its deeper, related second-order meaning system of moral platforms and archetypes. Together, these two meaning systems constitute a richly dynamic, emotional meaning system that found expression in blog content after Hurricane Katrina. It is what made the settling period meaningful in ways that were both very specific and also enduring, relatable, and generalizable to other people in the US and across the globe. In the depth and endurance of this meaning system, it served as an important resource for reestablishing predictability and routine, as the cultural codes and referents of the first-order meaning system were thrown into disarray. From here, new social goals and motives arose, resonating with new referents and codes within this unfolding context.

Second-Order Meaning System of Blog Content: Moral Foundations and Archetypes

Having highlighted the first-order meaning system of specific cultural codes and referents, I now address the more abstract moralities and archetypes on which the meanings of cultural codes and referents are built. They are related to the cultural codes of democratic societies in that they explain why civility and anticivility matter. Why might people care about the motives of actors or the relations they form or the institutions they create? Why do active/passive, rational/irrational, or calm/excitable motives matter? Why do open/secretive, trusting/suspicious, or altruistic/deceitful social relations matter? Why do inclusivity/exclusivity, equality/hierarchy, or impersonal/personal institutions matter? More generally, why do we care about justice, the broad theme around which these oppositions revolve? The answers to these questions might lie in moral platforms. These are the shared meaning systems we have developed not as people of distinct cultures, statuses, and other socially constructed domains (the location of first-order meaning systems) but as people confronted with the same problems across domains—problems and questions of survival, safety, suffering, cooperation, and living together that we all must address simply as human beings. I use Moral Foundation Theory (MFT) as my theoretical guide for examining moral intuitions/platforms in the blog content.

These moralities come to life in, and take shape through, archetypes, the common, abstract characters who perform moral and immoral actions according to loose themes such as the hero, wise person, great mother, warrior, trickster, villain, and fool. It is through these archetypes that abstract, free-floating moral platforms like MFT are converted into concrete examples and applied in real situations.

Morals are senses of right and wrong, "prescriptive judgments of justice, rights, and welfare pertaining to how people ought to relate to each other" (Turiel 1983, 3). They differ from norms in that they refer specifically to our treatment of people as people, rather than to our expected

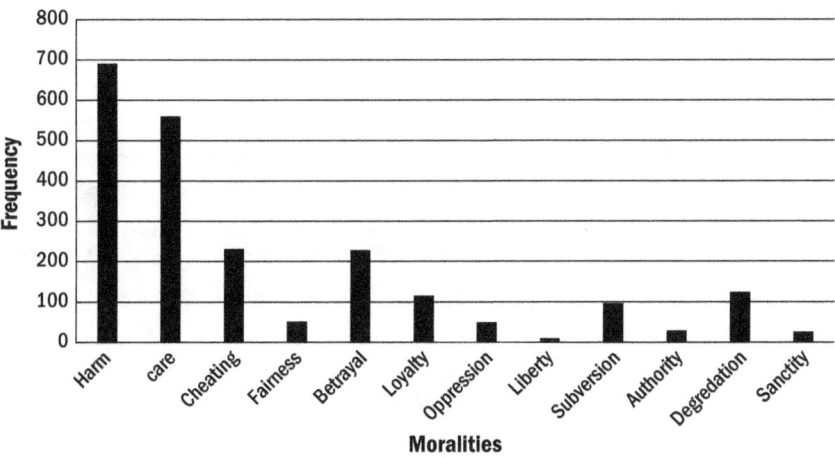

Figure 5.1. Frequency of moralities in blog content ($n = 2{,}181$)

behaviors within particular roles and based on particular statuses.[2] Morals focus people's attention and provide the reasons and justifications for action, and they are manifest in the expressed discourses associated with our action. MFT is a moral platform theory; it is a theory of moral topics on which more culturally specific moralities, cultural codes, value systems, and so on exist. This makes it significantly different from theories of moral judgment. As a moral platform, it shifts the focus away from culturally subjective areas of judgment and onto the collective topics of concern associated with our shared humanity. People construct meanings differently around these topics, which, I argue, is where we may locate civil and anticivil cultural codes and referents associated with democratic societies (i.e., first-order meanings). MFT proposes six moral platforms on which more culturally specific moralities and meaning systems emerge. They include care/harm, fairness/cheating, loyalty/betrayal, liberty/oppression, authority/subversion, and sanctity/degradation (Haidt and Graham 2007; Haidt 2012).

There were 2,181 moral expressions associated with MFT in the New Orleans blog-content data. The most common were harm ($n = 690$), care ($n = 560$), cheating ($n = 231$), and betrayal ($n = 228$). Figure 5.1 provides the numerical frequencies of each of the moral foundations recorded across the sample of blogs.

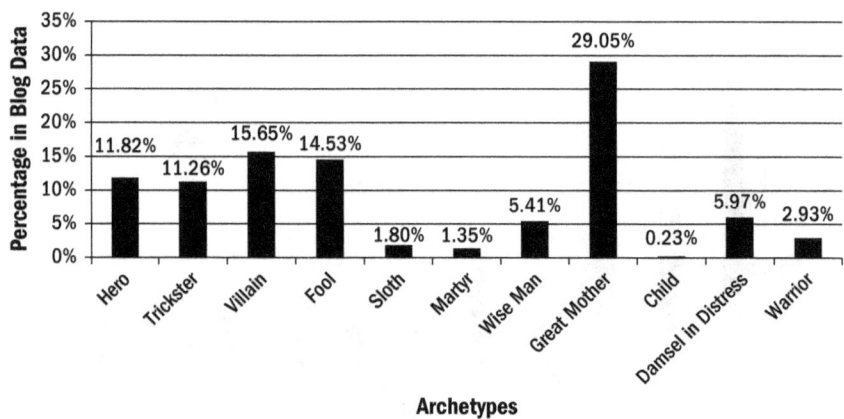

Figure 5.2. Percentage of each archetype in blog data

Just as the cultural codes noted earlier are expressed through the use of cultural referents, moral foundations are similarly expressed through the use of archetypes. There were 888 examples of archetypes in the analyzed data.[3] The most common archetypes were the great mother (258) and hero (105). These represented about 41 percent of the total number of archetypes communicated. They were used to signify civil codes and morally pure foundations. The villain (139), fool (129), and trickster (100) were common as well and together also represented 41 percent of total archetypes. These were used to signify anticivil codes and immoral foundations. Figure 5.2 illustrates the percentage of each archetype recoded in the total blog data.

Consistent with the interview data on the reasons people started blogging, the sources of these moral violations were typically the national media, private interests (contractors and insurance companies), and public authority figures (first national figures and later local figures). For example, Oyster, a native New Orleanian who's blog, *Your Right Hand Thief*, was a popular outlet and resource for many people, highlights a sense of being cheated by private contractors: "After fighting with insurance companies for over a year, Lisa hires a contractor to fix her house, and he promptly screws her over to the tune of many thousands of bucks" ("Things Have Been Bad," June 12, 2007).

Cliff of *Cliff's Crib* uses a personal story of his grandmother to illustrate his sense of betrayal at the hands of the US government: "It's hard not to feel anger towards America when I can't get FEMA to cremate the remains of my grandmother who drowned in her AMERICAN home that she worked to pay for behind a flood wall that the government of AMERICA designed" ("Day Three," February 2, 2006).

Liprap offers a similar story about betrayal, tying it into a variety of sources:

> The news coming down the pike concerning the political messes and the recovery hijinks in these parts continues to be overwhelming. The brain is not only addled by the rising temperatures and the air you could cut with a knife, it is also under pressure from being under a constant state of siege. If it ain't the idiot politicians or the law enforcement failures, it's the stress of rebuilding your place of residence with or without (uhhh, increasingly without) the help of the Winding Goat Path Home or from less-than-reassuring insurance companies. Not to mention finding a good, trustworthy contractor to do the job and do it well without gouging you to within an inch of your retirement fund's jugular. It doesn't help that people who have no clue still persist in dissing the efforts to keep this city on the globe. Grrrr. . . . It is truly akin to playing Whack-A-Mole armed with a teeny jeweler's hammer. (Monday, July 9, 2007)

Importantly we cannot fully appreciate the importance of cultural codes without understanding their resonance with more widespread and historically enduring moral foundations, and we cannot understand moral foundations without understanding their manifestation in distinct cultural codes and referents. Their mutual coexistence allows for their substance. Just as a picture is worth a thousand words, the collective blog discourse is composed of rich and dynamic texts, carrying multiple meaning systems simultaneously and existing at multiple levels of interpretation and significance. Blogging provided an outlet to express and consume moral sensibilities through the telling of personal stories composed of cultural codes and referents. Civil and anticivil codes and referents served as a means to engage moral foundations within a particular interpretive context, turning the abstract and general into the concrete and specific. To illustrate the simultaneity of first- and second-order meanings around the same text, I return to some of the examples I drew on in the first section of this chapter.

Returning to the January 22, 2007, post on *People Get Ready*, we see the moral foundations of loyalty and care signified with the New Orleans Saints for "committing themselves to New Orleans" and "being the vehicle of our hopes and prayers, and for keeping us in the consciousness of the nation," at a time when residents felt national interests were shifting into either hostility or apathy. Likewise, the first couple to return to their neighborhood and start rebuilding also signifies loyalty to the city and its residents. For a comparative reference, the final sentences illustrate the oppositions of loyalty and care (i.e., betrayal and harm), focusing on policy makers as the signified referents. These moralities are signified through the archetypes of hero (referring to the loyal and honorable Saints and the loyal and active couple returning to the city to rebuild their home) and the villain (policy makers who threaten the recovery and rebuilding work of city residents). This post on *People Get Ready* communicates cultural codes of civility and anticivility through specific referents by signifying honorable relations with the city and its residents, active and autonomous motives of the rebuilding couple, and the presumed passive, suspicious, and arbitrary actions of policy makers. Yet it simultaneously communicates moral and immoral foundations of loyalty/betrayal and care/harm through archetypical characters of the hero and the villain. These first- and second-order meanings systems coexist in the same text, linking the generally abstract with the culturally specific and the culturally specific with the generally abstract. This way people in other parts of the world can empathize with suffering residents, and suffering residents can effectively communicate with people in other parts of the world, arguably regardless of their political systems, civic cultures, or other culturally specific systems of interpretation. Outsiders might have no idea who Mayor Nagin is or why anybody would trust their authority figures, yet they might still empathize because of the deeper, second-order meaning system of care/harm or fairness/cheating communicated across blogs. That is, they know what it means to be put in harm's way and to be cheated by those who were once trusted.

Another example from earlier should add further clarity to the coexistence of cultural codes and moral foundations. Returning to Liprap's post from March 13, 2007, we see the moral foundations of harm and cheating signified through the culturally specific referents of insurance adjusters who make their judgments "from behind their car doors,"

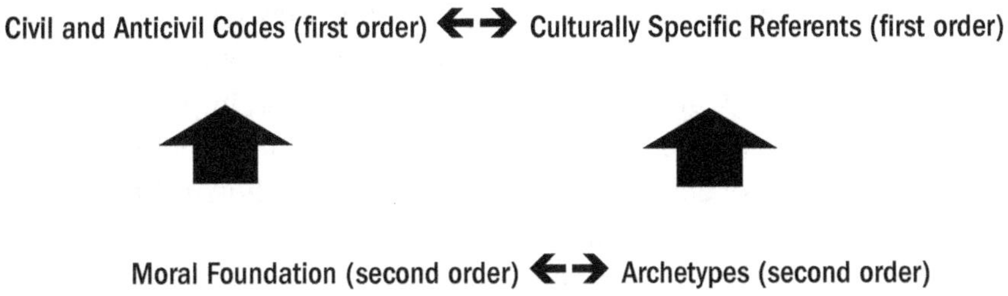

Civil and Anticivil Codes (first order) ⬅➡ Culturally Specific Referents (first order)

⬆ ⬆

Moral Foundation (second order) ⬅➡ Archetypes (second order)

Figure 5.3. Dynamic emotional meaning system

where they "happily cancel policies." These immoralities are signified with the trickster archetype in their dishonesty. Again, this text communicates both cultural codes and referents and moral foundations and archetypes simultaneously. As previously noted, we see the insurance adjusters serving as the cultural referent, acting in ways that appear irrational and distorted, suspicious and greedy, and arbitrary and factious. These resonate with the moral foundations of care/harm and fairness/cheating, as such actions cheat people out of their payments and threaten their livelihoods through the harm that may arise from homelessness. They are signified through more widespread and enduring archetypes, specifically that of the trickster.

We can understand the first-order meanings of cultural codes and referents with the second-order meanings of moral foundations and archetypes as a *dynamic emotional meaning system*. Here, we see the simultaneous existence of a much broader meaning system underlying a more distinct, culturally and historically specific meaning system. The moral topics associated with moral platforms like MFT and their related archetypes inform and resonate with the distinct cultural codes and referents of a given time and place, like civil and anticivil codes of democratic civil societies or civil spheres. In figure 5.3, I offer a simple visual representation of this relationship as part of a dynamic emotional meaning system.

The Emotionality of Blog Discourse

So far I have provided a largely "meaning-centric" analysis, but there is more to this discourse than strict meanings, even if they are dynamic and layered. The discourse of blogs in settling New Orleans was also wrought with emotionality. Emotionality is a key source of cultural power and action (Collins 2004; Jasper 2018) and an important factor that links the general meanings associated with moralities with the more specific meanings of cultural codes. *That is, emotionality sufficiently captured in writing and expressed through blogs (and other media) serves to effectively link moral foundations and cultural codes in internally consistent ways.* For example, anticivil codes and immoral platforms are related in part because they elicit and reflect the same unpleasant emotions, such as fear, anxiety, worry, and anger. Likewise, civil codes and morally pure platforms are related in part because of how they resonate with pleasurable emotions, such as happiness, joy, and pride. Moreover, effectively expressing emotionality in blog posts may transfer to readers. Just as when we read a book or news article that makes us cry, laugh, or get angry (Wahl-Jorgensen 2020), blog posts in the wake of Hurricane Katrina may do the same. As such, these emotions help foster a relationship between reader and writer, nurturing social ties and motivating collective actions related to the moral foundations/archetypes and cultural codes/referents. This was the case for both those who directly experienced the flood and its aftermath and those who were experiencing it from afar.

Emotions refer to the affective states of consciousness. They are feelings we experience based on our internal, bodily environment, the manifestation of endorphins that compel us to action or drain us of energy. Emotions are the real motivators of action (Collins 2004; Goodwin and Jasper 2006; Jasper 2011; van Troost, van Stekelenburg, and Klandermans 2013). They provide the energy needed to put one foot in front of the other. Without emotions, there is no action; we are only motionless bodily masses that think. This is particularly the case for activating emotions. These are emotions that fuel energy, where action may serve as a means of coping. Common activating emotions include pride, anger, happiness, and fear. Emotions are also fundamentally important in the telling of stories and among social movement leaders (Polletta 1998). They help focus attention, foster collective solidarity, and motivate collective actions (Goodwin, Jasper, and Polletta 2004; Jasper 2018). Written in a highly emotional context of a settling New Orleans and the shifting traumas that characterized it, blogs were wrought with emotionality.

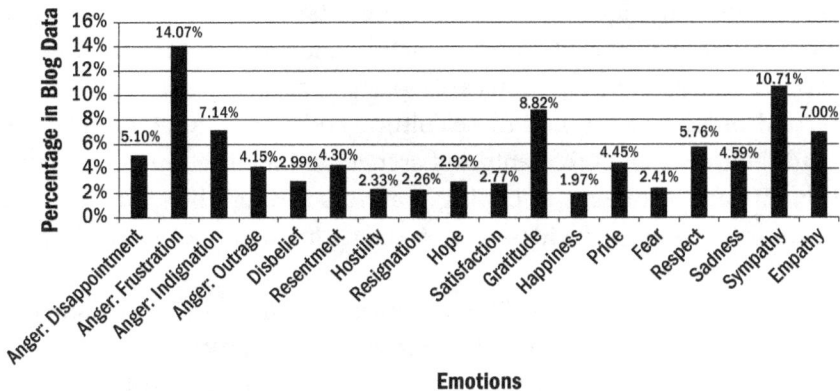

Figure 5.4. Emotional expression in blog content

There were 2,355 emotional expressions in the 2,334 units of text among seven blogs that were coded. In total, anger accounted for 944 of them (or roughly 40 percent).[4] The fact that anger represented so much of the total emotional expressions recorded in blog content was not surprising, as senses of incivility and immorality would resonate with feelings of anger. Anger is considered a secondary emotion and closely related to anxiety and fear. It may arise from a sense of loss of control, attributions of blame on sources of anxiety, or extended activation of one's fight or flight system (Esposito 2016). In the wake of Hurricane Katrina, many people's anger was ultimately rooted in collective trauma and the ongoing cosmological series they experienced. It was rooted in (1) threats to a shared cultural identity due to public humiliation (thus anger with the national media and "outsiders" passing judgment on the city and its resident) and (2) problems and concerns over the rebuilding of the city's infrastructure and institutions (anger over the harmful, greedy, and suspicious actions of political figures in their relationship with residents in need). These were sources of ongoing uncertainty, risk, and humiliation, threating how residents' lives and the lives of loved ones might unfold, given how the social and cultural traumas endangered the recovery and rebuilding periods and the image of residents as deserving of compassion, support, and help.

These sources of collective trauma were common during the settling period, as the national spotlight shown on the city and its residents and as authority figures and private interests took part in the recovery and rebuilding of the city's infrastructure and social institutions. From this, we can see how emotions are closely related to the first-order and second-order meanings, as these cultural codes and moral foundations (and their associated referents and archetypes) are the sources of emotionality and the focus of coping practices through blog writing and reading. Figure 5.4 provides data on the commonality of each emotion examined in blog content.

Dambala's post from the blog *American Zombie* provides a good example of anger (expressed as frustration) and its linkages to first- and second-order meanings. Here, he expresses his anger with city leaders and their inability to adequately address the city's crime problem, a constant source of fear and anxiety that rose to heightened levels toward the end of 2006 and into early 2007. It was also a source of public humiliation given the national attention it received and what it suggested about the city's residents and their ability to recover. Calling out Mayor Nagin and Police Superintendent Warren Riley, he wrote, "I don't know about the rest of you . . . but I feel incredibly frustrated with our city's leadership and their utter failure on so many fronts, violent crime being the most obvious. . . . The blog community is obviously outraged, as is I suspect, the community in general. In the same week Nagin and Riley are publicly stating that we're making progress. . . . We have almost twice as many New Orleanians murdered than American soldiers in Iraq" ("A War against Tourism??," January 6, 2007). Dambala is frustrated, and his frustration is linked to the dynamic meaning system I just discussed. Cultural referents are the city's leadership, namely, the mayor and police superintendent. Anticivil codes include passivity and irrationality, as both Nagin and Riley appear not to be taking enough or the correct action on the problem of violent crime. The moral foundation of harm is reflected in the concern over victimization associated with the high levels of violent crime in the city. Archetypes include either fools or tricksters, as the mayor and police superintendent might be either incompetent or deceitful.

Liprap provides another example of anger, this time with insurance companies:

> An Allstate "relations manager" claims that because Allstate has been around 75 years and insures more than 17 million households, they

are acting neither unethically nor illegally. She says that after Katrina changed the world and insurance industry, it is Allstate who is "stepping to the plate first to find solutions that help protect and prepare citizens, while making sure our company can continue to insure as many customers as responsibly possible." . . . Folks, the above is an idiotic and very unethical response for a number of reasons. I can talk about two of them without cursing until I am blue in the face. (May 13, 2007)

Like Dambala, Liprap is also angry, which is also linked to the dynamic, emotional meaning system. Her anger has a clear target and reasoning. She is angry at the insurance company and its representative, the "relations manager." This is the cultural referent. They are seen as suspicious, deceitful, and greedy in their relations with city residents (much as the "drive-by" adjusters noted earlier). These are the anticivil codes. They are also seen as cheating and betraying their customers, as insurance settlements were notoriously problematic. This is accomplished through the archetypes of the trickster, promising one thing but not delivering on it when the time comes.

Next is a post from *Cliff's Crib*, where Cliff sarcastically voices his frustration with an internet provider that did not follow through on its promise in the wake of the flood. He also touches on a related theme of cultural trauma, involving the perception of New Orleanians among people outside the city. These were both sources of anger and motivators for blogging. They were widely shared meanings and feelings and helped cultivate ties among similarly situated others.

> I would like to take this time to recognize EarthLink for being the latest company to go back on a promise it made to the city. They announced that they will not be expanding their free internet service throughout the rest of the city, giving everyone outside of Uptown and the French Quarter another reason to feel envious. I guess I should not be writing about this. I probably owe everyone at EarthLink and around the country an apology. I forgot that New Orleans is the only city where anyone who expects people to live up to things they committed to is a whiny, lazy, and shiftless bastard that can't do anything for themselves and is constantly looking for a handout. Foolish of us to expect that when someone stands

up in front of the public and tells you they are going to do something you are supposed to believe them. ("Another Broken Handout," September 4, 2007)

Finally, I provide Ashley Morris's post "FYYFF." Ashley is a friendly guy, passionate about the city, and, as I was told, always willing to invite you to his house for a beer and cigar on his porch. His post would become a famous post among these bloggers. It effectively captured their shared senses of cheating, betrayal, and harm and feelings of humiliation, anxiety, and anger, linked clearly and decisively to specific anticivil referents. Bloggers circulated this post widely, talked about it among each other, and mentioned it as important for their movement into offline action as it served as a kind of unifying expression.

Fuck you you fucking fucks.

I don't give a damn what the hell you Yankees/Texans do, do it in your own yard, and shut the fuck up. We don't care what you do, and we don't want your damned PVC sided beige square houses uglying up our town. Go home, and quit looking at my home as simply a chance to line your wallets.

I'm so glad all you Chicagoans have figured out exactly how to fix New Orleans. Look at your own nasty city and explain why you can't deal with the snow other than to throw tons of salt on the road, and why you can't buy a beer for under $5. Fuck you, you fucking fucks.

What about you fucks that don't want to rebuild NOLA because we're below sea level. Well, fuckheads, then we shouldn't have rebuilt that cesspool Chicago after the fire, that Sodom San Francisco after the earthquakes, Miami after endless hurricanes, or New York because it's a magnet for terrorists.

And fuck Kansas, Iowa, and your fucking tornados.

Fuck you, San Antonio. You aren't getting our Saints. When I get to the Alamo, I'm taking a piss on it. You probably go to funerals and hit on the widow. Classless fucks.

Fuck you Houston and Atlanta. No matter how many of our residents you steal, how many of our events you pilfer, you still ain't got no culture. One of our neighborhoods has more character than all of your pathetic cookie-cutter suburbs laid end to end. Fuck you, fuck you all.

Fuck you Tom Benson. I hate you on so fucking many levels, but the main one is this: they aren't your Saints, they're ours. The NEW FUCKING ORLEANS Saints. All you had to do was say that you were coming back. But you didn't. You had to fuck around to try to get more money. Fuck you, you greedy bastardo. Don't think we haven't noticed that you have phased out all of the merchandise that has the state of Louisiana on it. Don't think we haven't noticed how hard it is to get some Saints merchandise that actually says "New Orleans" on it. Fuck you, Fuck San Antonio, Fuck your whole fucking family. And if you and Rita think that anybody is going to patronize your car dealerships, then you got another thing coming, fuckface.

Fuck you New York. You lose a neighborhood and get scads of federal aid. We lose an entire FUCKING COAST, and the freespending W administration finally decides to become fiscally responsible. And fuck you all for taunting the New Orleans Saints fans, who have to deal with playing a home game in the Meadowlands. Fuck you, you classless motherfuckers. New Orleans donates a fire engine to the FDNY after 9/11, and you give us shit. Fuck you, fuck your town, fuck your residents, fuck your politicians. You. All. Suck.

Fuck you governess Blanco. Get your act together. Get a clue, or at least hire somebody who does.

Fuck you army corps of engineers. You are so full of yourself, and you don't have clue fucking one. Building levees on jello. You should be tried and convicted of treason, or mass murder. Fuck you all, let's give our money to the Dutch—they seem to have this shit figured out.

Fuck the Bush administration. Putting Mike Brown in charge of FEMA, you clueless fucking scalawag. You said "we will do what it takes." Then do it.

Now.

Bitch. ("Fuck you, you fucking fucks," November 27, 2005)

Ashley Morris's post is an emotionally laden moral expression of treasonous betrayal, tricksterism, and outrage directed at greedy, suspicious, and deceitful cultural referents. Immoral and anticivil outsiders who see the flood as an opportunity to line their wallets while "uglying" up the city, politicians and a broader public that do not want to rebuild the city, cities that are eyeing the New Orleans professional football team and the team owner's (Tom Benson) lack of loyalty to the city, Governor Blanco's incompetence, George W. Bush and Michael Brown's incompetence, the Army Corp of Engineers' smugness and the harm it caused in the levee system it constructed and maintained to protect the city from flooding—these are the multiple sources of moral and cultural anger that many bloggers shared and communicated. They coexist in a rich, emotionally laden moral discourse of archetypes, cultural codes, and referents, one that reflects previously existing feelings and understandings and one that came to serve as a rallying cry for many in this local blogosphere to take action offline.

Compassion and Bonding: Sympathy and Empathy at Work

Not all emotional expressions were of anger. Others were common as well. Sympathy and empathy were also represented in the blog content. Together, these capture compassion. This is an emotion we give and receive. We extend compassion to others whom we see as deserving. Likewise, we earn compassion when we are seen as suffering from no fault of our own. Like anger, compassion is also a complex emotion, but in a different way. Compassion is a combination of sympathy and empathy. These are feelings others extend to us; compassion is a gift of validation, support, and encouragement. If anger, anxiety, and fear are emotions related to pragmatism and the unfolding questions and concerns of uncertainty, compassion reflects the normative dimensions of emotionality. They speak to issues of social belonging, pride, and similar social goals. Note their relationship to anger and the anxiety, fear, and humiliation that grounds them. Compassion, as a prosocial emotion, is possible only as it is related to anger, anxiety, and fear, these more pragmatically grounded emotions. There is an intimate relationship between pragmatic and normative motives and how they operate together as cultural work.

Common expressions of compassion were directed at other bloggers, journalists, and writers and other city figures. For example, writing only a month after the flood, the *GulfSails* blogger expresses his gratitude to then–Police Chief Eddie Compass (along with other members of the New Orleans Police Department, NOPD), linking him clearly to the hero archetype: "I also want to express my thanks, sympathy and understanding to Police Chief Eddie Compass. You are indeed a hero, as are the vast majority of the NOPD" ("Brownie Introduce Me to My Hackles," September 27, 2005).

Next, Liprap expresses her appreciation for the small amount of progress that is taking shape and nearing completion, as well as the generosity of her neighbors:

> I'm able to deal with our neighborhood, more or less. There are some blue roofs around, the apartment house across the street is going through major renovations, which are nearing completion (and which are a joy to behold for a three-year-old in love with Bob the Builder cartoons), some piles of debris in front of other houses in the throes of renovations and repairs, and fewer trees in the park we frequent to let my dog do her thing and play with other neighborhood pooches. It helps that I love our house and that we have good neighbors, with whom we shared some crawfish pies and the recipe for them last night, after they offered us the extra crawfish they had leftover from a boil they had the night before that. I am thankful for those things, and for the efforts people are making in the immediate vicinity. (no title, March 6, 2006)

In the following example, Ashley Morris expresses his compassion for New Orleans's musicians, many of whom lost not only their homes but their livelihoods with the loss of their instruments. Here, he puts out a call for people reading his blog to do what they can to help, as do so is not only beneficial for the individual musician but for the city more broadly:

> Today, I dropped off an alto sax at Tipitinas,[5] where I met Lips. The Tipitinas Foundation is caring for the general welfare of many New Orleans musicians, and providing them with instruments whenever possible.
>
> Many musicians lost their instruments in the flood, and while it's bad enough that they lost a piece of their life, they also lost their means to make a living.
>
> It's easy to donate an instrument. Either contact the Tip's foundation and set something up, or drop by during the week before 6:00. You can deduct it from your taxes, and you'll be helping New Orleans stay New Orleans, and help New Orleans musicians stay IN New Orleans. ("NOLA Musicians Still Need Your Help," May 22, 2006).

The emotionality expressed in blog posts was an important element of this richly meaningful collective discourse. It served two critical rolls. First, it helped link the first-order and second-order meaning systems in internally consistent ways, providing a theoretical tool for understanding their relationship and an explanatory factor for understanding motivated action based on these meaning systems. Second, the data on emotions reveal that anger and compassion were the most common in the blog posts. This combination is important because it was key to the interactions among blog users (writers and readers), the development of trust and the voluntary social relationships that ultimately led to the cultural work of offline organizing and collective actions (see chapter 6).

Conclusion

This chapter builds on chapter 4 to illustrate how collective traumas and the cultural work they energized not only manifested themselves in blog content but informed a "storytelling network" fomenting an emotionally laden, moral discourse of archetypes, cultural codes, and referents. Here, I provided a thick description of this discourse as a complement to the thinner description captured in the frequencies and rates data presented in chapter 4. I used the thick description to argue that this discourse consists of multiple meaning systems and complex emotionality. I noted how it expresses simultaneously both a first-order meaning system of cultural codes and referents and a second-order meaning system of moral foundations and archetypes and that these must be understood together, in tandem, where each is made relevant and important because of its relationship to the other. I then explained how the distinct cultural codes and moralities of these meaning systems are embodied in specific referents and that these referents signify common archetypes that help in guiding interpretation. Here, I claimed that in a settling New Orleans, in the first-order meaning system, Mayor Ray Nagin, President George W. Bush, and other authority figures and private interests (mostly contractors and insurance companies) were common cultural referents for anticivil codes of greedy, self-interested, suspicious, and irrational. As second-order meanings, they represented the archetypical tricksters, fools, and villains associated with immoral foundations of harm, cheating, and betrayal. These are the first- and second-order meanings that make up the dynamic emotional-meaning-system framework.

Then I discussed the emotionality expressed in this same discourse and how it related to the meaning systems and was an important mechanism in unifying these meanings into a comprehensive homologous relationship with potential causal power. Emotionality informed the system of feelings that emerged with these collective traumas and provided the linking mechanisms that connected second-order moral foundations/archetypes with first-order cultural codes/referents in consistent ways. The relationship of the expressed emotions with the two meaning systems and with different emotions are important for the offline cultural work that these bloggers take part in (the topic of chapter 6). Anger and compassion were the most common themes of emotionality. This makes sense given the collective trauma and use of blogs as coping mechanisms. Blogs were a place for people to vent their anger, anger arising from their ongoing fear, anxiety, and humiliation, and so they did. It was also a place to extend compassion to others, others who were seen as rightfully angry about their treatment in the recovery and rebuilding periods or who were seen as getting undue criticism from judgmental outsiders.

Blogs and the act of using blogs reflect both the transmission and ritual views of communication. Blogs were sources for needed information on the specifics of the flood and the recovery and rebuilding work. This reflects communication as the transmission of information and may be best reflected in the first-order meaning system. At the same time, blogs were also means of communication that cultivated fellowship, camaraderie, commonness, and community around shared understandings. This reflects communication as ritual, cultural communication and the "construction and maintenance of an ordered, meaningful cultural world that can serve as a control and container for human action" (Carey 1989, 15). This may be best reflected in the second-order meaning system. Both meaning systems exist simultaneously in the blog discourse and contribute in different ways in the coping process, (1) by providing needed information about specifics and (2) by reestablishing basic senses of right and wrong in a communal process of sharing.

This blog discourse is both an outcome and a motivator for cultural work. It is an outcome of cultural work due to the collective traumas people experienced and their need to cope with them through writing and consuming information over blogs. It is a motivator of future cultural work in that, through the development of some shared agreement on the appropriate codes and referents, morals and archetypes, and emotional expressions, it helped people cultivate trusting social relations and encouraged other coping strategies in the form of collective actions. These are both forms of cultural work. The emotionally laden moral discourse of archetypes, cultural codes, and referents is a result of cultural work occurring beforehand, as such work was necessary in order to make this discourse in the first place, and is evident in the reasons people began blogging. It is also a resource in motivating and directing the cultural work occurring later, after its initial development, as people worked together to take part in a variety of collective actions offline. This is the topic of chapter 6.

6

Blogging and Collective Actions

Mobilizing over the Settling Period

Blogs were helpful resources that a number of New Orleanians used to cope with the collective traumas they experienced due to Hurricane Katrina and the settling period that followed. They used blogs to vent their frustrations and express themselves and to find trusted information and verify thoughts and beliefs. In so doing, they created a richly complex collective discourse of meanings and feelings. While itself a manifestation of cultural work, this discourse turned into a powerful tool for subsequent cultural work in the form of community building and offline collective action. This took time, with blogs and the collective discourse I noted in chapters 4 and 5 serving as key resources in this process. Through blogging, users cultivated trusting social ties and voluntary social relationships and developed a social support network that nurtured a sense of community and collective identity as "Katrina bloggers." With these mechanisms in place, they organized a number of different collaborative actions geared toward different needs over the settling period. Some of these offline actions were about camaraderie and were intended largely for themselves; others were about asserting power over the city as it rebuilt, highlighting signs of progress and regress. Some were short-term one-offs, while others were about creating something more lasting. Some were the product of individuals working to serve broader social needs; others were more complex, involving both blog users and nonusers. These are also examples of cultural work, though cultural work that emerged later, after people's collective turn to blogs and the creation of a shared discourse. In this chapter, I show how the collective discourse that bloggers created served as an important cultural resource in their creation of a digitally mediated social support network composed of trusting social ties and relations and a shared identity and sense of community. Having built this sense of solidarity through their collective blog discourse and coping practices, many then took part in various offline collective actions.

Anger and Compassion

In the wake of Katrina, anger became not just a short-term feeling but a more entrenched and lasting moral emotion focused on long-term goals (Jasper 2018). What were episodic insults and injuries of cheating, harm, and incivility became a steady, continuous flow, the "furious rage as insults piled upon injuries" that Ray Shae noted in chapter 3—something almost to be expected and anticipated when dealing with social institutions, organizations, and agents as part of the rebuilding period. The constant fear, anxiety, worry, and humiliation of collective trauma and an extended cosmological series cultivated an ongoing current of anger. Anger may have started as more sporadic and reflexive, but over time, as people had to deal with the settling period, it became a more enduring, underlying moral emotion guiding shared action around shared moral and cultural codes.

Emotions are seen as short run, medium run, and long run, referring to how long they last. Most emotions are thought of as short run; they are fast-thinking emotions related to a specific stimulus. They emerge quickly and then disappear just as quickly. But other emotions are medium run, and still others, such as moral emotions, are long run and slow thinking; they are more constant feelings that guide long-term, more strategic action (Jasper 2018). As a medium-run emotion, anger clouds our approach to, interpretation of, and experience with each other, and it follows us around for a while. As a long-run emotion, anger is a constant state of being; it informs our slow thinking and our strategies on how to deal with ongoing grievances. *This is how shared emotions and meanings foment causal cultural action.* While the anger among New Orleans blog users had several sources (cheating, harm, and incivility and their respective referents), it is best thought of as having shifted from short to medium to long run, as the settling period progressed and the collective traumas persisted and unfolded. In this context, the moral emotion of compassion (composed of sympathy and empathy) was a welcome relief. Compassion is a moral emotion that informs affective commitments and the respect, trust, and admiration for others (Jasper

2018). Compassion is a gift people extend to each other. It confirms what residents thought and felt, their anger, fear, worry, and anxiety directed toward agreed-on referents. In so doing, it allows for a temporary relief of anger through validation and was a key source in the emerging social support networks that developed among bloggers. Further, as an affective commitment, a gift extended to others, compassion was a key force in the development of trust, social ties, and relations. *It was the combination of anger and compassion, as they relate to each other in the long run and around agreed-on moral and civil codes, that became manifest in their cultural work.* It cultivated their senses of solidarity and the offline collective actions that many took part in as they sought to engage New Orleans in the settling period.

Collective Actions

The collective actions I discuss in this chapter are the result of two related emotional/meaning systems, one strictly of the need to act, to move and "do something." I call this the *Need to Act* theme. The other is about developing relationships with like-minded others and bonding. I call this the *Bonding* theme.

The Need to Act theme is energized by people's anger. It reflects a meaning system of immoral platforms (harm, cheating, betrayal) and anticivil cultural codes (secretive, suspicious, etc.). It is characterized by archetypes like the villain, trickster, and fool, commonly manifest in the distinct cultural referents of Mayor Ray Nagin, Fox News, George W. Bush, Michael "Brownie" Brown, District Attorney Eddie Jordan, and others. It is people's anger with these characters and their immoral and anticivil interpretations that motivate their action. But here, action is still largely individual, even if collective. It is the result of collective traumas and the problems and concerns that arose in the settling period as a collective of individuals experienced them and felt compelled to act on them. There are no connections with others yet. The Bonding theme grows from the Need to Act theme so that much of people's collective action was collaborative. That is, much of their collective civic action was not the result of them just coincidentally showing up at the same place and doing the same things, which is the case for much more impromptu digitally mediated protests and mobilizations, where participants rarely know each other (Bennett and Segerberg 2013). Rather, it required coordination beforehand, and this was possible because of the trusting relationships and social bonds they created with each other over several months of online interaction. These bonds were cultivated through compassion. They reflect a meaning system of moral platforms (care, fairness, loyalty) and civil cultural codes (altruism, etc.). They are characterized by archetypes like the great mother and hero, manifest in distinct cultural referents of other bloggers, local reporters, and city residents.

It is the combination of both themes that explains the quality and character of bloggers' collective civic actions. The Need to Act theme explains why people felt compelled to act in relation to the immoral and anticivil and the anger they experienced. But by itself, this only explains why they acted individually and independently, despite the fact that the impetus was in the collective traumas of a settling city. The Bonding theme explains why they worked together as, or in the name of, "Katrina bloggers," to organize and collaborate their collective civic actions. It is the combination of these themes that explains the collective actions that "Katrina bloggers" took part in. Both were important for the different kinds of offline, physical-world collective civic actions they organized and took part in over the settling period.

Many of the blog users I spoke with and observed took part in different contentious and noncontentious collective civic actions. One of the most significant was the Rising Tide convention. Staged to coincide with the hurricane's anniversary, Rising Tide was a convention organized and run by social media users, mostly bloggers. It ran from 2006 to 2016, missing only one year. Tracing the formation of this convention backward allows for a retrospective account of how it developed. It began with the storm and its subsequent collective traumas and then the turn to blogs as coping tools (chapter 3) and the development of a shared emotionally laden, richly meaningful discourse over blogs that captured, shaped, focused, and constructed people's collective attention and understanding (chapters 4 and 5). Later, their interactions through blogs and around this discourse helped in their developing an online social support network, starting to meet informally offline, and then planning and organizing a convention to take place during the first anniversary of the flood and to keep it going for a decade after.

In what follows, I explain this process as another facet in how people coped during the settling period. It is a manifestation of cultural work rooted in shared moral emotions of anger and compassion informed by shared interpretations of (im)morality and (anti)civility, focused on shared referents and archetypes and arising from the shared discourse that people created across their blogs. I then offer other examples of mediated cultural work and their different manifestations in collective actions. These examples involve a blogger's collaborative work with television news agents (*Squandered Heritage*) and then the creation of a new journalistic organization (The Lens); a blogger's investigative reporting and collaboration with his readers (Dambala), which led to the arrest of key figures in city hall, including the mayor and the director of the city's communication infrastructure; and the involvement of a smaller group of bloggers in a protest over former district attorney Eddie Jordan and their involvement in a large, citywide march on city hall designed to combat the city's approach to crime and violence. Some of these collective actions involved other bloggers, while others involved single bloggers who collaborated and organized with nonbloggers. All are examples of cultural work, in that they were informed by a shared system of feelings and meanings that energized and guided bloggers' collective actions, and they reflect different ratios of Need to Act and Bonding characteristics. In all cases, blog use was a fundamental aspect of their cultural work.

The Rising Tide Conference, 2006–2016

Perhaps the most impressive, organized, and lasting example of these bloggers' cultural work is the Rising Tide conference. The Rising Tide conference was an annual social media event held in New Orleans, and it is an impressive example of cultural work among blog users in the settling city.[1] It started in 2006, one year after the hurricane, with around fifty people in attendance, mostly the participants on panels and organizers. It ballooned into well over two hundred attendees only a few years later. It was a daylong convention that consisted of a series of panels and speakers, workshops, and a keynote speaker. Keynote speakers were often associated with media in some way. Sometimes this was another blogger, and other times it was someone in legacy media, either local and national (Mac McClelland, Chris Rose, David Simon). The conference included a number of panels that lasted about an hour and a half each. Their focus was on issues of civil and political society, including public safety, environmental sustainability and the Gulf Coast, journalism, crime and criminal justice, education, academics, neighborhood associations, and the like. Panelists included a number of representatives from these institutions, such as neighborhood leaders, local journalists, education reformers, and the police chief. Further, the conference included workshops specifically geared toward social media users. Examples include "Advanced WordPress Techniques for Bloggers" and "Know Your Intellectual Property Rights for Online Content," which were designed to protect bloggers and other users of social media from copyright infringement, libel suits, and other issues that might arise through their more politically oriented blogging. The name of the conference came from a book by the author John M. Barry (1998) on the history of attempting to control the Mississippi River and the engineering and politics that led to the 1927 Mississippi River flood in Greenville, Mississippi. The convention celebrated and included all users of digital social media, but blog users started it and were the most involved in running it.

The first convention took place in August 2006, as close to the hurricane's anniversary as possible. It was organized in about a month. Held on Lake Pontchartrain, it drew about fifty people, many of whom were organizers or panelists. While the numbers might not seem large (many people had not yet returned to the city, and the blog network was in its infancy), these blog users nonetheless found an offline outlet for their emerging collective discourse, and the conference grew in the subsequent years. A lot had to happen for this to be possible, but over time, several blog users put together an annual, organized event of speakers and panelists on the city's "progress and regress." Rising Tide stated its mission this way: *"For everyone who loves New Orleans and is working to bring a better future to all its residents. Leveraging the power of bloggers and new media, the conference is a launch pad for organization and action. Our day-long program of speakers and presentations is tailored to inform, entertain, enrage and inspire. We come together to dispel myths, promote facts, highlight progress and regress, discuss recovery ideas, and promote sound policies at all levels.* We aim to be a 'real life' demonstration of *internet activism* as we continue to recover from a massive failure of government on all levels" (emphasis in original) (Rising Tide 2015).

The blogger Oyster was the first to pitch the idea of a blogger convention in New Orleans. The idea originally came from the national blogger Scout Prime, who had been covering the flood and its aftermath for the national blog *First Draft*. Oyster had been reading Scout Prime's blog, as it was one of the few places on the national scene where people were still writing about New Orleans several months after the initial flood.[2] Oyster took some pictures and sent them to Scout Prime, which led to Scout Prime investigating Oyster's blog and blogroll. Scout Prime was impressed with the number of bloggers and the quality of their writing. She began communicating with Oyster on a more regular basis and eventually suggested that the New Orleans blog community organize a convention. People had recently used the web to organize the national conference Netroots Nation and for Howard Dean's presidential campaign. She suggested that the New Orleans blog community do something similar. Oyster agreed, and on July 5, 2006, less than one year after the flood, he put out a call on his blog to organize. Titling his post "Katrina Bloggers Activate!,"[3] he wrote, "Form of . . . a convention in New Orleans. Think of it: bloggers from all over could get together, and talk about the Katrina aftermath, and blog, and argue, and party, and share information, and podcast, and effect political change, and meet each other in person, and have a 'work day' in a flooded neighborhood, and actually *do something*, and have panels and guest speakers and t-shirts and stickers" (emphasis in original).

The idea was well received, with suggestions and assistance offered in the comments section: "I'll webcast. . . . Name panel on time and place. . . . I have video production and webcast in hand" (Dambala); "A blogger summit! I like the idea, so you can count me in on this one. At the very least, I can help out with some aspects of the PR, with promotional items (t-shirts, stickers and more) and possibly with artwork and with wrangling some entertainment, once we have some kind of budget and plan" (LisaPal). Typical questions followed: Can we get it done in time? How organized should this be? Will we just hang out or have panels and speakers? How do we reach others with this news? They agreed to meet in person and hash out the details. Being digitally networked already, some bloggers posted information about the convention on their blogs, helping to spread the word, and Oyster wrote subsequent posts for further discussion and organizing ideas. Shortly after, from August 25 to 27, 2006, these bloggers hosted the first of what became an annual conference. Oyster and many of the other bloggers were moving their collective action offline. Many were ready to do so. Around the same time as Oyster's post, the blogger da po' boy discussed his interest in coming together and working with other bloggers toward the broadly defined interest of community. He wrote, "Now that there is a blogging community in New Orleans, I think I have reached the limits of what blogging anonymously can do for me. We can certainly do more together than any of us (especially me) can do on our own. It seems we all have the same goal: community—both in the blogosphere and the biosphere. And, by uniting our different voices and different ways of achieving that same goal, we 'can' achieve it" ("Being Anonymous Sucks," July 18, 2006).

The first conference focused on several themes, mostly organized around bloggers' collective trauma. Ashley Morris emphasized "Preserving New Orleans"; da po' boy noted "community"; Dangerblond emphasized the memory of the city and its residents. In an interview, Last Magnolia noted a concern with being forgotten and the threat that could follow: "[The] theme was like 'everybody else in the country was tired of hearing about us, but we're still here and it's not okay.' So that was kind of the thing. Everybody had things that they wanted to talk about, about the city, and I think that was what made me [attend the conference and then start a blog]."

The creation of this conference did not materialize out of thin air. It took time for the ties, relations, and senses of solidarity that made it possible to develop. This occurred largely through blog use but not exclusively. It started with blogs and the connectivity and networking they afforded users, then it moved offline in the form of initial meetings at citywide public events and then more organized socials and potluck dinners hosted by and for bloggers. This was the background work that helped strengthen the social ties and relations among these bloggers, cultivating a collective identity as "Katrina bloggers" and sense of community that they activated for more formal organizing like the Rising Tide conference.

Geek Dinners

The turn to blog use that I noted in chapter 3 was not all that was needed for these bloggers to take action offline and to organize. Before they did so, they first took part in a number of "Geek Dinners." These were informal potluck dinners held at a blogger's house. They provided an opportunity for other bloggers and blog readers to meet face to face in an informal environment of camaraderie and socializing. These Geek Dinners were an important mechanism linking individual, largely anonymous blog users with known, collective blog organizers. They provided an opportunity for online personalities and avatars to meet, get to know each other better, and strengthen their ties and relations. The motive to do so had been growing among this group of bloggers. After months of interacting online, sharing stories and offering support, many felt it was time to take their digital relationship offline.

Maitri, a geoscientist born in Kuwait who moved to the US with the Iraqi invasion in 1990, is the host of *Maitri's VatulBlog*. She noted this desire to meet in person: "We had some people who almost carried each other in those months after, you know. So, um, we wanted to see each other in real life, and go, 'Who are you? You're like one of my best friends now. I need to meet you. I need to talk to you.'" The blogger Alan of *Think Progress* initiated the idea to start a Geek Dinner. He and a few other bloggers were organizing community workshops on how to use blogs and thought it would be nice to meet other bloggers. There was a strong drive to do so because, as Maitri and others noted, people carried each other in the first couple of months and they wanted to see each other. The Geek Dinners helped satisfy this need. Indeed, B.rox posted about this sentiment on July 18, 2006 ("A Festive Weekend"): "Imagine walking into a party full of people you've never met, but whom you know more or less intimately because they've been pouring their hearts out into their writing. That's what the Geek Dinner was like." Maitri echoed this comment in her July 16, 2006, post ("Day 322: Now That the Cake Has Been Eaten"): "Big News: Friday night's Geek Dinner was a blast! A big thank-you hug to Alan for throwing open the doors (all of them) of his Esplanade Ave. geek quarters to us, with room for food, drink, great conversation and techno-nerdery. While I have met and interacted with a majority of the attendees over the past year, I was finally able to put faces to some bloggers and geeks."

The blogger Loki in his July 15, 2006, post ("A Boggle[4] of Bloggers") echoed what Maitri and B.rox stated but added a little promotional note: "I would love to say something about each of these digital maniacs but I am going on too long as it is. If you are reading this and have not already, I encourage you to visit all of the links in this post. You will find a wild and wooley variety that, taken as a gestalt, will provide you a window into the reasons We Are Not OK and what we are doing to change that. Visit them, leave a comment, stay informed."

These Geek Dinners were fundamentally important mechanisms for the more formal and organized offline collective actions that many of these blog users would take part in and organize months and years later. They provided an essential link between online narratives and offline organizing, serving as a place of camaraderie and socializing, where trust, social ties, and ongoing, voluntary social relations were further cultivated and nurtured around general themes of community and "we are not OK." Yet, while the Geek Dinners were an important offline event for many blog users to meet and get to know each other more personally, some had already done so. Several months earlier, the city celebrated its first post-Katrina Mardi Gras. While a point of contention for some outsiders, as Ashely Morris noted in chapter 5, it was an important event for rekindling connections with the city and reestablishing some sense of normalcy for residents whose lives had been anything but normal for the previous six months. This was also part of the gradual process of converting digital interactions into offline social ties and relations that were ultimately activated to create the Rising Tide conference.

The Rising Tide conference represents the most organized and lasting example of these bloggers' collective cultural work. Rooted in collective trauma, it was the result of a shared system of meanings and feelings around the flood, the city's controversial rebuilding work, and the fear that the nation would forget that the city and its residents were not okay. But this is not the only example of bloggers' cultural work. Bloggers also collaborated with other bloggers and nonbloggers, taking part in different protest events and organizing in ways that would have lasting impacts on the city's civil and political institutions.

Collaborating with Nonbloggers

Love of New Orleans—and anger at those who would so stupidly destroy it—got me up in the morning and kept me up late at night.[5]
—*Squandered Heritage*

Karen first started blogging after Katrina in an effort to document the demolition of different homes in the city. She was concerned with issues of memory and remembrance, and in the wake of Katrina, a number of homes and buildings that captured the city's unique architecture were being destroyed. She wanted to document these places for posterity before they were gone forever. Before starting the *Squandered Heritage* blog, she was collaborating with several members of her neighborhood association, taking part in their online community. They would discuss shared problems and issues they were facing. She explained,

> I'm sort of a community meeting watcher, and I monitor a lot of the online boards, community boards, and . . . this was one of the things I did when I was still with my neighborhood blog. My heat would go out. My gas would go out the year after Katrina every two weeks, and then I'd have to wait for the gas guy, and they'd pump water out of it [the gas line]. And so I would monitor all these different community boards, so I could see people complaining about the same thing. And so then I was able to sort of contact all those people and say, "What are we going to do?" Because Entergy is telling me it's just me. People sent me emails like, "Oh, what I do is I unscrew the thing, the gas, and then I put the vacuum cleaner in." Like, no way! Are you going to shock back up into your gas main? So, yeah, it was insane, right?

As she noted, she a "community watcher," and her blogging underwent different transformations that coincided with the settling period. First, she took part in her neighborhood blog, and discussions focused largely around shared problems in her neighborhood, like the gas problem. Then she shifted to create her own blog (*Squandered Heritage*) after a fire destroyed an entire block of city houses. As we were discussing a vacant block in the Carrollton neighborhood, she recalled,

> So that was a huge, huge fire during the flood. . . . And my daughter used to wait for the bus there. And so, for me, it was vividly imprinted because that Friday before the flood, I had stood on that corner with her waiting for her bus to her first day of high school, which is, as any parent knows, one of the milestones of your transitions of your children. But I could, for the life of me, only remember one house in that entire block. I think there are sixteen houses gone. So the *Squandered Heritage* blog was an attempt to sort of re-create blocks of houses so that when people . . . had the same grasping desire to remember what was there [they can] access it with this very easy—in this very easy format.

Karen's work garnered her a small following and took her into city hall, where the policies on housing demolition were unfolding with little oversight of public involvement.

> So what we did was we decided—once again this little ad hoc group—that we were going to rewrite the ordinance for that committee and push it downstairs into city council chambers and have it be broadcast on TV and recorded. And that was about a year's campaign, which was successful. So the blog became—*Squandered Heritage* blog became very influential in land-use matters. And along the way, I discovered a number of things about the way the city was managing the demolition program. And that was—in order to meet a certain number that had been green-lit for demolition, there had been a, you know, "you can tear down two thousand houses." Well now they had to find two thousand houses.

In order to find homes to demolish, the city was being generous in its assessment of housing damage. Homes that were assessed at 50 percent damaged were suddenly assessed at 90 percent and slated for demolition. The city mailed out notifications to home owners, but the notifications were sent to their homes in New Orleans. Many residents had yet to return, and so they never received the notification. The bureau chief of the *Wall Street Journal* had been reading *Squandered Heritage* and decided to run a story on this topic (August 9, 2007). Soon after, Anderson Cooper and other national television personalities were contacting Karen about the story.

Karen's work on housing demolition led to her collaboration with a local television news reporter and a series of award-winning stories on the New Orleans Affordable Homeownership program (NOAH). The city had been allocated several million dollars in community block development grants (CBDG) to gut and clear properties that flooded, focusing specifically on housing for the elderly. Karen decided to look into this program. She was able to access a list of properties that would receive money and was immediately suspicious.

> And so I—my first foray to go look at these properties, it was like stunning, what I was seeing, that the addresses didn't exist, so fake addresses; properties owned by LLCs, so corporations; properties owned by the chief of police, public figures; owned by the redevelopment authority. And this was supposed to be a program for, specifically, the elderly or disabled. So you would have had to own your home. So right then, without even setting foot outside the door, there was a lot of red flags. But when I went out and looked at the houses, nothing had been done. So it was not only—it was a double insult.

She would go out and photograph the property, note the amount of money spent on the property, and note the property owner. Fortunately, a local television news reporter had been looking into this phenomenon as well but had not been given the okay to fully pursue it, as it was seen as too work intensive. Karen started working with him and eventually produced over fifty stories.

> And then I knew Lee Zurik was the TV reporter, and Lee had been onto this story but hadn't been given a green light because it's very heavy research. And so he and I would talk back and forth about it, and finally one day he said, "You know, the news director gave me the green light on it. Let's—let's do this story." . . . So we did the first piece, and the response was immediate and aggressive and hostile from the mayor. He called an immediate press conference at five o'clock at night. We went; he yelled at us, literally. I have the raw tape; he's yelling at us. And so we hit a really strong nerve. Well, [what] we didn't realize, and we did in the days to come, is that the executive director had created these corporations to

clean out these houses with her friends. So she just funneled the money to herself virtually. It was a very twisted and tangled story but one that, you know, went on to win a lot of awards.

Eventually, Karen slowed down her writing at *Squandered Heritage* and shifted her attention onto a new project, something more formal and lasting. She teamed up with the investigative reporter Ariella Cohen and created a new news organization called The Lens (Ostertag and Tuchman 2012). The Lens is a formal, nonprofit news organization focused on investigative and explanatory journalism in New Orleans. It was founded in late 2009 and, as of 2016, has eight full-time employees and revenues totaling over $600,000. The organization remains true to its roots in the investigative reporting on *Squandered Heritage*, "focus[ing] closely on New Orleans, in the areas of government accountability, criminal justice, coastal restoration, land use and public education" (The Lens, annual report 2017) and hosting various community events on such topics as how to file a records request. It has also diversified its funding sources since its inception. Whereas once it received approximately 80 percent of its budget from foundations and shared office space (and stories) with the local Fox affiliate, it now receives 46 percent of its budget from foundations. Investments, membership, gifts, and other sources of income account for the rest, and it has its own office space.

Karen's creation of The Lens involved several relationships with non-bloggers. First was her work with the local, legacy newsmaker noted earlier. This allowed her to generate the social capital necessary to create a new organization and access funds from interested foundations. In order to be seen as a legitimate enterprise and access these grants, however, she and Ariella had to bring other legacy news workers into the fold. This included a local journalist with years of experience working for the local daily, the *New Orleans Times-Picayune*, and a veteran journalist who became the editor in chief and CEO from 2010 to 2017. Now, almost ten years after its inception, The Lens has become a valued source of insightful news and information. As of 2017, it boasts 323 members and 3,824 subscribers, both having increased from the previous year (The Lens, annual report 2017). It has also made space on its website to house the archives of *Squandered Heritage*, so that this important work does not disappear like many of the homes its founder sought to document.

A second example of collaborating with nonbloggers is Dambala of the blog *American Zombie*. Dambala was more of a lone wolf than Karen; but he often reached out to his readers for help, and his work was squarely situated in the collective traumas that so many residents and bloggers continued to face. Dambala was a documentarian. He had been trained at the Smithsonian Institute in Washington, DC, and, upon moving to New Orleans, created a documentary on the city's public school system. He started blogging because of the graft and corruption he noticed when conducting research for his documentary. But what really got him involved was the audacity he noted among some city officials in the wake of Hurricane Katrina. In the following interview excerpt, he comments on Greg Meffert, the city's chief technology officer, who was responsible for creating and maintaining the city's communication infrastructure, an essential tool for first responders and other emergency personnel:

> Yeah, yeah so DOJ [Department of Justice], um, Meffert starts fucking with it trying to get a kickback to himself, as he did with everything. Um, and, ah, DOJ realizes what's going on, and they pulled the grant. Um, they, ah, pulled the $7 million back 'cause they knew that he was screwing around with it. So then what happens to, you know—two years later, the biggest natural disaster in history hits the city, 80 percent of the city goes underwater—what's the first thing that happens? All of the communication goes down. None of the first responders can communicate with each other, you know. To me that has—that's—the guy has blood on his hands, you know. Many people died from lack of that communication system that he tried to kick back to himself, so the irony is that he went down to Office Depot and stole a bunch of fucking—basically looted Office Depot and took a bunch of 80211 G Routers and set up a small ad hoc Wi-Fi. He didn't do it, actually; the guys who were with him did it. . . . Anyway, he wins an award because, you know, he "went to extreme measures during the, you know, the storm." When I saw that, I was just like, "Oh, you got to be fuckin kidding me," 'cause I knew what was going on, and, um, that's what, um—that's what got me started on Meffert in particular, but I also knew what was going on with C-Ray [i.e., Mayor Nagin] and all that

other stuff, so that kind of—I focused on that story, and then it just lead to everything else, all the other stories.

Greg Meffert was eventually arrested and spent thirty months in federal prison for taking kickbacks from contractors. His plan was to create a business that he and then-Mayor Nagin would control once the mayor's term ended. The goal was to get the company up and running while they were in positions to direct city contracts its way. Once their term ended, they would take over a thriving company. Dambala discovered this and started blogging about it. He was contacted by the FBI and other federal agents because of the information he was posting. At the time I interviewed him, in late 2010, the Meffert trial was under way, but there was still much to write about. Dambala remarked that this indictment ultimately led to Mayor Nagin. Three years later, Nagin was arrested and sentenced to ten years in federal prison. He was convicted on twenty of twenty-one counts of bribery, wire fraud, tax evasion, and other charges.[6] Dambala's investigative blogging uncovered material that the local press had not, and it kept interest on a story that could have easily gone away.[7]

While Dambala's work at *American Zombie* was his work, it was also collective. First, he had to collaborate with others to gather pertinent information. Second, the topics he was addressing and the grievances related to them were widely shared through the blogging community and the collective trauma they were experiencing. Third, others, such as Karen (housing programs) and G Bitch (education) were doing similar investigative work, which, while focused on other topics, nonetheless was related to the collective experiences of the settling city. Further, sometimes these bloggers would use their blog to ask for help. Hoping to access the collective wisdom of his readers, Dambala often posted questions about things he was trying to figure out during an investigation. While these bloggers may have been working individually in the day-to-day, their work was resonating with a broader collective sentiment and need for information, given the secretive, suspicious, and conspiratorial relationship between city government and its residents in the settling period. In this sense, it was collective and cultural work, even if the specific topics of their work differed and they were working with people who did not blog.

Working with Other Bloggers

Bloggers also worked with each other, using their blogs to help organize their work. This was the case with the Rising Tide conference noted earlier but also for their participation in other, less institutionalized events. Here, unlike with the Rising Tide conference, bloggers did not create a new organization among themselves but rather took part in an event organized elsewhere, but they did so largely through their blogging and as bloggers. This mostly involved participation in protest events, such as a demonstration against District Attorney Eddie Jordan, and a citywide protest against violence held on the steps of city hall.

In the years after Hurricane Katrina, violent crime in the city reached a tipping point as the institutions and routines that structured social life disappeared and ongoing suffering, neglect, and inequality became too much to bear. While usually isolated to people "in the life," violence had become less predictable, less isolated, and more random. District Attorney Eddie Jordan was the city's lead prosecutor during these years. His tenure as district attorney was saturated with controversy and critique but also pride among many of the city's Black residents. Jordan's problems actually began before Hurricane Katrina, but the flood and its wake exacerbated them. They started when Jordan, the first Black district attorney for New Orleans, fired forty-three white employees upon taking office in 2002–3. He was subsequently sued, and in spring 2005, a jury decided against him, claiming that the former employees were fired because they were white. (This was indeed an ironic finding, given how challenging it often is to legally prove whites' racism toward people of color in the US court system.) The court awarded $2.5 million in back pay and damages, which Jordan could not pay. Jordan appealed, resulting in the award growing to $3.7 million due to interest and lawyer fees. He turned to the city for the money, but it refused. This was an ongoing point of contention that would shroud Jordan's tenure as district attorney, but it was not the only controversy. In the summer of 2007, as the city's crime problem was reaching a breaking point, Jordan was also criticized for failing to effectively prosecute several cases. He dropped the charges against David Bond, the alleged killer of Dineral Shavers, a local brass-band musician, and Michael Anderson, who was accused of killing five teenagers in June 2006. A judge also threatened to release twenty suspects from prison due to Jordan's office taking too long to bring the case to trial. The final straw came that October, when Elton Phillips, suspected of robbery, home invasion, and shooting a New Orleans police officer, was found in Jordan's home. Jordan first told a reporter that he did not know Phillips and was just trying to help someone in need. He later stated that it was his girlfriend who knew Phillips. The tide of public opinion was turning rapidly. Once-supportive bloggers, such as Cliff, found themselves struggling to continue their support, while others had enough. In an October 26, 2007, post titled "Eddie!!!!!" Cliff wrote,

> What the hell are you doing brother?
> What happened to the dude in the cool hats prosecuting Edwin Edwards?
> What is going on with you?
> You wouldn't have gotten this far in your career if you displayed the bad judgment you are displaying now. You know once you fired those people without a legitimate reason everything had to go right to keep things together. Until this drama blows over, don't let anyone visit your house that you don't know personally.

While Cliff remained supportive, some other bloggers did not, and several came together to protest Jordan's performance and call for his resignation.[8] Last Magnolia was involved in this effort and in an interview stressed the role of bloggers in this protest event:

> We did protest Eddie Jordan in front of the Cabildo, and that was like NOLA bloggers only. He was the former district attorney. . . . There was all kinds of problems with him. I mean, there was that sexual harassment thing. There was also overzealous prosecution or whatever, where they convicted an innocent person and then they had this huge multimillion-dollar settlement, and of course it's not in their budget, you know. But he was . . . just horrible, and, ah, yeah, the bloggers, there was a couple dozen, and it was mainly blogger driven. [And we] went down there, and the idea was we would protest with signs because I think *Good Morning America* was at the Cabildo for something. . . . This had to be . . . before October 2007.

In late October 2007, Eddie Jordan resigned as New Orleans district attorney, amid calls from city council members, the mayor (Nagin), and a broad public including many bloggers.

During this time, the city's crime problem had been escalating, and neither he nor any of the other authority figures seemed able to do anything about it. Public outrage was peaking and directed at all authority figures, including the mayor and police chief. It became manifest in a massive demonstration on the steps of city hall in early 2007. Two incidents in particular really sparked this march. One was the murder of Dineral Shavers, the much-loved drummer for a well-known local brass band called The Hot 8. Shavers was a talented musician who was active in helping the city's youth use music to stay off the streets. He was murdered in late December 2006 in what was largely believed to be an accident, with the intended target being his fifteen-year-old stepson.[9]

The second incident involved the local filmmaker Helen Hill. Hill was murdered a couple of weeks after Shavers, on January 4, 2007. An intruder had entered her home in the early-morning hours. She, her husband, and their toddler son were in the house. The intruder shot and killed Helen. Her husband jumped on top of their toddler to protect him and was shot three times. He survived, and the toddler was physically unharmed. In what were two horrific examples of the city's crime problem over the settling period, Hill's and Shaver's murders sparked a massive march on city hall. The March for Survival drew around five thousand people and was organized in less than a week. It took place on January 11, 2007. The primary organizers were not bloggers; but bloggers organized their own involvement, and some bloggers spoke at the event. B.rox was a friend of Helen's and spoke at the event. As he recalled in an interview,

> There are people being murdered unfortunately, and that is a real problem in the city. But in particular, there were two high-profile people who were killed around that time, and one of them is a friend of mine. So as a result of that, I ended up writing about her death. Ah, the circumstances were quite sensational about the whole thing, um, and then I was—I spoke at this rally, which was televised, and it was still a part of the narrative of the recovery of New Orleans. So CNN came down. Anderson Cooper marched with us actually and interviewed me afterwards.

Many of the bloggers involved in organizing the Rising Tide conference organized their involvement in the march. Last Magnolia was there and explained,

> It was that core NOLA bloggers group, the Rising Tide group. They all were going to get together and march. But, like, Bart marched from his house, so he marched kind of separate from that. And there were marches from different places, and [my group] decided to get together at the foot of Canal Street. So that's where we started, but um . . . everybody blogged about it, about you know, "Go to the crime march" whatever. I'm not sure if that really made it that successful, because there was other publicity about it from the Silence Is Violence people.

The Rising Tide conference, Geek Dinners, the work of the *Squandered Heritage* and *American Zombie* blogs, and the contentious protest events that bloggers took part in are all collaborative forms of cultural work. They reflect the varied ways bloggers sought to cope with the ongoing collective traumas that they experienced as the city settled in the years after Hurricane Katrina. These varied manifestations of cultural work emerged from the shared systems of meanings and feelings that bloggers experienced with the collective traumas of the settling period and that they built through their collective blogging: the morals and cultural codes, archetypes, and referents and feelings of fear, anxiety, and anger that made their unfolding experiences meaningful and energized their cultural work of the settling period. Their collaborations, however, were not based solely on these activating emotions, as activating emotions energize behavior but do little regarding collaboration and relationships. Bloggers' later cultural work was not composed of a collective of solitary individuals working independently. Rather, they worked together, in collaboration with each other. This required something else, something that bonds them, something like compassion. Compassion for each other helped bloggers create social ties and voluntary relationships with each other. It was fundamental in their building a social support network and sense of community from which they could ground and build these collective actions in meaningful, largely agreed-on ways.

Solidarity: Compassion and Social Support

Much of these bloggers' cultural work was possible because of the social support network they created and their reputations as trustworthy people posting reliable and needed information. As we saw in chapter 3 with the collective traumas, manifest in the collective discourse noted in chapters 4 and 5 and reflected here most clearly with Karen from *Squandered Heritage* and Dambala, anger (due to humiliation, fear, and anxiety over being cheated and put at continued risk) led many to start blogging. But they were also fearful of being forgotten by the nation. They feared that outsiders who might help would believe that everything is fixed in New Orleans and that their attention and help is no longer needed. Fear and anger worked together to motivate blog use, and it was through fear and anger that bloggers extended compassion and were able to bond with each other.

Over time, much of this local blogosphere developed into a social support network. This involved the creation of social ties and voluntary social relations, oriented around shared understandings of the flood and its aftermath and solidified through trust, "the expectancy of others' virtuous conduct towards ourselves" (Sztompka 1999, 5). Compassion was key to these developments. Compassion is a complex social emotion composed of sympathy and empathy. It is an emotion we extend to others. Sympathy is the ability to share in the sorrows, fears, and anxieties of others due to having similar experiences. One can emotionally relate because one has experienced similar or the same situation(s). Empathy is the attempt to appreciate the sorrows, fears, and anxieties of others despite not being able to share in the same or similar experiences. Both are social bonding emotions (Scheff 1990) that inform affective commitments (Jasper 2018). They involve the extending of one's emotional self to others. In so doing, we expose our weakness and vulnerabilities. We open ourselves unto others. It is the result of being able to trust as sincere and honest the feelings and understandings of others. With this, we may cultivate the social ties and voluntary social relations that inform senses of solidarity. From here, collective, collaborative action emerges.

In chapter 5, I noted anger as a key moral emotion, the result of fear, humiliation, and ongoing anxiety associated with the collective traumas and cosmological series of a post–Hurricane Katrina settling New Orleans. Yet indicators of compassion were also evident, constituting the second most common emotion. This might appear as odd at first, but it is not. Compassion corresponds with anger. Compassion is a recognition and appreciation of another's feelings. If people are angry, then compassion is a welcome response to their anger. It is an emotional statement that says, "I believe you, and I'm with you." As such, it is key to the development of social ties, voluntary relations, and the senses of solidarity that were essential for the different collective actions noted in this chapter. Bloggers' social relations and collective actions involved cooperation, the willingness to work together toward a shared goal. To get to this point in the context of high-anxiety, post-Katrina New Orleans, where few authority figures could be trusted, required compassion.

Compassion is extended in both direct and indirect ways. Sometimes people are more explicit with their compassion than at other times, yet it is often what is left unsaid that is powerful (Polletta and Callahan 2019). As such, compassion is often communicated indirectly, through feeling "sorry" for another and wishing one was not grieving or that an event did not happen. Sometimes it is about rooting for one's resilience and fortitude. One need not say, "I sympathize/empathize with you," to extend compassion to another. Often it is subtler and softer but nonetheless implies a general agreement and validation of one's feelings, the meanings of those feelings, and the sources that generate them.

Compassion is a twofold emotion involving sympathy and empathy. Importantly, it was commonly expressed in readers' comments to blog posts. Collective evidence of compassion can be seen in the moral oppositions of MFT and anticivil codes. While many bloggers emphasized the immoral and anticivil nature of the flood and its aftermath, as this was the source of their fear and anger, supportive others were more likely to emphasize the moral and civil, directing them at the bloggers and similar, like-minded others. That is, *the immoral and anticivil was more commonly expressed in the blog posts, while the moral and civil were more commonly expressed in the blog comments.* These complemented each other so that blog posts emphasizing the immoral and anticivil of various referents might be commented on so that the bloggers and similar others were framed as moral and civil, fostering the creation of a social support network.

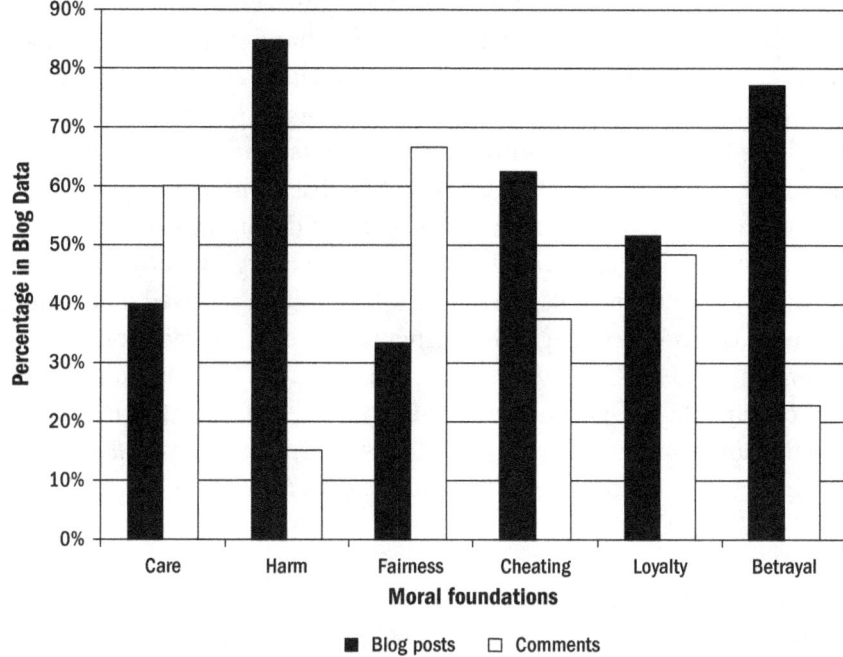

Figure 6.1. Percentage of each moral opposition in blog posts and comments

We can see evidence of this dynamic in figure 6.1, which highlights the percentage of each moral opposition as it was expressed in the blog posts and comment sections. Looking at the care/harm opposition, 40 percent of the blog content that touched on care was expressed in the blog posts, while 60 percent was expressed in the comments, indicating that commenters were more likely to express caring sentiments than were blog writers (in the form of validating supportive feedback and reciprocity). Likewise, looking at harm, 85 percent of blog content on harm was found in the blog post, while only 15 percent was found in the comments, again supporting the notion that by and large, blog posts were outlets for bloggers to express their fear and anger at the immoral and anticivil elements of the flood and its aftermath, while blog commenters were more likely to offer compassionate moral and civil responses. This is important in the validation it offered blog writers and in the development of a sense of community that eventually emerged and fomented their offline cultural work.

Some of those who commented on blog posts, especially in the early months, did not experience the flood firsthand but rather through media, rumor, and various sources of news. This was when national attention was heavily focused on the city and its residents, before interest shifted elsewhere, sparking many residents' fear of being forgotten and their rallying call of "We Are Not OK!" The commenters were more likely to be empathetic, which they expressed through their comments. The *GulfSails* blogger, because he was actively blogging during and immediately after the storm, had a large following and received many early comments. As others began blogging, their posts also got comments. However, because *GulfSails* was so popular due to its being one of the few offering on-the-ground news, information, and other thoughts during the hurricane and to people outside New Orleans, he garnered many comments from people living around the country and the world.

> Gidday Troy,
> I'm from New Zealand and have been reading your blog daily since around August 27 when you commented something like "Looks like this is going to be a big one."
> Reason I keep coming back here is that you give the real man on the ground position. I have a profound mistrust of mainstream media; they are all owned or controlled by vested interests, so to see you reporting the reality is refreshing, if sometimes heartbreaking and disturbing.
> I have huge admiration for people like you who have been able to stay and see the distance, despite personal loss, and, more importantly, to become involved in the recovery and assistance work.
> Kudos to you, Troy. And strength.
> Alison (comment, October 4, 2005)

Allison was commenting from New Zealand. In the following comment, Lois, from Madison, Wisconsin, offers her support. Here, we already see evidence of the national tide turning toward one of victim blaming, almost two months after the city flooded:

> Well, you didn't participate in the initial evacuation. So, for some reason, maybe people don't understand your experiences because it wasn't part

of the MSM disaster porn going on at the time. Don't know what your access to TV was then, but for about two weeks it was pretty much non-stop on CNN, et al. The coverage was all the murder and rape rumors going on at the Superdome and Convention Center, and rampant looting (which all turned out to be pretty much untrue.) On top of this was the FEMA vs. state responsibility blame game. Troy, an unfortunate aspect of life is that most people adopt the "deer in the headlights" look when an awkward topic of loss or sadness comes up in conversation. Yes, we have empathy for your situation, just spare me the details. These people have no soul. It is hard and sad not to find people that are open to talking about the rawness of living. You'll figure out who is worth talking to and who isn't. Just like anything else, it will take time to figure out. I wish you the best with this. Lois Madison, WI (comment on *Gulf Sails*, October 13, 2005)

Over time, as others began blogging, they too received comments of support and validation. I offer two examples from *Liprap's Lament*, both of which were written over a year after the hurricane struck the city:

Wow, good writing on your part. So sorry for what you are going through. This was an interesting read. (comment on *Liprap's Lament*, November 17, 2006)

Yikes. How sad indeed. I think it's hard to wrap the mind around it when you haven't seen it/lived in it/been neck deep in it, etc. (comment on *Liprap's Lament*, December 20, 2006)

A year after Liprap's examples and over two years after the flood, a commenter on Ashley Morris's blog expressed solidarity with the collective trauma perpetuated by private parties. Referring to the city's primary energy company, Entergy, this commenter wrote,

From one who has audited the billing of almost every power company in the U.S.
ENTERGY IS THE WORST!
ENTERGY IS A PURVEYOR OF FRAUD ON A MONTHLY BASIS!
(December 3, 2007)

Sometimes compassion and solidarity were expressed in more assertive ways, such as in response to a previous comment that might have been critical of the blogger's line of thought. As the months passed, the national media abandoned New Orleans, and the national discourse shifted to contempt and victim blaming. Some commenters reflected this shift in what they had to say about a post. Other commenters, who might know more about the response and recovery, would sometimes rebut. In the following example, the commenter responds to a previous comment that criticized the people of New Orleans for (allegedly) not taking part in their own recovery and waiting for the handouts of other taxpayers. This framing of New Orleans and its citizens after the storm was not uncommon and was a source of residents' cultural trauma. In a reflection of one of the various ways people shared compassion, offered support, and built solidarity, this person responded to a previous commenter with the following:

> Snooch, you have no idea what you are talking about. There is so much still up in the air that people don't know what to do. FEMA hasn't even released new flood maps, 7 MONTHS LATER. We have no idea when block grants will be awarded. Some people don't have insurance money yet. Schools are closed, there are no hospitals, thousands of cars still need to be towed.
>
> Despite all of that there are hundreds of thousands of people back in the metro area, fixing homes, working their jobs and moving along.
>
> My wife and I lost EVERYTHING at our home in midcity. We were lucky because we both have decent jobs that were able to keep us on and we found a place to rent that was DOUBLE our old rent. We were able to get back to the city relatively early, back in October. There are thousands of people in this city like us.
>
> You have no idea what you are talking about. (comment on Ashley Morris's blog, April 6, 2006)

Compassion was a common component of the comments but was not uncommon in blog posts either. It was an important quality of the interaction among blog writers and readers as they developed trust, social ties and relations, and a sense of community, which ultimately became manifest in

Table 6.1. Moral Oppositions in Blog Content (Posts and Comments)

	Moralities						
	Care	Harm	Fairness	Cheating	Loyalty	Betrayal	Total
Blog post count	210	385	14	55	48	54	814
Blog post percentage	15.46%	28.35%	1.03%	4.05%	3.53%	3.98%	59.94%
Comment count	316	69	28	33	45	16	544
Comment percentage	23.27%	5.08%	2.06%	2.43%	3.31%	1.18%	40.06%
Total count	526	454	42	88	93	70	1,358
Total percentage	38.73%	33.43%	3.09%	6.48%	6.85%	5.15%	100.00%

Note: The moral oppositions of liberty/oppression, authority/subversion, and sanctity/degradation were removed due to their small numbers in the blog content (posts and comments) and to simplify the table for easier interpretation. As such, the numbers as they are presented here do not equal 100 percent.

various forms of offline cultural work. Table 6.1 provides further evidence on the frequency of moral content as it related to the immoral content of blog posts and comments, capturing the interactional, supportive, and rewarding qualities between blog writers and commenters. Table 6.1 shows the three most common moral oppositions associated with MFT (care/harm, fairness/cheating, loyalty/betrayal). In each one, we find that a majority of the immoral narratives (harm, cheating, betrayal) were found in the blog posts and were therefore an expression of the blog writers. Yet a majority of the moral narratives (care, fairness, loyalty), which would serve as indicators of compassion, were found in the comments. As this table illustrates, moral narratives (and their homologous civil codes) were more commonly expressed in the comments sections, while their immoral oppositions (and their homologous anticivil codes) were more commonly expressed in the blog posts. These oppositions supported each other in the dynamic collective blog discourse in such a way as to encourage continued writing and to nurture senses of trust, social ties and relations, and the solidarity underlying their collaborative cultural work. As Maitri and Liprap noted, bloggers supported each other in the months and years after the flood. They formed a sense of community that was therapeutic in dealing with the ongoing collective trauma associated with the recovery and rebuilding periods.

Conclusion

The interaction among bloggers and commenters was important in helping people cope with the collective traumas of the settling period. It also had a secondary outcome, the creation of trusting social ties, relationships, and a sense of solidarity. This was due to the ability to offer supporting narratives and words of encouragement and verification to each other around sorrowful personal stories and posts in the collective interest. These relationships became manifest over time, through continued interaction. Most of this took place online, especially in the early months. But, as people moved back to the city and began interacting across blogs more regularly, they became closer and developed a need to meet in person. Different public events and informal get-togethers provided the opportunities to do so, further strengthening their connection with each other. From here, and as they continued to confront the ongoing collective traumas, many of these bloggers decided to take action offline. They created new organizations, hosted an annual conference, and took part in contentious and noncontentious political actions. Some took it upon themselves to investigate and report on different events of the recovery and rebuilding periods, doing so individually but in the collective interest and also collaborating with others. They all shared the same general set of motives: a moral outrage in the form of anxiety, fear, and anger at how they were being treated, by the federal government, the national media, ignorant outsiders, and their own elected officials at city hall. This outrage informed the cultural work they took part in, manifesting itself in various ways but sharing the same background of anxiety, fear, and anger and the immoral and anticivil actions of key figures and institutions involved in the recovery and rebuilding projects. These emotions informed their need to act, compelling them to do something to alleviate these feelings. Yet much of their work was collaborative, which requires bonds and trust. Through compassionate narratives of support offered on each other's blog posts, bloggers developed bonds with each other and a sense that what they were thinking and doing was right. These narratives combined to explain their sense of camaraderie and solidarity and the different collective actions they took part in during the settling period.

And yet, as close as some of these folks were and as strong as some of their ties (for example, Oyster was a pallbearer at Ashley Morris's funeral), the relationships did not last forever. For many, their blog use and therefore connections with other bloggers waned. As the city began to settle, as did people's lives, they found themselves with less time to write, less need to do so, and fewer things to say that mattered to others. Many found their writing dwindling along with their participation in this blogosphere. The blogosphere itself diffused with this collective movement toward settlement. Chapter 7 addresses what happened as "time went on" and the settling period of post–Hurricane Katrina New Orleans morphed into relative settlement.

7

As the City Settles

Predictability, Routine, and Fatigue

As the settling period in New Orleans progressed, months turned into years, and as life became more stable, priorities changed. New responsibilities emerged, controversial projects were well under way or completed, people's lives returned to routine and predictability, and the national media's interest in the flood and its aftermath largely disappeared. The collective traumas and collective cosmological series that motivated people's cultural work and blog use waned. The Rising Tide conference continued until 2015, its tenth year, but did not return after that. People's blogs went silent, and updated posts were far and few between. Some of those who used their blogs like personal diaries continued, but their writing shifted to more personal issues. Some even wrote a final blog post, a kind of send-off signifying the end of an era. It is a considerable amount of work to host a blog and update it frequently, and if it is not updated frequently, then people are less likely to visit, read, and comment. The blogger G Bitch spent hours writing a post, inserting hyperlinks to relevant sources of data, proofreading, and such before she would post it. She started a series she called "Who is?" in which she would spend weeks researching someone involved in one of the city's primary institutions, education being her main focus, creating a kind of exposé on this person. As she stated in an interview,

> It's a serious investment, which is why I kind of dropped off a bit. When I wasn't working, I had that time. And I was reading a lot more mainstream and alternative news sources, and that's where a lot of the inspiration would come. I'd read something and be like, "Oh, I got to put this on my blog." And since, I've kind of pulled back on that a bit. Just because I started working and my dad needed more attention, I've kind of fallen back. . . . I mean, if it doesn't fit in your life, then you drop it for a while,

and then you go back to it. Like, it's going to be really light this semester, and I'm taking next semester off, and I'm back on, so to speak.

G Bitch touched on a few themes on why her blogging dwindled, having to do with the settling period and the stimuli to blog. First, as she said, "It's a serious investment." Like many bloggers in my sample, G Bitch had high standards for blogging. She felt that a blog post needed to be thoroughly researched and clearly written. It was serious work and needs to be respected. With the settling period, the free time to do this kind of work dwindled. G Bitch went back to work, which reduced her free time both to do the reading that would provide the stimuli to post and to sufficiently research and write the post. As she returned to work, her time to blog diminished, as did the time she had to spend reading other sources and therefore learning about things to blog on. Adding to this, she also had family responsibilities and needed to spend more time taking care of her ill father. Something had to be dropped, and it was not going to be work or family.

Others reduced their blogging because of similar reasons. Blogging is time-consuming, and when not done for pay, it may be difficult to sustain when other life obligations arise. Dangerblond echoed G Bitch in her reasons for reduced blogging and the changes in stimuli:

> Yeah, I used to keep mine up all the time, and real-life kind of got in the way. And I also don't like to dash things off. I like to put more thought into it. So I kind of—I have some ideas that I don't put on there because I haven't had time to really think them out, and I don't want to put something that's really bad or not thought through. . . . It takes time to put in all the links and stuff. . . . I don't have that kind of time anymore, and I don't feel like I have that kind of inspiration now that Nagin is gone.

Like G Bitch, Dangerblond noted that writing a blog post is considerable work and investment of time and that "real-life kind of got in the way" of her continuing to write frequently. As life routines became more normalized and stable, work, family, education, and other "real-life" responsibilities returned to the fore, and blog writing took a backseat. Other stimuli also changed, which reduced the need to write as well. As I noted in chapter 3, people started blogging because it provided a suitable outlet to express their moral anger and vent. As the response stage turned into the recovery and rebuilding stages, and the federal government returned decision-making power to the city, the stimuli shifted to local sources. Mayor Nagin was a consistent source of anger and therefore a constant stimulant for writing, especially as key decisions about the recovery and rebuilding were still being debated and newly under way. However, as Mayor Nagin's tenure ended and a new mayor took control of the rebuilding work, the constant stimuli that had been provided to these bloggers diminished. For many of the bloggers in my sample, Nagin was seen as immoral and anticivil, a trickster who could not be trusted and who was largely greedy and incompetent. The next mayor, Mitch Landrieu, enjoyed widespread support from city residents. He enjoyed a family history narrated in civil and moral ways, as his father, former mayor Moon Landrieu, was involved in significant decisions on desegregating the city's political institutions. With this, one of the primary sources of trauma, and therefore one of the primary motives to blog, disappeared. Part of the settling period involved changes in authority figures, and the resignation of District Attorney Eddie Jordan and the election of a new mayor to replace Nagin signified these changes.

With the settling city well under way, changes in the sources of collective trauma and diminishing time needed to write a blog post due to newly emergent priorities reduced the motives and time available to blog. On top of this, people were tired and burning out. How long can someone remain mad at a particular subject before they have to shift attention elsewhere, if only to remain sane? Fatigue was a reason for both reducing blog writing in general and a reason for shifting to other topics. Adrastos, a proud Greek who loves to throw out the word *malaka* once in a while, pointed this out in explaining why he does not blog much about the city's levee system and its reconstruction in the rebuilding period:[1]

> It [the city's flood-protection system] has been [a common topic of his blog writing] in the past, but, um, there's a lot of burnout over the subject and a lot of frustration over the subject. Um . . . and the guy who was really on top of that story was Matt McBride and his blog, which I don't even know if it still exists, called *fixthepumps*. So the archives are out there, but basically what happened is that people got, you know, people

got burnt out, and a lot of people moved on to their own lives. . . . Not that we care less, but just that it's just such a massive project.

As the settling period moved on, most people's blogging became less and less frequent. Some bloggers just stopped writing, maybe posting something every six months or so, or stopped updating altogether. Some blogs were no longer accessible, as the host website removed them for whatever reason. Links went dead, both on blogrolls and hyperlinks to other blog posts and documents provided within a post. The upkeep became too much as other priorities of work and home life returned and as some of the stimuli for blogging disappeared and people grew tired of the constant trauma and anger. Sometimes they would compose a send-off post, something signifying the end of their blogging. Tim of *Tim's Nameless Blog* nicely captures this and the shifting problems and concerns that led to his decision to stop writing. On December 31, 2010, five years after his first post, he wrote his final post:

> As 2010 comes to a close, I must admit this blog does not get the attention it used to—not from me and as a result not from readers.
>
> This is not a bad thing. I started blogging in the dark days after Hurricane Katrina, when the city of New Orleans was still mostly deserted, when the power was not yet on in many neighborhoods and the heavily damaged parts of the city were off-limits in daytime and at night. I blogged because I had a story to tell. I knew I was living through something unique, something terrible, yes, but something people needed to know about nonetheless.
>
> But the main reason I started blogging was for my own sanity. My mind was filled with images and ideas that I had to put into writing. My mind was screaming with despair for what had happened but also with hope for what would come.
>
> But I guess my life is more "normal" now. I don't expect anyone will want to read about what I had for lunch, and I don't feel a need to wax poetic about the new TV we bought earlier this year. Hence, this space is left quiet.
>
> I hope everyone remembers that just five years ago, there was talk that New Orleans should not be rebuilt. Many, in Congress, on the news and especially on the Internet said it would be "stupid" or "a waste of time

and money" to rebuild New Orleans. This talk has subsided, but the sentiment remains. Just yesterday I heard myself defending the existence of New Orleans yet again, telling a Virginian my well-rehearsed line about how New Orleans is almost 300 years old—what makes you think it won't survive 300 more?

Today, New Orleans is growing and thriving. Like every other city in America we have our challenges. But we face them, head on. What kind of cowardice has taken hold of America when someone can seriously propose that a major port city should not be continued?

New Orleans is no place for cowards. We steadfastly struggle with nature, ourselves and everyone else on a daily basis. Someone wrote to *The Times-Picayune* a few years ago that everyday in New Orleans is 24 hours long and 48 hours hard. You're damn right.

So everyone who doubts us, everyone who says or thinks we're not worthy, piss off. This is New Orleans, This is America, and WE ARE STILL HERE.

And we are moving forward into 2011 with your help or without it. Doesn't matter to me.

Peace, and Happy New Year.

Tim's post captures a range of elements associated with settling times. He points to his personal and social reasons for blogging and how it helped him cope with personal and collective traumas that emerged from the disaster and aftermath. He touches on how outsiders asked whether New Orleans should be rebuilt and the importance of letting others know that New Orleans is part of the United States and that it is still here (recall the comment from Sam of *NOLA Slate* about abandonment from chapter 3). He frames the city's residents as courageous and agentic, touching on the broader trend of civil repair that many of these writers took part in (Ostertag and Ortiz 2013), reminders of the key themes that mattered for him and other bloggers, as he closes this chapter of his life.

Separating from the Rest of the Pack: Organizing, Monetizing, and Visibility

While much of the New Orleans blogosphere diminished over time, it did not completely disappear. Occasional events would spark short boosts in use, especially if these events were flood or hurricane related. In 2012, Hurricane Isaac hit New Orleans and the Gulf Coast. It was "only" a category 1 hurricane but nonetheless sparked renewed stress and anxiety in many of those who survived Hurricane Katrina, seven years earlier. Some used their blogs as an outlet to give warnings and advice (e.g., keep an axe in your attic and have plenty of clean water and batteries) and to cope with their posttraumatic stress that seemed to return every hurricane season since Katrina. Other, physical-world events also brought many of these blog users back together, even if their blogging diminished. The Rising Tide conference was still going strong and provided an annual event to reconnect (as did the informal gathering of drinking and camaraderie that organizers hosted the night before, or what Loki called a "boggle"). Blog users would also get together to celebrate book launches. A couple of books compiling blog posts had been published, and these provided another opportunity for people to get together and renew friendships. For example, in 2010, the bloggers Sam Jasper (*Katrina Refrigerator* and *NOLA Slate*) and Mark Folse (*Wet Bank Guide* and *Toulouse Street*) put together an anthology of writing (mostly blog posts and poems) about the hurricane and flood. In the summer of 2010, they hosted a book launch party at a local bar, where roughly forty people attended, including the soon to be winner of the annual Ashley Morris Award: Cliff of *Cliff's Crib*.[2] Several years later, Cynthia Joyce put together another edited volume of Hurricane Katrina–related blog posts, *Please Forward: How Blogging Reconnected New Orleans after Katrina*. A local bookstore hosted a book launch and invited a few of the bloggers included in the book to take part.

The final Rising Tide conference was Rising Tide X, hosted in 2015. After this, the conference proved too much work, given the shifting priorities and diminishing blog use. The blog at the Rising Tide website remained silent for 2016, but in 2017, one blogger sought to renew its energy for a new, related purpose. On November 29, 2017, the blogger Mark Folse, of *Wet Bank Guide* and *Toulouse Street*, wrote, "I'm thinking of putting the band back together. After a long, drunken conversation about the long term future of New Orleans in a rising sea level world in which the oil companies have a preeminent place, I think it's time. Rising Tide are you ready to rise again?" Unfortunately, there was not much interest. Oyster was the only person to comment, responding eight months later, on July 28, 2018, with, "I don't know, Mark. Maybe there will be more interest for a 15th or 20th anniversary type reunion." Ironically, the final Rising Tide conference in 2015 came at a time when it was becoming more organized and formal, having been incorporated as a 501(c)3 nonprofit organization and creating a list of fifteen board members and key organizers, called the "Conference Krewe," drawing on the Mardi Gras parade Krewes that are so celebrated in the city. In its final year, the organizers were also able to waive the conference attendance fee, thanks to a sponsorship from a local bank. Yet they still sought to raise funds so they could offer some food, live webcasts of the panels, and other services that cost money. The organizers created a GoFundMe page and sought to raise $3,000 from donations. They created the page in late July 2015, a month before the conference.

> It's the tenth year of the Rising Tide Conference and the best year yet. This year we are making the conference completely free to anyone who would like to attend! Unfortunately it still isn't free to put it on. We'd like to offer all those things you've grown to love like breakfast muffins, lunch, a live webcast, etcetera. There's also less sexy stuff like security and programs to pay for. We've got some amazing content for you—let's make sure the rest of the conference is just as good.
>
> Thank you so much from all of us!
>
> (Monnot 2015)

By August 5, 2015, the Rising Tide organizers had already reached 10 percent of their fund-raising goal, and they seemed enthusiastic: "I'm so excited to announce that we have already reached 10% of our goal!! Thank you so much for your support and thank you for supporting Rising Tide X." A week later, August 12, 2015, the excitement appeared to wane a bit: "Hey everyone! We're this close to hitting the 20% mark. We really want to be able to buy everybody lunch so I'm crossing my fingers that we get there soon!!" There were no more updates, and conference organizers were able to raise $1,920 of their $3,000 goal—not too bad in the little amount of time they sought donations but still considerably short of their goal. Indeed, thirty-two people donated money, most in the $25 and $50 range. However, it was not as much as the organizers needed, and the money that was raised did not go to fund the conference. That is, the conference remained entirely volunteer driven. It is amazing that it ran for ten years given the amount of work involved. Its final year involved forty-four people sitting on panels, running workshops, or giving presentations, including 2016 presidential candidate Dr. Jill Stein. Plus, organizers arranged for lunch, had to find suitable space, and figure out other logistical things as they organized the conference. While impressive, it proved unsustainable without some paid staff, especially once the outrage from which it emerged dwindled and fatigue set in.

While the coordinated collective work among bloggers may have been hard to sustain for the long haul, two individual bloggers were able to go the distance, drawing on skill sets, reputations, and external investments to create something more lasting. This was the case with Karen of *Squandered Heritage* and Dambala of *American Zombie*, both examples of bloggers who collaborated with nonbloggers, as noted in chapter 6, and both illustrating their ability to adapt and effectively mobilize their available resources (in this case, largely nonmaterial resources). Karen drew on the reputation she built through her collaborative blogging with a local news station and the award-winning reports she helped produce with the legacy news reporter Lee Zurik. This was beneficial in two ways, both of which speak to her ability to adapt and evolve her blogging. First, she was popular and respected to such a degree that people sought her out. Ariella Cohen, who cofounded The Lens, moved to New Orleans to work with the newspaper *City Business*. Cohen eventually sought out Karen in an effort to work together to create something new and innovative. They envisioned something snarky and web based and applied for funding through different grant agencies. The Open Society was interested but wanted them to create something more formal, with a board of directors and some staff with legacy news experience. So they adapted and created The Lens. The Lens is a formal digital news organization, complete with bureaucracy and funding structure. While it confronted its own struggles with regard to funding and its status as a nonprofit (Ostertag and Tuchman 2012), it allowed Karen to shift from a volunteer blogger to a paid employee and to mobilize the financial and human resources necessary to create a more sustainable model of news making.

American Zombie is a different story. Dambala was trained as a documentarian and has always been a "media guy." His blogging was perhaps the most active and investigative of the bloggers studied in this book, leaving the web to hunt down people and speak with them. Initially, he sustained his blogging through ongoing moral outrage, a constantly renewed sense of anger at the extent of and incessant political corruption that both insulted city residents and sacrificed their safety and well-being. At the time of our interview, in October 2010, he was thinking of different ways to sustain his blogging. He wanted to keep it going, knew people were interested in it, and invested a substantial amount of time and effort into it. He also knew he could not keep it up forever. He had bills to pay and a family to help support, and the volunteer blog work he was doing was not helping him with these needs. He was brainstorming how to monetize his blog so he could continue. One idea was to webcast high school football games. Using Texas as his template, where high school football draws large sponsors like Coca-Cola and Nike, Dambala was considering doing something similar in Louisiana, then using the money he raised from these webcasts to fund his investigative blogging. Another possibility, one that speaks more directly to his visibility as a blogger, was to draw on his reputation and exposure to find employment with someone else but to continue with investigative blogging, in New Orleans or elsewhere. In the following excerpt, he is talking about a report he was about to publish on then-future-congressman Cedric Richmond.[3] Richmond was in the process of campaigning for his congressional run, and there were a few scandals that threatened it. Given the national significance of this campaign, Dambala thought that his story might generate enough national attention that he might find employment in Washington, DC.

> Yeah, so if—if I publish this, when I publish this—hopefully I get that up by tomorrow, um, you know, and I can somehow affect the outcome of this congressional election, and Cao (the local challenger) actually wins this, then, you know, that catapults me into I think a whole new level, in terms of the national stage. Obama endorsed this guy, the only politician in the country running for office that he did a television commercial for. You know, so you know, hitting a national story like that can only be good for me in terms of exposure. Now how do you equate that into money, you know? I don't know, you know. Maybe I get hired eventually by somebody, I don't know. But once again, I would have to have free rein

of what I was doing. But if I can get resources, I mean, jeez, put me in Washington, DC, and give me the fucking resources. I'll go—I'll be dead is what I'll end up, but . . .

But even Dambala ran out of steam, as the social validation and reward for his hard work disappeared over the settling period and the work to investigate and blog was no longer worth it. He was upset at the lack of interest and serious investigation by other journalists on the city's corrupt political and judicial systems, and his feeling of discouragement with not having any lasting impact on these frustrations took its toll. In the decade after the flood, Dambala had a large following, larger than any of the other bloggers in my sample, by orders of magnitude. However, it was not what it used to be, and this was also frustrating to him. While he may have been actively writing for much longer than many of the other bloggers in this study, his writing slowed almost to a stop. In December 2018, his blogger account was hacked, and emails from his blog were sent out to those who were linked to it. His next post was three months later, in March 2019. In a post titled "tap . . . tap . . . ," he simply wrote, ". . . anyone here?" Nobody commented. His final post (as of this writing) was in August 2019, titled "Requiem." It captures his frustration and why he did not blog much anymore. He begins with the following:

> I stopped posting on this blog because of the severe emotional and financial burden it became.
>
> I also realized . . . there is no recourse. You can tell people all day how corrupt things are but at the end of the day . . . nothing will happen to change it.

Even for Dambala, perhaps the most active, involved, and energetic blogger I spoke with and one who acquired a significant reputation for investigative reporting and a skill set of media documentation due to his training at the Smithsonian Institute, the struggle became too much, the lack of significant impact too discouraging, and the dearth of continued validation and similar social rewards too insignificant. The work took its toll.

A few examples in this blogosphere serve as illustrations of cultural work that extended beyond the work of many other individual bloggers.

Bloggers were able to continue hosting the Rising Tide conference for a few years after this local blogosphere began to diminish. Yet, while the event was well organized, its infrequency (held only once a year) and the organizers' inability to convert their work into a paycheck or even to generate funds to help organize and run the conference proved too much, and the Rising Tide conference ended. Dambala also continued his investigative work on *American Zombie* long after many other bloggers stopped posting and most of this blogosphere had dried up. But again, the inability to monetize his blog, the diminished visibility and social support that occurred over a decade after he started blogging, and the emotional and psychological toll of his blogging forced him to stop. Without the visibility and support of his readers, it just was not worth it. Karen of *Squandered Heritage* was the only blogger who was able to convert her individual blogging into a paid endeavor and a formal organization, taking on a life of its own. This was possible because of the visibility and reputation she garnered as a blogger, especially while working with a local legacy television news organization. This gave her the experience, credentials, and legitimacy to turn her individual blog work into a formal news organization, though not without some hitches (Ostertag and Tuchman 2012).

As the settling period progressed, the core questions and problems that people confronted transformed. Priorities changed, as family, work, and school settled and other obligations took precedent. People grew tired as fatigue set in. The work required to blog and to do it to the standards that many bloggers expected of themselves and of each other became too exhausting. While blogging initially helped people preserve their sanity in the early months, the constant attention and focus on the city's problems took its toll, and some needed to direct their attention and work elsewhere. Finally, changes in city institutions also mattered, as Mitch Landrieu replaced Ray Nagin as mayor in 2010, District Attorney Eddie Jordan resigned, and "progress" was made in the city's education system, tourism industry, construction of a new jail and medical complex, and flood protection; other sources of collective trauma also disappeared, changed, or were being improved to such an extent that there seemed no purpose to continue venting about them. With this, the social validation and support network that arose around blogging also diminished, as readers stopped visiting sites and comments shriveled or disappeared altogether. With these changes and bloggers not being able to adapt and monetize their blogging, many shifted attention elsewhere, and blogs went silent, with the only sign of their continuing life being a brief statement in the vein of "Never Forget 08-29-05" posted across many of these blogs each Katrina anniversary.

Cultural Work in Sleep Mode: The "Stickiness" of Katrina

We should be cautious in how we think about this dissipation of collective cultural work, especially considering how it arose through digital social media. While the moment of post–Hurricane Katrina blogging has passed, the shared experience remains a powerful heuristic that may remain important. These bloggers created strong social ties with each other. Many respected each other and enjoyed each other's company. They supported each other during an extended time of great need. These connections do not disappear altogether; they leave a mark, a footprint in their collective memory. They become a form of "sticky" culture (Fine 2013) that may be significant for reorganizing and remobilizing should future conditions warrant it.

Indeed, as sticky culture, some aspects of this blogosphere may have taken hold of the bloggers' collective memory and may be drawn on years later as useful tools for re-forming social ties and engaging more current events. Adrastos, who continued to write, though on different political topics and for the national blog *First Draft*, offers one example. On September 14, 2018, Adrastos wrote a post for *First Draft* as part of his "Your President Speaks" series. With this post, which he dedicated to his friend the late Ashely Morris, he drew on Ashley Morris's classic blog post, "Fuck you you fucking fucks" (FYYFF), to critique President Donald Trump and his response to the people of Puerto Rico, who only a year earlier had suffered and continued to suffer from the devastation of Hurricane Maria. Interspersed with screenshots of tweets from Trump in which he tried to blame Democrats for the poor response and from others who tweeted their experiences, Adrastos wrote,

> It goes without saying that none of this is true. Fuck you, Donald.
> It goes without saying that this is obscene. Fuck you, Donald.

It goes without saying that Trump thinks Hurricanes Maria and Florence are about him. Fuck you, Donald.

It goes without saying that he is desecrating the memory of those who died in Puerto Rico and those who might die as a result of Florence. Fuck you, Donald.

The real reason this president never cared about the deaths of some 3,000 Puerto Ricans is that they were never going to vote for him. It's a horrible thing to say about anyone but it's true. Fuck you, Donald.

As someone who lived through Hurricane Katrina and the Federal Flood, I take this very seriously. When a major storm makes landfall, I feel twinges of PTSD and I was one of the lucky ones. You shouldn't play politics with hurricanes. This is about human suffering, not about a ridiculous man who sits in the White House live tweeting Fox News. Fuck you, Donald.

Having said that, I disagree with those who think Trump should be thrown off twitter. I want to know what the enemy is up to. I believe in turning over rocks and exposing the evil underneath. Besides, the Insult Comedian keeps saying damaging things on twitter. Let the stupid fucker tweet to his heart's content.

Hurricane Katrina, as with other disasters and crises, lives in the collective memory of those who experienced it. While this memory differs based on how people's experience are structured by race, class, and other social forces and locations, as well as their personal idiosyncrasies, it nonetheless serves as a shared "sticky" cultural object, capable of being drawn on years later in an effort to make various points and construct new and reformed collective meanings. It is true that many of these bloggers stopped blogging, but the collective memory of Hurricane Katrina remains intact, and it may be drawn on for various reasons. Should New Orleans experience another flood like the one that followed Katrina, or perhaps some other disaster followed by an extended settling period, the digital networks and social ties that these bloggers built with each other may be pulled out of sleep mode, reactivated, and reenergized as they are put toward newly developing collective problems.

Indeed, signs of this collective memory emerged in 2020, during the COVID-19 pandemic. On March 28, Loki, who runs and writes for the group blog *Humid City*, reactivated the blogger listserv put together in the early days after Hurricane Katrina and before many people started blogging. Sending out an email to the listserv titled "[Bloggers] Still out there," he wrote, "Testing, testing, are these groups still functional?" Over the following few days, about twenty people responded in the affirmative, with some suggesting organizing another Rising Tide conference. However, not much followed, as the longevity of the pandemic at the time, the sources of anger and fear (especially local ones), and the availability of other social media outlets like Facebook all were part of a different context. There was not much "settling" going on, as the disruptions and collective traumas brought forth by the COVID-19 pandemic differed considerably from those of Hurricane Katrina.[4]

More recently, and perhaps more closely related to Hurricane Katrina, was Hurricane Ida, which struck New Orleans and the surrounding region on August 29, 2021, literally the same date as Hurricane Katrina sixteen years earlier. Hurricane Ida was one of the most powerful storms to ever hit the US. While the city's flood protection did its job (at least for New Orleans), the severe winds (150 miles per hour) knocked out the city's power grid, leaving over one million people in and around New Orleans without power. Many were without power for weeks, and some for months. Reminiscent of post-Katrina, the city began to smell, as rotting food mixed with ninety-plus-degree humid air. A bird's-eye view of the city and surrounding towns would reveal a sea of blue tarps covering damaged rooftops for mile upon mile.

One would think that this blogosphere might be reignited following Hurricane Ida, but it was not. While the similarities between Katrina and Ida are shocking (same date, severe winds, loss of electricity, massive evacuations, though not mandatory ones), the key difference was the longevity and lack of social and cultural trauma. Recall that this blogosphere did not really take shape until months after Hurricane Katrina's floodwaters receded and the devastation from the flood was more omnipresent and observable. The damage from Hurricane Ida was hard to see, as it was mostly due to loss of electricity. For the most part, the physical damage was not present or as visible, unless from the sky. People could still stay in their homes if they needed to. Further, electricity was largely restored to the city a month after the hurricane. While a month is a long time to go without power, it was not the months that followed Katrina. Finally, the city's social institutions remained largely intact (besides its power grid). There were no massive rebuilding projects under way, projects that could generate the suspicion, opportunism, and secrecy that characterized post–Hurricane Katrina New Orleans, and the national news did not swarm down to New Orleans to report on the devastation. The conditions in which people turned personal trauma into collective trauma and personal work into collective, cultural work were not present. The only sign was a post by Loki sent across the dormant listserv: "I rode it out, through the third day without power. Then I bolted to Cincy where I have tribe from living here before. I am coming back with a U Haul and relocating there. I just can't take it anymore and for my own mental health am going someplace a bit more boring. I feel like a traitor sneaking out, but for once I'm going to do something purely for myself. Love you all and I will be back to visit" (September 7, 2021). That is a decision that many people, including myself, can understand.

Conclusion

As the stimuli producing collective trauma became less stimulating, due to fatigue, acceptance, or removal, and as people's routines and lives returned, they found themselves with less time and desire to continue blogging. Many stopped, though some continued but shifted their writing to other issues, some very personal. Nonetheless, there was still some inertia that maintained their networks and relations. The Rising Tide conference and several other offline events (book launch parties, Katrina anniversary events) brought them back together to renew their connections. Yet these were only sporadic and not enough to sustain continued writing or ongoing physical-world meetings. However, this does not mean that their social ties dissolved; rather, they may have just become dormant. Certainly a few blog users did not get along and grew annoyed with each other, but most did not; and although some bloggers were frustrated with the blind spots and areas of concern of others (e.g., racism), many nonetheless continued to share similar frustrations and concerns.[5] Should another devastating, long-term event strike New Orleans, it is entirely possible that these networks and ties will be reactivated. These bloggers shared in the trauma, and that is not something that disappears quickly; and they created digital meeting spaces that would serve as convenient places to congregate. Further, they created another cultural resource in the form of collective memory, documented and made possible through their writing. If the circumstances develop and resonate with their collective memory of Hurricane Katrina and the settling period that followed, and if other options for expression are limited, it is possible that they may take up blogging again.

8

Communicating Culture

Ritual, Drama, and Blogs

It is clear that blogs were important resources for people to vent their frustrations over their fears, worries, and anxieties, to post news and opinion, and to offer validation and social support to each other in the wake of Hurricane Katrina. They served as digital outlets for cultural work motivated and oriented by the collective traumas of a postdisaster settling period. This was before the iPhone, Twitter, and many of the social-networking media common today. But what was it about blogs that users found useful in alleviating their fears, worries, and angers and being compassionate with each other? In this chapter, I address the question of affordances and suggest that it was the combination of both mechanical and cultural affordances of the blog platform that users enjoyed as an outlet for their cultural work. As digital social-networking media, blogs allowed for the creation of networks and the expression of stories with feedback, enabling unacquainted users to create meaningful, affective connections with each other and the sense of community and collaborative cultural work that followed.

Affordances

Key to the development of community among Katrina bloggers were the affordances of the blog platform. While the specific definition of "affordances" varies somewhat, the term essentially refer to the kinds of action (or potential for action) that a particular technology or artifact favors, enables, and/or constrains. Work on affordances originated in ecological psychology, where the term was devised to refer to the relationship between an organism and its environment: "the affordances of the environment are what it offers the animal, what it provides or furnishes, either for good or ill" (Gibson 1979, 127). Donald Norman (2002) built on this original conception with the notion of "perceived affordances," noting that affordances must be perceived as such for them to afford in the first place.

A sizeable amount of scholarship has developed around the idea of affordances, with strands focusing on various disciplines. In communication, the notion of "communicative affordances" (Hutchby 2001; Schrock 2015) refers to how communication technologies favor, enable, or constrain various kinds of action (Wellman et al. 2001; Schrock 2015; Khazraee and Novak 2018). Importantly, affordances must be "imagined" by users if they are to affect practices and performances (Nagy and Neff 2015).

The scholarship on affordances may be broken down into two general forms: those that enable the creation of a social network and those that enable a rich discourse thick with meaning and emotionality. The ability to create a social network refers to a communication technology's "mechanical affordances," which is a much more common topic in the affordances scholarship. The ability to create a thick discourse refers to a communication technology's "cultural affordances," which is a less common topic. Both are present with the blog platform, which speaks to why blogs became such an important communicative resource in the settling period.

The mechanical and cultural affordances of the blog platform were such that they enabled users to narrate and consume stories in the form of social drama and to share and respond to these stories across a growing network of users. Much has been written about mechanical affordances and the networking capabilities of digital social media (Bucher and Helmond 2017). For blogs, such affordances foster the creation of digital networks because they allow users to hyperlink to each other in their posts, enabling readers to follow the flow of communication and discover other active bloggers. Blogs also foster digital networks because the blog platform commonly includes a list of other blogs (a "blogroll"), so that users visiting one blog can discover and explore other blogs that the host has made available. Further, blogs allow readers to comment on posts, where they may include additional hyperlinks and introduce themselves as bloggers as well. Finally, blogs are open sources, not hidden behind paywalls, friendship requests, or other boundaries that limit the discovery of others and the growth of a networked blogosphere.

Through hyperlinks, blogrolls, commenting, and open access, the mechanical affordances of blogs are such that they allow for the rapid growth of digital social networks among users. Indeed, this was the case among bloggers in New Orleans.

While digital networks are important, they are not the only thing that is important. Zizi Papacharissi notes that "technologies network us, but it is our stories that connect us" (2015, 30). Mechanical affordances address networks but not stories and therefore leave much to be desired with regard to developing meaningful, affective connections with users. Without adequately addressing those connections, we are left struggling to sufficiently explain the cultural work that emerges from social-networking media like blogs and the social bonds and relationships people form through blogs. Not only do the networking capabilities matter, but the discourse communicated and consumed also matters. What people say with their blogs and how they say it is important for the quality of social connections they make through blogs. This speaks to the cultural affordances of blogs, a communication technology's capacity to effectively narrate an ongoing, richly meaningful, and emotive story. The cultural affordances of blogs allow for "cultural communication" (Carey 1989, 15), so that the discourse communicated with blogs was not just about information but also about sharing and fellowship. The cultural affordances of blogs provide for the celebration of commonness, communion, community, the "representation of shared beliefs," and working "towards the maintenance of society in time" (Carey 1989, 18). Blogs are useful resources in facilitating cultural communication. They allow users to create a richly meaningful, affective, and ongoing story across the digital network that users have created. This takes the form of a social drama, a story form that includes a cast of characters, background, and plotline, all involved in (im)moral, (anti)civil, and emotive performances, performances that are not only expressed narratively in the blog posts but performed by the bloggers themselves in the act of blogging.

Social Drama across Blogs: Narrative and Performance

Social dramas are stories of conflict, narrated in communication, including antagonists, protagonists, and a supporting cast of characters involved in an unfolding story line. They encourage social bonding and boundaries around shared understandings and sentiment. Social dramas begin with a breach, an event that substantially disrupts social life at a material and ontological level, and then move through several stages to their eventual conclusion, or they fizzle out. Hurricane Katrina was a beaching event but one that was played out in the settling period. These were times of extended uncertainty and conflict, rife with collective traumas, constituting an unfolding collective cosmological series.

Social dramas are constructed through communication in the form of morality tales. Most work on social drama focuses on legacy media. This was the case with the coverage of Aldo Moro, the Italian political figure kidnapped in the 1980s (Wagner-Pacifici 1986) and more recently with the racist murder of Stephen Lawrence in the United Kingdom (Cottle 2004). There are exceptions. Victor Turner's (1980) original formulation of social drama involved indigenous tribes without a mass media system, and Ron Eyerman's (2008) analysis of Hurricane Katrina involved a mixture of media in showing how social drama may be converted into cultural trauma. Social dramas may also be constructed by amateur news makers, in the context of a city settling from a massive destruction. This was the case with bloggers in the wake of Hurricane Katrina. The construction, narration, and performance of social drama through and across this network of bloggers constitute an important cultural object (Griswold 2014), serving as a central tool for unacquainted but networked individuals to build trust with each other, establish voluntary social relations, and form a shared identity and sense of community as "Katrina bloggers." By extension, the bloggers cultivated shared interpretations and understandings and ultimately meaningful, voluntary, affective connections with each other.

Narrating Social Drama

Drawing on the collective discourse that these bloggers created, we may recognize how the emotionally laden moral discourse of archetypes, cultural codes, and referents is communicated in a pattern reflecting a social drama. As people turned to blogs as an outlet for their cultural work over the settling period, they focused collective attention on and fomented shared understandings of collective threats, humiliations, and sources of blame. They came to know each other online and later offline, at the Geek Dinners, the Rising Tide conference, and other physical-world events. Their collective narratives told a story of conflict over New Orleans's recovering and rebuilding from Hurricane Katrina. Antagonists were plenty. In the early months, they largely involved the national media, authority figures, and judgmental outsiders seeking to blame residents for their own struggles. As time went on and the responsibilities for recovery and rebuilding shifted to the city, antagonists included local authority figures and private interests such as insurance companies and contractors. Judgmental outsiders remained a consistent concern, as the national media would periodically return as antagonists with each Katrina anniversary special and other periodic updates.

These figures were frequently cast as immoral and anticivil, framed as harmful cheaters and betrayers whose motives, relationships with the city and its residents, and control over social institutions were anticivil. As cultural referents, these actors included former president George W. Bush, former FEMA director Michael Brown, national news figure Anderson Cooper, and Fox News, as well as congressional figures like Speaker of the House Dennis Hastert and the many nameless and faceless outsiders who criticized city residents in the comments on blog posts or other outlets. Locally, actors included Mayor Ray Nagin and city communication director Greg Meffert, District Attorney Eddie Jordan, the Army Corp of Engineers, which was responsible for building and maintaining the city's flood-protection system, and other figures running the secretive and suspicious recovery and rebuilding work out of city hall. Also cast as antagonists were the private insurance companies, contractors, and other companies (e.g., cable, energy) that, in their greed, deceit, and self-interest, skirted their responsibility to help people in need. These were the fools, villains, and tricksters who acted immorally and anticivilly as they made decisions on how to allocate resources that had immense implications for the lives of city residents.

Returning to some of the examples noted in chapters 4 and 5 to illustrate, recall Liprap's post on insurance adjusters canceling policies from the comfort of their cars. For Liprap, insurance adjusters are the antagonistic actors—companies and an industry that she narrates with anticivil codes—as many people needed their insurance payouts as they sought to rebuild their damaged properties. She simultaneously framed insurance companies as immoral, in that they cheated and betrayed residents, exacerbating the collective trauma they were already experiencing. As such, these actors were characterized archetypically as tricksters and villains who could not be trusted.

Recall *Cliff's Crib* from chapter 5 as well. In Cliff's March 2, 2007, post on President Bush's visit to New Orleans, he likened the president to a friend who owes you money but never repays. Here he drew on anticivil codes framed with immoral platforms that may also be understood as part of the collective social drama that spread across this blogosphere: This post used former US president George W. Bush and the federal government he was leading as cultural referents. They were framed as immoral in their betrayal and cheating of city residents in need of their leadership and support. They were cast as anticivil in their suspicious actions, flying to the city for a photo op but largely unwilling or neglectful in their lack of help in the city and as residents recovered and rebuilt, despite ongoing promises and obligations to do so. Archetypically, they were cast as tricksters, saying they will do one thing but doing something else instead.

Bloggers developed trust and social bonds with each other around their collective anger with these key figures and their agreement in how to understand them as antagonists in this unfolding social drama. By commenting on each other's posts, linking posts from one blog to similar posts on others, and corroborating and validating each other's conception of antagonists and their cultural referents, bloggers began to form trusting social ties with each other. By seeing each other as largely on the "same page" with regard to understanding each other's anger, reasons for their anger, and sources of blame, they could start to see themselves as like-minded, start to trust each other, and start to meaningfully and affectually connect with each other.

Yet this was only half of the story. They also developed trusting social bonds through the narrative construction of protagonists. Here, bloggers highlighted progress, agency, and other moral things that reflected civil codes. These were sources of pride. Returning to Liprap's January 7, 2007, post in chapter 5 about the local author and *New Orleans Times-Picayune* journalist Chris Rose, Rose is framed in civil ways, both overtly and by implication. By claiming that Rose is "buck[ing] tradition" and "going for the jugular," Liprap is drawing attention to Rose's solidarity with city residents and indicating that he can be trusted. By extension, she presents him as disdaining the same secretive and self-interested "powers that be" and that threaten the fairness and security of city residents in the settling period. Further, by referencing Rose's donations to charities in New Orleans, Liprap frames him as altruistic and honorable. He is someone to be trusted, appreciated, and celebrated for his civil purity among these bloggers.

In another example that I also highlighted in chapter 5, on January 22, 2007, Schroeder of the blog *People Get Ready* wrote about the New Orleans Saints (the city's NFL team) and one couple that was rebuilding their home, noting their loyalty and dedication to the city and their civil motives and relations with its residents. This post is rich with moral platforms and civil codes, narratively linked to the Saints and courageous and dedicated residents who are willing to rebuild. Archetypically, the Saints and these residents are heroes, leading the way to return to the city and serving as examples for others who may be considering where to live next.

Moral platforms and civil codes in the blog posts tended to have a local focus, noting specific or general city residents as cultural referents, including some people at city hall, other bloggers, critical journalists, and locals who were clearly going above and beyond in altruistic fashion and whose loyalty to the city was unquestioned. Archetypically, these were the heroes, wise people, and sometimes the great mothers who went above and beyond to care for the city's residents in need, as their actions toward the city and its residents were reasonable, trusting, altruistic, and truthful.

Immoral platforms and anticivil codes were both local and national in focus, including public and private interests, which were commonly cast as harmful cheats betraying the city and its residents. These were the villains, tricksters, and sometimes fools, deceitful, greedy, secretive, and incompetent in their actions toward the city and its residents.

Moral and immoral platforms, civil and anticivil codes, and their archetypical cultural referents often coexisted in blog posts, building off each other to strengthen the point. The main characters sometimes had supporting actors whose presence helped illuminate the moral and civil qualities in the unfolding social drama of postdisaster New Orleans.

Performing Social Drama

Blog users could bond over the narratives they constructed and shared over their blogs. Agreement in the framing of those who were involved in the city's recovery and rebuilding work served as a trust-building mechanism and helped bloggers create meaningful, affective digital connections with each other. Yet there was more to their bonding than the narrative construction of others in the form of social drama. It also involved their performances as bloggers. In blogging, they performed their own morality and civility for other residents who were reading and relying on what they wrote. Archetypically, they performed as warriors, strong and aggressive in their framing of others as antagonists and protagonists; great heroes, leading the charge against the impending threat from anticivil and immoral decision-makers, private interests, and judgmental outsiders; wise people in their calm, rational, and carefully thought out and crafted posts; and great mothers in their care and concern for the city and its residents. Bloggers performed multiple archetypical characters with each post, sometimes being more hero than wise person or more warrior than mother. Nonetheless, their performances were part of the unfolding social drama, as the public nature of blogs meant that they could not remain in the shadowy background and only narrate the unfolding story of post–Hurricane Katrina New Orleans, even when using an avatar and blogging anonymously.

Much like Liprap's post about Chris Rose, a local newspaper reporter, many bloggers saw each other as satisfying similar needs for news, information, and critical commentary in a context of constant uncertainty and immoral/anticivil bombardment by the powers that be. Bloggers worked to highlight the immoral and anticivil among those who were involved in the recovery and rebuilding period. They also highlighted signs of progress and promise, sharing stories on how city residents were actively involved in the recovery and rebuilding work. In the process, they were working to construct a form of civil repair against the negative coverage from the national media and other outsiders (Ostertag and Ortiz 2013), coverage that in many ways framed the city and its residents archetypically as fools for not evacuating, sloths in their apparent lack of work toward their own recovery, and tricksters in their dishonesty in requesting the help and need of others. They were cast as immoral, as cheating the nation out of taxpayer money, as degrading to the nation in their perceived lack of self-work, and as anticivil by being passive and dependent on the handouts of others. By writing on these issues and constructing their position vis-à-vis these issues, bloggers simultaneously wrote themselves into the story of post–Hurricane Katrina New Orleans (Robinson 2009). They performed their morality and civility by demonstrating their care and loyalty to the city and its residents and by doing so in ways that were trustworthy, open, and altruistic. Through their demonstrated care and loyalty, their openness and altruism, they archetypically cast themselves as heroes, great mothers, warriors, and wise people. They provided needed information that soothed the uncertainty and anxiety of others, and they did so through careful and thoughtful analysis and commentary. As such, users were better able to build meaningful, affectual relationships with the bloggers, learning to trust them and bond with them not only because of the social dramas they narrated across their blogs but also because of how they performed as protagonists in these ongoing social dramas.

Conclusion

Blogs became useful social media tools for users to communicate and consume an unfolding social drama on the settling period of post–Hurricane Katrina New Orleans. With their mechanical affordances, blogs enabled the creation of digital social networks, which helped people discover each other. With their cultural affordances, blogs enabled the communication and consumption of a rich, thick, affectual discourse of moral and immoral platforms and civil and anticivil cultural codes, populated with cultural referents performing the roles characterized by different archetypes, all within the context of New Orleans and the collective trauma of a city settling from the "federal flood." But why blogs? It is true that the context of my study takes place at a time before many social-networking sites that are common and popular today, like Facebook, Instagram, and YouTube, existed, but this does not mean that people had to turn to blogs. Using blogs to the extent that they were used in the wake of Hurricane Katrina was not predetermined or mandatory. People could have limited their expression to writing emails, talking to others, contributing to local and national newspapers and other outlets, and similar forms of communication, or maybe they could have kept it bottled up. But they did not. They turned to blogs on a large scale. Why? This chapter has argued that it was the combination of mechanical and cultural affordances of the blog platform, as users discovered and celebrated them, that helps explain why they used blogs. With blogs, users had an outlet to communicate useful and much-needed information but to do so in ritualistic fashion. As a form of cultural communication (Carey 1989), blog users could be storytellers as they vented their frustrations, shared news, and offered thoughtful analysis and opinions, in a format that allowed them to elaborate, to contextualize, and to paint the simple facts with affectual color, guiding interpretation and meanings, and they were able to do so with a platform that reached strangers and friends alike. They may not have started blogging intending to construct a social drama, wanting only a suitable outlet to reach others and express themselves, but the storytelling genre of social drama structured their writing nonetheless, as they shared needed information and joined each other in communion and fellowship.

Social drama is a tool of cultural persuasions. With social drama, and the cultural and mechanical affordances that enabled its construction through and across blogs, users were able to foment greater agreement with each other over the social needs and questions that arose in the wake of the flood. They were able to foment relative agreement over cultural referents, their casting as antagonists and protagonists, archetypical characterizations, and related affectual meaning systems. Social drama turned into a bonding mechanism, fostering the trust and social connections that users developed with each other and that helped them work together to organize and take part in many of the collective civic actions noted in chapter 6. If technologies network us but the stories we tell connect us, as Papacharissi has claimed (2016), then the ability to construct and share stories in the form of social drama with blogs helps explain the connections that many users had with each other and why they were willing to invest in each other and work together to leverage some say over how the city rebuilt and the nation witnessed from afar.

Conclusion

Rethinking Culture and Action

As I stated in the introduction, this is a book about collective desperation and strength—the desperation that arises when everything you hold dear and all that is familiar and comfortable is destroyed, when all aspects of life, for you, your friends and family, and everyone around you, is destabilized and in constant flux; and the strength that arises when, despite the challenges, threats, and work that must be done to create that stability and return life to "normal," you, your friends and family, and everyone around you nonetheless muster the energy to get up each day and do something.

Hurricane Katrina struck New Orleans and the Gulf Coast on August 29, 2005. It rapidly grew from a category 1 hurricane as it swept across Florida into a category 4 "super storm," hastily gaining power over the Gulf of Mexico before hitting the region. Roughly 80 percent of New Orleans flooded, forcing evacuations and rescue efforts for most of the city's 452,000 residents and destroying the infrastructure that was so fundamental to the city's daily operations. While the hurricane was hugely traumatic in its own right, also traumatic was the long-term recovery and rebuilding work that city residents confronted up to a decade after the hurricane and floodwaters receded (Mayer 2017; Kroll-Smith, Baxter, and Jenkins 2015). I refer to this extended time period—a period seldom examined, or examined closely in the disaster literature (Frailing and Harper 2015)—as the *settling period*. This is when a disaster turns into a crisis, as the initial destructive event sends shockwaves across a region that continue to be felt years after (Gotham and Greenberg 2014). It is characterized by consistent and continuing uncertainty, fear, and anxiety, shifting problems that seemingly pop up everywhere (like "Whack-A-Mole," as Liprap noted), and ongoing moral dilemmas with ever-changing targets and topics. These conditions characterized life in post–Hurricane Katrina New Orleans. The basic ontological understanding of society and social life underwent substantial, continual, and evolving threats. Under these conditions, people are compelled to reestablish routine and driven to re-create familiarity, to create some semblance of order and reproduce themselves in the ongoing process of embodied autopoiesis. In post–Hurricane Katrina New Orleans, people discovered blogs as important communicative tools that they could rely on to cope with their desperation and trauma, as they worked toward creating order and consistency in their lives.

While the settling period was one of constant uncertainty and anxiety, it was also a period rife with collective agency, of people working together to restore life to "normal," forming new routines and practices based on newly devised systems of meanings and feelings, creating new resources forged in their need to return to ontological stability and security. This extended period of disaster recovery and rebuilding, the settling period, is revealing for how we understand culture, as discourse and as practice, as automatic and deliberate, as public and private, as a resource, and, most interesting to me, as a source of collective causal power. I call this power *cultural work*, collectively compelled action motivated by shared emotional energies, guided by shared meaning systems of moral foundations and cultural codes, performed through enduring archetypes, becoming manifest in culturally relevant characters and representations. This is the story told in *Connecting After Chaos: Social Media and the Extended Aftermath of Disaster*.

The Story So Far

Let me briefly summarize my findings and argument before discussing how this project advances scholarship in cultural sociology and why it is useful for sociology in general. I argue that Hurricane Katrina and the settling period that followed not only massively disrupted basic ontological understandings of society but did so for months and years on end. The long-term nature of this ontological disruption created an extended and collective cosmological series by interrupting embodied autopoiesis, an organism's fundamental need to reproduce itself by interacting with the surrounding environment. Because that surrounding environment was rendered so completely chaotic and uncertain for so long, the familiar tools and practices that people had come to rely on for embodied autopoiesis were no longer available or useful. This created a crisis situation, not just physically but ontologically, existentially, psychologically, and emotionally, and not just individually but collectively. It became a shared human condition, uncomfortable in the short run and unsustainable in the long run. It had to be dealt with in some way.

These conditions of the settling period were traumatic: traumatic in the breakdown of social order and institutions, traumatic in the representations of the city and its residents on display for the nation, traumatic in the questionable actions of decision-makers running the recovery and rebuilding work, and traumatic in the abuse and exploitation of private interests seeking to make a quick buck from people in need. It is under these conditions of collective trauma, rooted in the unfolding and extended settling period of post–Hurricane Katrina New Orleans, that cultural work manifested itself most clearly. Emerging from the shared problems of uncertainty that people faced and guided by shared goals and rewards that grew from those problems, cultural work took shape. Anxiety, fear, and anger associated with uncertainty energized one part of their cultural work, while senses of pride, social belonging, and self-enhancement generated by helping others deal with their collective uncertainty energized the other part. That is, their cultural work was both pragmatic and normative.

Under these conditions, blogs became useful outlets for cultural work. They began as mechanisms for coping with collective trauma, as they allowed people to find and share news and information, vent their frustrations, fears, and vulnerabilities, and offer support and validation for each other. Over time, more and more people started to blog, users discovered each other, and what might be understood as a local blogosphere emerged. In the process, they created a collective discourse and social support network for blog writers and readers. I characterized this newly created resource as an *emotionally laden moral discourse of archetypes, cultural codes, and referents*. Complete with antagonists, protagonists, an unfolding plotline of the settling period, and a background of years of controversy over the city's flood protection and political leadership, this discourse took shape as a collective *social drama* across much of the local blogosphere (Ostertag 2021a). Under these conditions, the cultural work that became manifest in blog use reflected both the need for information and the longing for connection and communion that was shattered with the flood (Carey 1989).

This discourse and the social drama form it took was possible not only because of bloggers' cultural work but also because of the shared mechanical and cultural affordances of the blog platform. Blogs provide a mechanism for users to satisfy their initial needs of news seeking and venting and then subsequent needs of community building and collective actions through a story format that the bloggers not only narrated but also performed (Ostertag 2021b). Social dramas are tools of social bonding and cultural persuasion, turning the collective discourse communicated and consumed across this local blogosphere into a useful, dynamic cultural resource, an outlet for coping with collective traumas, a mechanism for constructing a shared identity and sense of community as "Katrina bloggers," and a tool for organizing and staging a variety of physical-world collective civic actions that were both contentious and noncontentious.

As the settling period progressed into relative settlement, social institutions were rebuilt, and social lives returned to the familiar and predictable. With this, the collective traumas that created an extended cosmological series and interrupted collective embodied autopoiesis dissipated, and therefore so did bloggers' cultural work. People blogged less frequently and on fewer traumatic issues. The once-active blogosphere diminished, as did the physical-world collective actions that many of these bloggers organized and took part in. Yet, while their cultural work dissipated, their social ties might not have disappeared altogether. Rather, they lie dormant, in sleep mode, ready to be reactivated should a similar unsettling event and long-term settling period strike the city and its residents again. We may witness again how the cultural work of residents operates through social media, as they seek to connect after a different but in some ways similar form of chaos.

Contribution to Cultural Sociology

With this project, I put several literatures in conversation with each other, all directed toward the building of a framework for thinking about culture and causality that I call *cultural work*. In so doing, I build on a growing interest in cultural sociology that is revisioning notions of culture and action. This work, most innovative in the cultural cognition branch (Vaisey 2009; Lizardo 2017), is moving beyond discredited structural functionalist frameworks of coherent value systems driving long-term goals (Small, Harding, and Lamont 2010; Vila-Henninger 2014), which continue to serve as anchors for criticism (almost seventy years later). I build on an understandably timid and cautious (but growing) sociological engagement with the biological sciences that acknowledges the importance of how the body operates internally and what this might mean for sociological questions of collective action and meaning-making/maintaining (Massey 2002; Freese, Li, and Wade 2003; Wright and Cullen 2012) and without adhering to overly deterministic claims rooted in non-biological social constructs. I also build on work on emotions as motivators of action (i.e., activating emotions) by recognizing their compulsive powers and highlighting the reciprocal relationship between emotions that motivate actions of avoidance (e.g., anxiety and fear) and those that motivate actions of attraction (e.g., pride and happiness).

Culture is a notoriously tricky concept in sociology. It may be symbolic or material, meaning based or noted in practices; it may reside deep in the human conscious or more on the surface and accessible in our narratives; it may motivate or be used to justify action; it may be personal or public (DiMaggio 1997; Swidler 2001a, 2001b; Alexander 2003; Vaisey 2009; Griswold 2014; Lizardo 2017; Simko and Olick 2020). Christina Simko and Jeffrey Olick (2020) recently synthesized the various strands of cultural sociology into a four-part typology. They argue that most cultural sociology focuses on either practices and action or discourses and meanings and that this work tends to focus on these as either explicit, publicly performed and available or implicit, hidden in the habitus, practical consciousness, and similar areas of the subconscious. These strands of cultural sociology are represented in four lines of common scholarship, with scholars often stressing their difference from each other. Yet these need not be treated as mutually exclusive, nor do the differences need to be the focus of attention. Rather, they may be integrated in different ways so as to offer several innovative research and theoretical trajectories that capture the dynamics and nuances of culture without getting bogged down in overcomplexity and particular distinctions. Indeed, recent scholarship is starting to highlight that these distinctions may have been overemphasized and that the different approaches are actually more commensurate than we usually assume (Vila-Henninger 2014; Norton 2020; Mast 2020; Simko and Olick 2020).

Using Simko and Olick's typology as a guide and in the spirit of commensurability, we can understand the problems that this book seeks to address and what the notion of cultural work offers the scholarship on culture and action. With a massive disaster and the period of unsettlement that immediately follows, taken-for-granted background assumptions, cognitions, practical consciousness, and such are threatened. The new environment is no longer familiar or predictable. As the unsettled period shifts into the settling period, the national discourse on the disaster, the city, and its residents shifts from one of compassion to fatigue and victim blaming. These are evident in the speeches, vocabularies, stories, and other cultural objects that populate the national media, that are expressed by authority figures, and that become manifest among other third parties, framing residents and the city in anticivil ways. Basic cultural codes, meaning systems, and cultural structures are threatened from outside and from within. Outsiders construct residents and the city in anticivil ways, threatening people's ability to settle and creating the need to defend, reconstruct, and repair their selves. From within, and as the rebuilding work transitions from the national to the local level, authority figures handling the recovery and rebuilding projects act in suspicious and secretive ways, demonstrating anticivil motives and relations as they rebuild or build anew the city's basic institutional structure. In the process of responding and acting toward these discourses and practices, New Orleans residents discovered blogs as useful resources for constructing alternative, affirmative narratives of themselves, for critiquing people in charge of the local recovery and rebuilding work, for sharing and analyzing news and needed information, and for building a social support network among like-minded others who shared in their understandings and desires, all explicit and justifiable actions focused around their general sense of abandonment, that they were "not OK," and that they needed to keep attention on authority figures as they rebuilt.[1]

These are the multiple ways that culture may be implicated over the settling period, as people desperately seek to return to predictable, routine, familiar life. But why? What motivated people's action in New

Orleans? This is where I seek to build on recent developments in cultural sociology and return to questions of culture and causality with my notion of cultural work. Cultural work draws on the scholarship in cognition, biology, and emotions to build an argument about culture and action (Collins 2004; Vaisey 2009; Small, Harding, and Lamont 2010; Vila-Henninger 2014; Lizardo 2017; Jasper 2018), and it follows up on criticisms of the past that found fault with a cultural sociology that shifted attention away from motives (Campbell 1996, 1999) and toward talk about action (Albas and Albas 2003) and cultural capacities (Swidler 2001a). Recall that *cultural work is collective agency around a shared system of emotional energies and meanings that operate together to motivate and orient collective action.* It answers questions about motives and efforts and why people use explicit culture in the first place and how they use it. Capacities for action that inform our strategies of action and draw from our cultural repertoires speak to how culture influences action but not to how culture motivates action per se. Capacities for action speak to our cultural resources, as it is these resources we draw on to construct lines of action, but again, our focus on resources offers little to explain why we choose to use the resources we do or why we collectively act toward these resources in the first place. These are not mutually exclusive positions; they are different and complementary aspects of cultural action. However, it is not enough to say that problems that threaten our identities as member of various social institutions explain our action. Here, what it is that actually compels that action goes unanswered, and it ignores all those who might be dealing with similar problems but not acting. If you are sampling largely on those who are already acting, then you can ignore questions of motives and instead focus on capacities, resources, and culture in action.

We know complete, holistic value systems do not really exist and do not inform action in the form of long-term, normative end goals. That has been clear for a long time. However, the turn away from structural functionalist approaches to action and the fear that cultural explanations inevitably lead to victim blaming resulted in sociologists abandoning interest in culture and causality entirely. This is unnecessary and limiting (Small, Harding, and Lamont 2010). Goals may be short term, immediate, and context specific (Agnew 1992), as are the meaning systems that motivate actions toward these goals (e.g., short-run, medium-run, and long-run moral emotions [Jasper 2018]). Carl Bankston has noted that a "causal explanation . . . is wrong because it is poorly reasoned or does not fit the evidence, not because it would have undesirable implication if it were true" (2017, xix).[2] With cultural work, I return to questions about culture and causality, avoiding the pitfalls of victim blaming and biological determinism that led to sociological abandonment of culture and causality over half a century ago. Cultural work focuses attention on the emergence, maintenance, and dissipation of collective behavior, with my case being the context of extended disaster recovery and rebuilding. This is the context in which shared problems and a related system of social rewards emerged to guide and motivate cultural action. In this sense, culture is an adaptation, something that many cultural sociologists recognize, but an adaptation with agency and causal powers and absent the moral judgment that earlier versions of cultural causality tacitly assumed.

I find Orlando Patterson's conception of culture most useful for recognizing the intricacies of cultural work. For Patterson (2014), culture is composed of two layers: one, a pragmatic, deeper layer of practical consciousness, informed by the core problems we face as human beings living together, cooperating, surviving, and such; the other, an upper, normative layer identifying social goals and senses of belonging. These are related, as it is the deeply pragmatic layer of shared problems we try to solve that brings to light and informs the social goals and senses of belonging that constitute the upper, normative layer. This is a useful conception of culture because it helps us recognize the pragmatic and normative simultaneously and as related (Winchester and Guhin 2019) in a reciprocal relationship of avoidance and attraction, which is fundamental to human action (Elliot 2008).

Cultural work reflects this dual-layered notion of culture. Culture's causal powers, therefore, reflect how we experience and understand shared problems and the normative system of self-enhancement, social belonging, and other rewards that we associate with addressing those problems. The extent that this becomes manifest in shared emotional energies and meaning systems around which collective action is organized and motivated speaks to cultural work. Consciousness can, at times, override subconsciousness and the habitus (Vaisey 2009), but the question of when or under what conditions this happens remains undertheorized (Vila-Henninger 2014), with Ann Swidler (1986, 2001a) only giving lip-service to it (i.e., unsettled times) and as a context for introducing and explaining culture in action and building the cultural resource perspective. The context of settling helps shed light on this answer, suggesting pathways for theorizing about culture and causality. In post–Hurricane Katrina New Orleans, the context of settling created ongoing schematic failures and constant threats to embodied autopoiesis. In so doing, it introduced people to shared problems from which a shared normative system of social motives and rewards emerged. These, together, informed their cultural work, cultivating it and structuring it around how people interpreted and understood their problems and rewards, guiding and motivating their collective actions. The particular characteristics of their cultural work reflected these pragmatic and normative factors as they were experienced by a group of largely white, middle-class bloggers, in a particular cultural environment in the months and years that followed Hurricane Katrina. (For further elaboration, I discuss the scholarship in the sociology of action, culture, and causality in the appendix.)

Sociology and the Everydayness of Culture Work

How common is cultural work? The narrative on settled and unsettled times treats these states of social existence as distinct and wholistic, clearly demarcated from each other. A society is either settled or unsettled. I have shown in this book that there is a period of settling that exists in between, linking them on a nonbinary continuum. But I want to push this argument further and, in so doing, claim that my notion of cultural work is much more common than we might initially think.

Throughout this book, I situated my theory of cultural work as something that emerges in settling times, as people collectively cope with an unsettling event and its aftermath. I believe this was necessary, as doing so provided a social condition in which an argument for renewed thinking about culture and causality may be more obvious and therefore receptive. Yet I wonder how unique and unusual such conditions actually are in contemporary society. Given the scale of destruction brought forth with Hurricane Katrina, it is easy to see how an entire region, including all its social institutions and the routine activities of its residents, is completely destabilized and for an extended period of time. Culture work in these conditions seems straightforward and not that controversial. But must it arise only from such all-encompassing destruction? I am not so sure.

I believe there are a couple of ways of thinking about and recognizing the everyday, commonality of cultural work. Recall that in chapter 1, I noted that I want us to think of cultural work similarly to the way work is thought about in physics, the transference of energy into action. I want to push this analogy a little further. Culture work is kinetic energy in the form of collective action structured according to a shared system of meanings and feelings. All objects possess potential energy, but it is when that energy turns into action that it becomes kinetic. I think the same can be said about collectivities of people. We all possess potential energy and at all times, but when that energy is linked to the same sources, understandings, and emotions, it turns into action; it becomes kinetic. That is, it becomes cultural work. With this in mind, let us consider three cases that may help us recognize how common cultural work actually is in our everyday lives: (1) crisis ordinariness; (2) status and identity threats; (3) hate and the dark side of modernity.

Case 1: Crisis Ordinariness

Crisis ordinariness is the recognition that late modernity is characterized by ongoing, shifting crises (Berlant 2011), that there is no real settled time. In a sense, we are in a constant state of settling, roaming from one crisis to another and another and then back again. At one level, this is crises over war, disease, concerns over healthy food, clean water and air, climate change, political scandals, oil and energy costs, capitalism, and economic markets. At another level, this is crises over the cost of rent, gas for our vehicle, the increasing price of food, health care expenses, and the shrinking purchasing power of our paychecks. These all introduce an ongoing stream of inescapable, nonstop crises shifting from target to target. While at one time crises were things to "overcome," to "get on the other side of," to have them "blow over," they are now "normalized and diffused into everyday feelings of anxiety and unease" (Mayer 2017, 77). Crises are the new normal. Life of late modernity is characterized by roaming crises, with no place to really stand firm. As we come to the end of the first quarter of the twenty-first century, upheaval and chaos abound. Indeed, Nadya Hajj's remarks on our "broken world," from her work on Palestinian refugee camps, ring loudly: "There are ever-increasing numbers of refugees, migrants, 'informals,' and 'stateless' people fleeing violent conflict, climate disasters, and catastrophes like the novel coronavirus pandemic in all corners of the globe" (2021, 86). We exist, day in and day out, on social realities made of quicksand—not usually as porous as in the context of post–Hurricane Katrina New Orleans but quicksand nonetheless. We are continuously treading to keep our heads above and to temporarily stave off sinking.

To the extent that this is true, it begs the question, then, How common is cultural work? If the conditions I highlighted in postdisaster, settling New Orleans cultivate cultural work in a clear, obvious way, then how do we understand cultural work when crises are more subtle, lingering, slow moving? When they are a continuous feature of everyday life? When escape from crises and the ability to rest are only temporary and fleeting? To the extent that late modernity is characterized by crisis ordinariness, then cultural work should be an underlying feature of social life and therefore something in need of continued analysis, refinement, and implementation.

Case 2: Status and Identity Threats

Bringing the issue of crisis ordinariness to the level of identity is the breaking down of status binaries and the fluidity of social identities that characterize late modernity (Giddens 1991). This development has radically altered how people understand themselves, each other, and our relationships—core aspects of sociality. While emancipating and freeing in many ways, this change has also introduced continuous ontological threats and risks to self-identity and validation. People live life as members of various social locations, networks, and domains, simultaneously. We all occupy multiple statuses and identities at the same time. Some of these may be quite unstable, and perhaps even traumatized, while others may be relatively stable. We may experience trauma in some areas of life, as we take part in certain social domains, while avoiding it in others. For example, the constant threat of job loss that characterizes advanced industrial capitalism may create ongoing uncertainty and instability, while at the same time, family life may provide the stable support structures people need to help cope. These are not mutually exclusive: the instability of work life may coexist alongside the stability of family life. The conditions that generate intentional, motivated action by threats to embodied autopoiesis may be activated in the work domain but quelled in the family domain. Therefore, we may see cultural work more clearly emerging in work-related actions, while it is less obvious in family-related actions, where established routines and resources remain readily available and effective.

In another example, particularly relevant today, consider the experiences of the nation's Black and brown people with police, alongside family and perhaps church. Family and church may provide stability, familiarity, and support, while being out in public (especially for youth) exposes them to the whims and violence of local police officers. This characteristic of public space, and the constant uncertainty about police, may threaten embodied autopoiesis, cultivating cultural work that becomes manifest not only in organizations like Black Lives Matter but also in the more intimate, local actions of resistance, challenge, and organizing that we find across the nation's cities. Indeed, cultural work might help explain the less radical and active, such as the everyday collective impression management that goes into simply being a person of color in a white-dominated public. Is cultural work not part of this in some way? Are these actions not a form of collective agency rooted in shared activating emotions and meaning systems emerging from ongoing uncertainty about police encounters and the trauma that produces?

For a final example, consider sexualities. In the family domain, being gender and sexually fluid, for example, may be wrought with potential ongoing traumas. Parents may feel ashamed and be unsupportive, with some even refraining from talking to their children altogether. Would such qualities of family life not compel more thoughtful, intentional actions on behalf of the children due to the anxieties and anger generated? At the same time, supportive friendship networks may offer safe spaces to be oneself and recover from the experiences of family, with a host of cultural resources readily available to negotiate life. In the course of a few hours, visiting family and then hanging out with friends later, we may see cultural work rise and then diminish as people participate in unsettled family life and then in more settled friendship networks.

These conditions and social settings are not mutually exclusive. Borrowing from the literature in the sociology of deviance and labeling theory, our statuses overlap and oscillate as we go about our daily lives (Adler and Adler 1983). Some social spaces may be more threatening to ourselves and therefore ask more of us in the form of cultural work than other spaces, as we move in and out of them and other "going concerns" throughout the day (Gubrium and Holstein 2000). Perhaps cultural work is more common than initially implied with this study of disaster and its wake. Indeed, cultural work might be a quite common and regular part of everyday life, as threat and risk are ubiquitous features of our social lives, and usually at least one social domain that we take part in may be unsettled.

Case 3: Hate and the Dark Side of Modernity

From another perspective, culture work might help scholars better understand the ugly side of humanity and therefore better construct strategies for justice, inclusion, and equality/equity. For example, macro-level trends associated with modernity and globalization have brought forth a host of exclusionary, hateful actions. The recent growth in authoritarian populism in the US and Europe may be understood as resulting from cultural work, though clearly an ugly form of it. Authoritarianism is characterized by a search for collective security, in light of collective fears and anxieties around faith, family, and country, by scapegoating groups perceived as threats and working to exclude them from social belonging and citizenship (Norris and Inglehart 2019, 7, 77). Indeed, it is not hard to imagine a system of shared emotional energies motivating action according to a shared meaning system that reflects authoritarian values and the perceived "problems" that ground it. Such is exactly what Pippa Norris and Ronald Inglehart (2019) were referring to with their notion of "cultural backlash." Further, a similar argument may be said about the conservative reaction to many social justice movements, such as environmental, women's, LGBTQ, and the many "awkward" movements that seek cultural goals of new meanings and understandings (Armstrong and Bernstein 2008; Ostertag and Díaz 2017). Indeed, cultural work might help explain the conservative insurrection at the US Capitol that occurred on January 6, 2021, after Donald Trump lost the 2020 presidential election. Fascism, nationalism, white supremacy, and other harmful ideologies, and the collective actions associated with them, surely reflect a shared system of emotional energies and meanings, even if they are rooted in exclusion, hate, and similar despicable qualities. It is essential to understand this if we are to effectively confront hate movements, mobilize the many fence-sitters and apathetic people, and create lasting and effective inclusionary polices and practices.

ACKNOWLEDGMENTS

This book has been long in the making, and there are so many people who have helped in some way. I know I am forgetting some, as I have been working on this project since 2010, and I am truly sorry if that is you. But there are some people who have helped out quite a bit, and I want to thank them openly.

First, I want to thank the Katrina bloggers, everyone who spent time to open their hearts, relive their trauma, and talk to an outsider like me. Your passion, sense of need to capture your lives after the hurricane, and what you all created are inspiring and awe-inducing. I thank you for your time and energy.

Second, I want to thank David Ortiz. David was my colleague at Tulane University and a coauthor on a number of papers that laid the groundwork for this book. His hard work, dedication, and insights were and are appreciated greatly.

Third, I want to thank Gaye Tuchman. Gaye's willingness to read through paper drafts, hear my ideas, and open up opportunities to me all helped me improve this project and have made me a better scholar.

Throughout the years, I have tested some of the ideas in this book with numerous people who deserve thanks. Jeff Alexander provided publishing opportunities and chances to workshop ideas at the Center for Cultural Sociology at Yale University. In fall 2021, I was able to spend my sabbatical semester there as a Faculty Fellow and complete the finishing touches of this project. Wendy Griswold has been a supporter of this project since we first met at the University of Exeter during the European Sociological Association Culture section meetings. She provided a sense of confidence that I should continue doing what I was doing, even though so few sociologists were interested and many were dedicated to already-existing popular frameworks for thinking about culture and action. Robin Wagner-Pacifici read early chapter drafts and offered useful feedback as well. Kevin Gotham also read paper drafts that tested the early ideas of this book and consistently provided detailed, honest, and useful feedback, even when he had little time to do so. Michele Adams always opened her door for me to ask questions and test out ideas early in this project. She provided challenging questions that helped keep me grounded and put me back on track.

The Tulane University Department of Sociology's Cultural Workshop and Sociology Colloquium series provided spaces to test out early ideas, and I thank many of the organizers and attendees, such as David Smilde, Mariana Craciun, Camilo Leslie, and Christopher Oliver. I also want to thank the Center for Engaged Learning and Teaching and the New Orleans Center for the Study of the Gulf South, both of which provided small grants to support data collection for this project. In 2010, the International Communication Association awarded me its annual James W. Carey Prize, which helped me kick-start this project. Thank you.

I wish to thank Ilene Kalish, my editor at NYU Press. Ilene was encouraging and supportive of this project since she first read my proposal. After I had swung and missed with so many other presses, Ilene saw the potential and supported it all the way.

Finally, I want to thank my family and friends who have provided unwavering support and encouragement along the way.

METHODOLOGICAL AND THEORETICAL APPENDIX

Methods and Explaining the Study

In the weeks, months, and years after Hurricane Katrina and the "federal flood" (Eyerman 2015), many people discovered blogs as useful tools for communicating and consuming news and information about the flood and later the response, recovery, and rebuilding periods (Pignetti 2010; Ostertag and Ortiz 2013). They focused collective attention on and fomented shared understandings of collective threats, humiliation, and sources of blame. In the process, they grew to know each other, both their online personalities and in the physical world. They created a dynamic shared discourse and an online community and collective identity, with some taking part in physical-world mobilizations of various sizes and longevities and others creating new organizations. The intentions were to exert some influence over how people rebuilt their lives and the city and to remind people outside New Orleans that everything was not "OK," that there was still a lot of work to do, and that residents of the city were working hard to rebuild. This book reports on a study examining these processes as they unfolded over a roughly eight-year period, from 2005 to 2013. It draws on four primary sources of data: interviews with blog users, analyses of blog content, observations from events organized through and by bloggers, and analyses of institutions and organizations they created.

My primary source of data involved interviews with twenty-seven of these bloggers, which I collected from 2010 to 2013. By interviewing bloggers, I could learn about their motivations and reasons to blog, what topics they blogged on, how they got started, and where they were with their lives several years after the flood. Through reflection, interviews allowed me to extend my analysis back in time, to when they first started blogging and how they got involved within the context of a settling New Orleans. Interviews also allowed my respondents to reflect on the shared discourse they created and collective actions they took part in, helping illuminate those baby steps that are so essential to the cultural formations they created. Interviews also helped me uncover the system of meanings and feelings that motivated and oriented the culture that fostered these cultural formations.

To complement the interview data, I also attended, observed, and participated in several events organized by and for these bloggers and other users of social media, all of which had the flood as the initial impetus. This included attending three annual Rising Tide conferences (2010, 2011, 2012), in one of which I was invited to be a participant on a panel titled "Social Media, Social Justice" (Rising Tide 6, August 27, 2011).[1] Organized by "Katrina bloggers," this conference started in 2006 and continued every year until 2015. It was a daylong event designed to provide a platform for bloggers and other users of social media (and the general public) to discuss city progress, regress, and other storm/flood-related issues and concerns associated with the recovery and rebuilding periods. Each of the three years I attended drew around two hundred participants. I also attended a book launch party for an edited book called *A Howling in the Wires: An Anthology of Writing from Postdiluvian New Orleans*, an anthology of blog posts and other writings of the postflood settling period, selected to capture the raw emotions, pain, need to be heard, and sense of community that developed among bloggers (Jasper and Folse 2010). Further, I attended several events that the city and some of its institutions organized for the five-year anniversary of the storm (2010), in which bloggers were key speakers and/or panelists. These observational data allowed me to witness the social formations that these bloggers created years after the flood and the social ties and relations that they formed with each other and that were essential for their offline collective actions.

Some bloggers also created new organizations and local social institutions. The Rising Tide conference is one, and I analyzed it not only from my position as participant observer but also as itself a cultural object (Griswold 2014), with key figures, events, and stories that "stuck" as cultural memories and were drawn on later in practices of remembrance and bonding (Fine 2013). A second involved the creation of a new, innovative news organizations called The Lens. I spoke with and interviewed the founders, reporters, editor, and opinion writers for this new organization and attended several anniversary parties they created. For a time, I was also a member of the organization's board and was able to witness its gradual formation of a bureaucratic structure, its movement to resemble a legacy news organization, and its budget and finances. These observational and participation data helped me understand the results of the organization's cultural work, allowing me to link blogger narratives to real-world social formations and the shared meanings and feelings that cultivated them.

Finally, and in different waves, I analyzed blog content, including posts and comments. This involved a close, qualitative analysis of blog content (Altheide and Schneider 2013), in which I sought to investigate the cultural codes, moralities, emotions, archetypes, and collective traumas expressed in the posts. Along with my colleague David G. Ortiz, I assembled a small team of researchers (undergraduate students supported through several rounds of small university grants) and examined seven of the most active and important blogs in this local blogosphere, using the paragraph as the unit of analysis. These blogs were key nodes in this local blogosphere, active writers who were highly engaged with each other. In total, I examined 2,234 paragraphs associated with these blogs. The dates range from August 2005, before the storm hit New Orleans, through December 2007. This twenty-eight-month period allowed me to capture the growth in blogs as a means of communicating and consuming news, information, and commentary on the storm and its aftermath; the shifting topics and questions as they emerged over time; the creation of a richly meaningful, emotionally laden collective discourse; and the networks of interaction that developed among blog users. The blog content provided an invaluable digital archive for examining these phenomena, as well as a useful tool for verifying and clarifying statements from the interview data (e.g., motives to blog, cultural references, affective network formation, etc.).

While these data were collected over a span of just a few years, 2010–2013 being the most active period of data collection, they allow me to examine a much longer period of time, capturing shifting questions and concerns as the city went from settled to unsettled to settling and back to relatively settled. Interviews with bloggers and blog readers allow for a retrospective account of people's movement into blogging, including the motives to read/write and the process of developing relationships (and tensions) with others through digital social media. Observations and participation in collective events allowed me to witness how bloggers mobilized and organized years after Hurricane Katrina and to develop some sense of their impact on the city. Analysis of new organizations and institutions helped me consider the collective impact these bloggers were having on how the city rebuilt anew. Analysis of blog posts and related literature (books, etc.) provided a digital archive of content and digitally mediated interaction over time, as blog content often remained accessible years later. Together, these sources of data provided a rich pool of empirical information that allowed me to monitor and analyze how personalized social-networking media were used over an extended period of great need, including the cultural structures that underlie their use, the content communicated and consumed through them, the creation of a new cultural resource and its uses, and the various social implications that they enabled and afforded as personal needs shifted into collective questions, concerns, and problematics associated with the settling period.

Theory: Sociology of Action and Culture

Sociological approaches to action focus on three primary concerns: (1) the nature and causes of what is tacitly assumed to be rational action; (2) the rules and knowledge that underlie and control action; (3) the learning and negotiating of meaning between and among actors. Our actions are assumed to be purposeful, controlled, and autonomous. We act toward others and our broader environment intentionally and autonomously, anticipating future outcomes (Summers-Effler 2004; Mische 2009; Tavory and Eliasoph 2014; Hitlin and Johnson 2015) and using our bodies as instruments in ongoing negotiations among other people and things. This scholarship has roots in many early sociological traditions, including Weberian sociology, Parson's action theory, and symbolic interactionism.

Early Approaches to Action: Culture as Internalized

Today, we can see these trends manifest three different approaches to studying action (Abramson 2012). One focuses on the relationship between values and goals. This approach began with Max Weber's emphasis on subjective interests driving action toward instrumental end goals. Weber (1946) emphasized subjective meanings associated with interests and ideas as key factors in action. He distinguished action from behavior, or action that lacks meaning. Personal action becomes social action when other people and interests are taken into consideration by the actor. Weberian approaches to action view action as instrumental (Emirbayer and Mische 1998): we are actors seeking particular ends. Sometimes we do not care about the consequences or the means of our actions, and other times we might take these into account. In either case, our individual interests direct our action. Weber's interest-driven theory of action provided the bedrock on which much subsequent sociological scholarship on action developed (Campbell 1996). For Weber, interests direct action on the basis of cultural (subjective) motives, goals, and the means of achieving them (Swidler 2001a, 69).

In the mid-twentieth century, Talcott Parsons reformulated Weber's approach to action by focusing on normative values instead of subjective interests. Parsons's action theory (1937) stresses values and norms as key factors in explaining action. These play two roles. First, they identify end goals, things toward which to strive, in a way similar to Weber's interests, though with a greater normative emphasis. Second, they constrain action by constituting the informal rules and expectations that limit choice. Early Parsonian approaches were more goal oriented, focusing on the causes of behavior and their normative motives. Later, Parsons turned to questions about the rules and knowledge that underlie and control what was once treated as voluntary action. Like Weber, however, it is the rational individual who acts, but this time action is based on particular normative value systems, and interests are collective rather than individual.

For both Weber and Parsons, culture was located inside individuals, as were the motives to act. Goals, whether they be individual interests or collective values, were assumed to be long term, and meaning systems, such as values, were treated as coherent, cohesive, and consistent. These became problems in the second half of the twentieth century as scholars realized that interests and value systems are not so coherent or consistent, that the end goals associated with interests and values are poor predictors of action, and that it is better to think of culture as external, publicly available rather than individually internalized. These criticisms led scholars to move away from questions of values, goals, and cultural causality onto new sets of questions.

Culture and Action: Mid-Twentieth Century to Today

These new questions informed three strands of research on culture and action. One emphasized culture as a system of meaning externally accessible in signs, symbols, codes, and other collective representations. A second shifted attention to talk of action in the form of vocabularies that we use to justify and neutralize the meanings of our action to ourselves and in the eyes of others. A third focused attention on how people use the public culture they are familiar with as a resource or tool with which to build "strategies of action."

The first path is rooted in Durkheimian anthropology and is more notable in Clifford Geertz's (1973) notion of culture as "webs of significance" and how people make meaning from the explicit culture around them. For Geertz and those following in his tradition (e.g., sociologists still interested in culture after it was abandoned in the wake of structural functionalism), culture is "an historically transmitted pattern of meanings embodied in symbols" (1973, 89). It is a "defense against meaninglessness, making potentially incoherent experiences cohere" (Swidler 2001a, 40). It is with these symbols, in the form of rituals, art, ceremonies, stories, and such, that people build modes of understanding and act accordingly. Geertz's epistemological approach was to examine these meaning systems within the context of situations, such as events, or institutions, such as art and religion. This led to the treatment of meaning as appearing coherent, much as Parsons did before him (Swidler 2001a). A thick description of the social settings associated with these situations and institutions produced a narrative that favored cultural coherence. Yet, when approached through the actors, such coherence disappears. Interactionists recognized this problem and shifted their attention onto the vocabularies around action. Scholars drawing on the cultural resource perspective recognized it as well and shifted their attention toward questions about culture *in* action. Later, Jeffrey Alexander and the strong program in cultural sociology returned to questions of meanings and codes, situating them within broader structural systems and examining their significance for action, particularly related to boundaries (Alexander and Smith 1993; Alexander 2006, 2007).

These criticisms informed two strands of scholarship. In one strand, the study of action turned into the study of "parts of action," in the form of how we talk about and justify particular aspects and segments of action (Campbell 1996). The action was no longer the starting point for analysis, but the meanings and justification of action were. Action became a product of people's justification, sometimes before the act but often after. In a second strand, the study of action shifted to examine culture's influence on action, particularly on how people use their cultural environment (material and symbolic) to navigate life. Both, while still considered the study of action, manipulated the unit of analysis so that the cultural causality of action and the agency that makes it possible either were given little independence or autonomy or disappeared altogether.

Starting with vocabularies of motives (Mills 1940) and through techniques of neutralization (Sykes and Matza 1957), stigma management (Goffman 1963), and accounts (Scott and Lyman 1968), one path turned to how we justify our actions and neutralize unwanted reactions from others. Here, sociologists (especially interactionists) began to conceptualize motives as "answers actors give to challenges to their behavior, which have the potential to disrupt an ongoing interaction sequence" (Albas and Albas 2003, 352). The question is no longer about the motivations of people's action but instead the discursive work we do to normatively explain our action to ourselves and others and to neutralize any negative reactions. This "slippage" in the use of motives for understanding action, as Colin Campbell (1996, 102) called it, turned attention onto parts of action, "reasons given for action, rather than precursors to it" (Albas and Albas 2003, 349). Scholars also began to examine the role of identities in these narratives. Growing out of the symbolic interactionist tradition, identities are treated as important filters for interpretation and therefore justifications and action. We act in ways that resonate with our most salient identities (MacKinnon 1994). These identities affect how we interpret events, the meanings we generate, and the justifications we draw on to normatively narrate our action to ourselves and others.

Also growing out of the aforementioned criticisms is the emergence of the cultural resource and repertoire perspectives, where scholars examine culture *in* action. Continuing the shift away from questions about the causes of motivated action, this approach moved onto questions about culture's influence on action. The word "influence" is important here as, much like the shift to vocabularies, it represents a subtle manipulation in the framing of action. Here, culture is seen as facilitating, rather than determining or causing action (Swidler 2001a); it is an external resource that provides a toolkit of competencies for building and shaping strategies of action (Swidler 2001a, 105). The focus shifts toward the resources and other capacities and equipment used in orienting, shaping, and controlling action. Shared problems rooted in institutional contexts loosely inform which tools are appropriate for which strategies of action. Again, however, questions of motive and ultimately agency undergo a transformation as scholarship shifts the focus onto qualities of action rather than action per se. We might now understand that values are poor predictors of action; we use narrative devices to justify action, and we draw on and are limited by the familiar resources we have at our disposal in our action. Yet this continues to say little about action per se, that is, the actual act of acting: what we think and feel and how this compels us to collectively act. These questions are important because they offer insight on why we draw on certain resources and build certain strategies when multiple options are available or why we may choose to do nothing.

The downplaying of causality in cultural approaches to action is afforded by cultural sociologists' preferred epistemology of practice theory (Bourdieu 2008; Giddens 1984; Schatzki 1996; Vaisey 2009). Practice theory is a broad set of loosely related conceptions of action that "take orderly materially mediated doings and sayings ('practices') and their aggregations as central for the understanding of organizational and social phenomena" (Nicolini and Monteiro 2017, 110). While cultural practices may represent the action of culture (Simko and Olick 2020), questions of motive and what compels us to act remain largely unaddressed. This is because the basic premise of practice theory is that people are born and socialized into already-present, ongoing streams of variously meaningful action. We do not start practices from scratch but rather enter into already-existing practices. For example, we do not make journalism, religion, or education from scratch but enter into preexisting arrangements of journalistic, religious, or educational practices. From here, we draw on our cultural resources, justify what we do, and make or break boundaries. Tacitly assumed in this work is that these ongoing practices sweep us off our feet and carry us forward like a rafter down a river. We navigate this river with the tools we have and justify how we do so. Causality, and the work needed to act in the first place, is not examined because movement is treated as always ever present. Yet action is not involuntary and automatic like the beating of a heart or constant and always present like the current of a river. Indeed, there is plenty of inaction and counteraction, and action for every single one of us must have a starting point. This is so whether we are talking about the routine, automatic "thoughtless" action of habitus or practical consciousness or the thoughtful and deliberate action of intentionality and strategy. We are not carried forward on preexisting currents of action as if we are floating down a river or standing on a "people mover" in the airport. Rather, we must move our own bodies as if we are stepping into a busy sidewalk and keeping up with the flow of traffic. Sometimes this takes significant expenditures of energy; most times it requires little. Either way, the work required to enter, take part in, exit, challenge, or change cultural practices goes largely unrecognized and untheorized in the sociology of action scholarship. Yet it is vitally important for building on existing scholarship in these areas and better understanding culture and action.

A Return to Causality

As we settle in the twenty-first century, the cultural resource and repertoire approaches remain strong and are established frameworks for understanding action (Swidler 2001a). Yet, while recognizing the value of these approaches, some scholars are incrementally moving back toward questions of culture and causality (Small, Harding, and Lamont 2010), reconsidering "broad orientations towards 'meanings and values'" (Spillman 1995, 131; Vaisey and Lizardo 2010, drawing on new frameworks for conceptualizing action and culture from other disciplines, and recognizing that understanding people's ability to initiate and maintain a line of action (what Campbell calls "Type 1 agency") is not the same as, nor does it discredit, the independently constraining power of social structures (Campbell 2009). First is the work on meaning, signification, and representationalism (Alexander and Smith 1993; Mast 2020) associated with cultural sociology's strong program. The strong program directs attention directly on the intersections of meaning and action. Jeffrey Alexander (2003, 2006), in particular, has built a model for understanding culture as a causal agent of collective action, stressing the importance of shared meanings and feelings as these form around and resonate with cultural codes and referents situated within broader notions of civil society (i.e., the civil sphere). Scholars have drawn on this basic notion of culture to explain collective motivated action in contexts where such action cannot be reduced to institutional logics, constraints, or material forces alone (Kane 1991; Alexander 2007; Olick 2010; Patterson 2015; Ostertag 2016). Agency as a mechanism of social change, exercised against forces of control and cultural reproduction, is a central feature of this approach and is captured in the term "relative autonomy." Yet this work lacks a theoretically parsimonious framework for linking meanings and feelings together, in a relationship that orients and energizes action.

Second is the work associated with cognitive culturalists (Vaisey 2009; Lizardo 2017). Sparked by the earlier work of Eviatar Zerubavel (1996), Paul DiMaggio (1997), and Karen Cerulo (2002), these scholars draw on various conceptions of cognition and cognitive processing practices to understand action as reflecting multiple qualities. At a deeper level, one more aligned with automatic cognitive processes, culture takes the shape of such things as habitus, practical consciousness, and similar implicit, largely subconscious motives that cause action. At a higher level, one more aligned with deliberate cognitive processes, culture is more explicit, taking the shape of such things as narratives, vocabularies, ideologies, and similar resources we commonly draw on to justify action (Vaisey 2009; Vila-Henninger 2014; Simko and Olick 2020). These coexist as both motives and justifications for action (Vaisey 2009), mutually reinforcing each other with the conscious mental system sometimes overriding the subconscious (Vila-Henninger 2014), under the right conditions (such as an extended cosmological series).

These approaches to action are often treated as mutually exclusive, with scholars stressing the importance of one over the other. However, convincing arguments exist for their compatibility and integration in models of action (Norton 2020; Simko and Olick 2020). For example, Corey Abramson (2012) notes that motives, values, and orientations (what he refers to as "cultural inputs") provide attributions about aspects of the world, notions of good and bad, worthiness and worthlessness, right and wrong. These provide the ends that people value and pursue, arguably constituting the "broad orientations towards 'meanings and values'" that Lyn Spillman (1995, 131) and Stephen Vaisey and Omar Lizardo (2010) note. Our cultural resources help explain how people get to these ends, and our meaning systems inform how we understand and interpret appropriate ends, values, and means of achieving them given context and interpretive environment, whether they be short, medium, or long term.

The Conditions of Causality

The return to questions of motives brings cultural sociology back toward questions of causality. While I will elaborate on this later in the appendix, we may understand motives as existing at three levels; *deep* evolutionary biosocial drives, *subconscious* social psychological intuitions and orientations that direct action toward worthy goals, and more *conscious* discursive inputs on worthy pursuits. These are not mutually exclusive cognitive realms responsible for specific cultural components of action but rather are related and therefore potentially enlightening for understanding the relationship among different components of action. While most sociological work emphasizes the role of automatic cognition in motivating behavior and deliberate cognition in justifying behavior, Luis Antonio Vila-Henninger (2014) notes that these operating systems work much more closely together. He argues the following:

> We can conceptualize motive states as being combined with an actor's social knowledge and perception of situational cues to generate motives through the interaction of conscious and subconscious systems. In these terms, it is not accurate to claim that fully formed motives are generated by subconscious cultural schema. Instead, motive states are subconsciously generated and are then integrated with event/action sequence knowledge and social perceptual knowledge to create motivations, which then drive action. These motivations would then be available to varying degrees to an actor's consciousness. (Vila-Henninger 2014, 252)

Important questions follow, such as, When are motives most significant for action? As Swidler noted (1986, 2001a) and Abramson (2012) supported, motives are most significant for action during moral dilemmas and unsettled times. Why might this be the case? Because these situations pose threats to the certainty, familiarity, and routine of predictable social interactions and relationships. Rapid and substantial changes in broader environments (social and physical) introduce uncertainty to the basic ontological status of social life. Such conditions require much more intentional and deliberate action as people monitor their physical, symbolic, and social environments and seek to reestablish familiar routines. Existing knowledge and resources are available tools in this process. This is why the context of Hurricane Katrina and the months and years that followed, or what I have called the *settling period*, are important for a study of culture and causality. It is this prolonged period of instability and uncertainty that creates the context for collective motives to coalesce around shared meanings and emotions in a way that foments a form of collective agency that I have termed *cultural work*.

Introducing Cultural Work as a Theory of Causality

These approaches have largely structured the field of culture and action in sociology for the past half century (Campbell 1996), with recent scholarship in cognitive cultural sociology reengaging questions of culture and causality in ways that (1) avoid many of the pitfalls associated with Weberian and Parsonian approaches of specific, long-term end goals and cultural unity, (2) are not incompatible with the work on cultural resources or representationalism, and (3) that remain wide open to innovative developments and theoretical promise. But cognitive culturalists are not the only ones. Joining them (and in a teaser for what is to come), research into emotions and emotional energies is also engaging questions about causal action (Collins 2004; Jasper 2018), providing greater insight into the changes in the body's chemical states and how these compel or depress action. These two bodies of scholarship can be combined to create a model of cultural work, in which the power of culture lies in its ability to energize and orient collective action around shared understandings and representations (Campbell 1999). The theory of cultural work that I develop draws on and builds on this scholarship. It proposes that the cognitive sciences, cultural sociology, and work on emotional energies can be combined to build a causal model of culture and action that I call *cultural work*.

What Is Culture?

A model of cultural work will become clearer if we start with an appropriately dynamic definition of culture, one that captures the complexity of the term, accounting for the depth of meaning and motives of action under a single, umbrella conceptualization. Orlando Patterson's (2014) conception of culture is helpful here, as it acknowledges both the normative and pragmatic, the goal-seeking and problem-solving character of culture, their relationship and interdependency. Using this as a guide for what follows, Patterson sees culture as

> the conjugated product of two interconnected, componential processes. The *first* is a dynamically stable process of collectively made, reproduced, and unevenly shared knowledge about the world that is both informational and meaningful. Its basic processes are shared schemata that are internally embodied and externally represented. They provide predictability and regularity, coordination equilibria, continuity, and meaning in human actions and interaction and meet certain core motives such as belonging and self-enhancement. . . . The *second* is a pragmatic component of culture that grounds the first, and it has its own rules of usage and a pragmatically derived structure of practical knowledge and provides routine ways of interactionally using the constituted cultural structures. (2014, 5–7)

What is useful about Patterson's conception is that it captures both the normative and pragmatic qualities of culture and motivated action simultaneously, and in ways that resonate with popular resource perspectives, but it makes room for the renewed work on culture and causality. Moreover, it does so relationally, opening up the possibility for scholars to develop models of action based on this relationship. My theory of cultural work situates the normative as an adaptation to, or a reflection of, the pragmatic. Our normative goals of social belonging and self-enhancement motivate action on the basis of how we help others deal with the shared problems of practical knowledge that we might confront. Likewise, our need to maintain cognitive consistency associated with practical knowledge motivates our action to seek that help. Motives exist at the pragmatic and normative levels, but they are compelled by different stimuli, so that the relationship is not equal. It is the need to solve collective problems that generates and structures normative social goals. This is useful as we move forward and develop a notion of cultural work because it provides a way to think about culture and action in which action is normatively meaningful and guided but pragmatically rooted in and informed by shared problems associated with routine and practical knowledge.

This conception of cultural action that I am developing helps scholars traverse a long-standing problem in the sociology of action, namely, where to locate motives. We may recognize two basic kinds of motives identified in the scholarship. Jeremy Bentham, J. A. Hadfield, Max Weber, and others make the distinction between initial motives and end motives (Hadfield 1955; cf. Campbell 1996, 102). *Initial motives* refer to psychological pressures that compel action. *End motives* refer to the broad end goals we act in relation toward. Alfred Schutz offered a similar distinction, with "before" motives corresponding with initial motives and "in-order-to" motives equivalent to end goals (Campbell 1996, 104). Both exist simultaneously but were largely abandoned as objects of analysis as the scholarship on action shifted to focus on talk about action and resources that facilitate action.

Patterson's conception of culture is useful because it allows us to recognize both motives—initial and end—and their linkages to pragmatism and normativity, simultaneously and as related, so that disruptions in the practically rooted component of culture will lead to subsequent disruptions in its normative adaptations, compelling initial motives focused on reestablishing predictability, regularity, equilibria, continuity, and meanings (i.e., the constituted cultural structures) that underlie and inform senses of belonging, self-enhancement, and other broad, normative end goals and social rewards.

In applying this definition of culture to my notion of cultural work, let me briefly restate the argument I make in this book. In the context of disaster and the shifting collective traumas of the postdisaster settling period, the regularity and routine of collective life was disrupted.

This introduced new shared problems for people to confront and new meaningful goals of self-enhancement and belonging that resonated with these problems. It is the relationship between both layers of culture, identified in the aforementioned conception, that informs meanings, motives, and actions. Disruptions to routines introduce new shared problems, at a deep, implicit level, and people collectively address these disruptions. In so doing, they rebuild other, normatively meaningful goals of belonging and self-enhancement. The problem-solving and goal-directed aspect of people's collective action in New Orleans existed simultaneously, evolving to reflect the settling period of post–Hurricane Katrina New Orleans, in which people sought to create order out of the chaos of the flood and its aftermath. This is the general idea of action in my notion of cultural work. It is meaningful, relational, motivational, and most obvious in settling social conditions.

The Action of Cultural Work

I now provide the details of cultural work, the nuts and bolts that are the core components of my theory of cultural work. Three things matter: (1) embodied autopoiesis, which grounds action in core psychological and biological needs; (2) emotional energy sets, which provide general drives that make action possible; (3) meaning systems, which direct and orient action in patterned ways. I bring these three components of action together in my theory of cultural work and explain how the settling period is useful epistemologically for studying it.

EMBODIED AUTOPOIESIS

Psychologists and biologists refer to the continued production of oneself as a process of *autopoiesis*. It involves concerned interaction with the environment and is the basis for teleology and sense-making (Weber and Varela 2002). The creation of meaning involves the interaction between a living system and its environment. It is adaptive, reacting to the immediate environment, the past, and to some degree an anticipated future. Autopoiesis involves *embodied cognition*, with action emerging in real-time interaction between a larger nervous system in a body with particular capabilities and an environment that offers stimuli, opportunities for behavior, and information about those opportunities. The brain and body exist together in a relationship of embodied cognition rooted in autopoiesis that is called *embodied autopoiesis*. It serves as the core bodily mechanism that energizes and orients behavior at a fundamental human level. My theory of cultural work is based on embodied autopoiesis. It is on this grounding that pragmatic and normative motives emerge, energizing and orienting collective action within particular cultural contexts.

Embodied autopoiesis involves cognition, the "extraction of significance from the noisy informational barrage that the world generates" (Norton 2020, 51). Most of the time, cognition is routine, and therefore so is much of our action: practical consciousness, automatic cognition, minimal mental effort required or exerted to process stimuli, navigate our environments, and act in relation to familiar and predictable experiences and anticipations, cognition on autopilot, embodied autopoiesis on cruise control. The making of significance from our environment and the process of re-creating ourselves is fairly predictable, routine, and familiar. Here, we are very much "meaning-maintainers," as Patterson (2014, 7) aptly noted, reproducing our social worlds according to familiar scripts, resources, and practices. This informs the action of settled times. Actors rely on externalized, stable cultural scaffolding to guide behavior, taking advantage of cheap, cognitively optimal, and efficient action operating at the level of discursive consciousness (Lizardo and Strand 2010). Existing schemata effectively help us process our environments in predictable and familiar ways. Little in the form of motivation or intention is needed to act. Rather, meaningful action in these settled times largely involves justification (Swidler 1986, 2001a), with intentionality and motive as outliers, arising "when conduct is 'frustrated' in some way" (Campbell 1996, 107). This is action in settled times.

But what about unsettled times, or the "gaps" and "crevices" of settled times, where the cultural scaffolding that provides continuity, routine, and stability is disrupted, when our trusted and taken-for-granted schemata fail (DiMaggio 1997; Lizardo and Strand 2010)? In these conditions, what was once novel and regular is now problematic and must be reexamined (Hitlin and Johnson 2015; Cerulo 2010, 118). Embodied autopoiesis is no longer on autopilot. Cognition requires more attention in order to restore it. These are "problem situations," with the "potential to lay bare causal connections that often go unnoticed in the inertia of everyday life" (Edelmann 2018, 335). Military veterans returning to civilian life (Edelmann 2018), adolescents in the tenuous life stages between childhood and adulthood (Fine 2004), and other transitions over the life course in general (Hitlin and Johnson 2015) represent common "transitional moments" (Edelmann 2018), when we traverse the gaps and crevices between familiar institutions that usually provide continuity, routine, and predictability (Lizardo and Strand 2010). When the ontological and existential status of the world and ourselves is thrown into question, we must be more deliberate, intentional, and conscious of our action.

Disruptions in embodied autopoiesis and cognition provide a baseline for action rooted in changes in familiar, routine, and predictable environmental stimuli. How we respond to and act toward these environments will be based on a combination of our emotional and mental interpretations. Our emotions speak to changes in our bodily chemical states that drain or energize action as a response to stimuli. Our mentality speaks to how we understand these stimuli and what they mean to us.

EMOTIONAL ENERGY SETS

Emotions are the conscious components of our affectual system. Affects are states of bodily experience that register in levels of intensity (Massumi 2002; cf. Cavalcante 2018). Emotions are recognized and identified affect (Papacharissi 2015; Cavalcante 2018). They are feelings we experience and interpret based on our internal, bodily environment, the manifestation of endorphins that compel us to move or drain us of energy. Most sociological scholarship on emotions examines (1) how people's feelings are conditioned by cultural and structural factors (Kemper 1991); (2) the role of culture in defining what emotions are to be experienced, expressed (Hochschild 1983; Peterson 2006), and used (Clark 1997); and (3) the cultural construction of appropriate vocabularies and labels associated with our internal states. Some sociologists have extended this scholarship to question the role of emotions in social relationships (Scheff 1990; Schmitt and Clark 2006) and, more recently, to investigate the role of emotions in motivating action (Massey 2002; Collins 2004; Turner and Stets 2005, 2006; Goodwin and Jasper 2006; Jasper 2011; van Troost, van Stekelenburg, and Klandermans 2013). Their basic conclusion is that emotions play a fundamental, if not *the* fundamental, role in motivated action (Campbell 1999; Jasper 2011). It does this by providing the energy needed to put one foot in front of the other. Without emotions, we would have no energy to actually move, and while we might have movement without action, we cannot have action without movement.[2] Emotions provide the bodily chemical states that make movement, and therefore action, possible (Massey 2002; Freese, Li, and Wade 2003; Jasper 2018), as it is our shared human biology that drives "the arousal and flow of emotions" (Turner and Stets 2005, 4) and compels us to act (or at times not act).

One promising line of scholarship in this area is Interaction Ritual Theory (IRT; Collins 2004). IRT emphasizes the power of emotional energies to motivate action and argues that this energy is generated primarily through senses of pride and guilt, with the end goal being self-enhancement (Summers-Effler 2004; Boyns and Luery 2015). IRT is useful in explaining our actions toward things that attract us, such as social belonging and self-enhancement, our normative end goals and social rewards. Yet action is also rooted in avoidance (Elliot 2008) and is where we see the pragmatic grounding of action.[3]

Actions of avoidance reflect the problem-solving nature of pragmatism and resonate with uncomfortable emotional states we typically try to avoid, such as fear, worry, and anxiety. They may become manifest in anger if our fear, worry, and anxiety are seen as unjust. They are linked to our need to understand so we can establish meaning, certainty, and trusted prediction. These are not so much goal directed but rather seek distance from risk (Lupton 1999) and uncomfortable stimuli. Here, action is a coping mechanism (Wilkinson 2001), for anxiety, fear, and worry associated with ontological insecurity, schematic failure, and other threats to embodied autopoiesis. We are averse to these negative emotional energies and seek situations that, informed by history and memory, we anticipate will relieve us from them.

Actions of attraction reflect the goal-seeking nature of normativity and resonate with enjoyable emotional states we typically seek out, such as joy, pride, happiness, and satisfaction. They motivate projective actions (Emirbayer and Mische 1998) toward future situations (Collins 2004; Boyns and Luery 2015) that we believe will enhance our sense of self (Summers-Effler 2004). We desire positive emotional energy and seek out stimuli (e.g., situations) that we anticipate will yield it, on the basis of memory of past experiences. Actions of avoidance reflect a need to distance ourselves from uncertainty and the uncomfortable emotional states of anxiety, fear, and worry that such states foment. These are not mutually exclusive emotional states and actions. Rather, they exist simultaneously in the relationships between and among actors and their environments. For people blogging in the wake of Katrina, seeking and sharing information reflected both forms of action. They sought information to learn about what happened so they could avoid uncertainty and understand and plan in light of new pieces of data, factoids, and insights. They shared this information with others in need, earning respect and appreciation from the social approval of others.

MEANING SYSTEMS

While emotional energies of attraction and avoidance offer a notion of action rooted in normativity and pragmatism, the action of cultural work is guided by shared meanings. Meanings exist at different levels and reflect different needs. Like the rings on a tree, meanings are layered, some resonating with older histories and others resonating with newer experiences and conditions. Schematic failure and the transitional moments (Edelmann 2018) ushered in during times of significant change do not necessarily threaten all meaning systems equally but, rather, may be particularly threatening to those most relevant to our familiar cultural environment, as it is this environment from which we extract significance and maintain embodied autopoiesis. In unsettled times and the settling that follows, when our cultural environment changes and we struggle to extract familiar significance from it, a deeper meaning system nonetheless exists, and we may use it to help reestablish cultural familiarity. It is this meaning system that we draw on to solve problems and to reestablish order, understanding, routine, and predictability. From here, we build a more specific cultural meaning system within certain contexts, codes, referents, technologies, practices, and interpretive frameworks. This is how we use meanings in embodied autopoiesis and during schematic failure, as we seek to reestablish social order and the predictable, routine, and familiar of our social, symbolic, and material lives.

There are conceptual tools for capturing this complexity and situating it within a theory of cultural causality. Moral Intuition Theory and

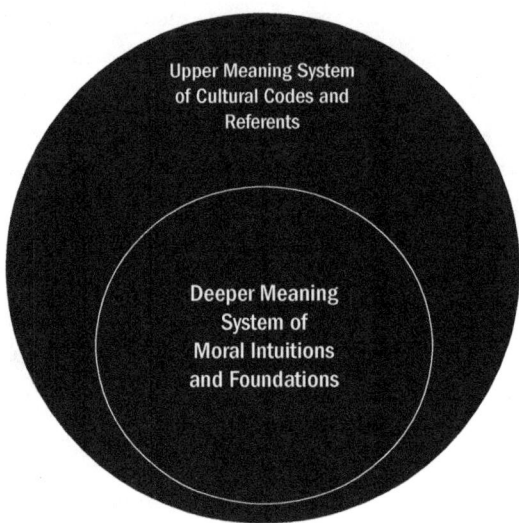

Figure A.1. Layered meaning systems

its focus on moral platforms (Abend 2013), for instance, offers one way of understanding the deep meanings that transcends specific context and that ground newly created culturally specific meaning systems in times of schematic failure. This is because, while filtered through cultural contexts, moral intuitions are not solely cultural. Shared moral intuitions exist across cultural contexts and social domains. Moral Foundation Theory (MFT), specifically, offers one system of meaning that is useful in such cases. This is due to its widespread, cross-cultural support and grounding in evolutionary human adaptations to universal problems of survival and cooperation. MFT proposes several moral topics that serve as consistent themes that draw people's attention, frame their interpretation of stimuli, and guide their actions. Presented in oppositions, these foundations focus on issues of care/harm, fairness/cheating, loyalty/betrayal, authority/subversion, sanctity/degradation, and liberty/oppression. While not all cultures attend to all of them equally and all the time, these foundations nonetheless appear rather consistent across cultural contexts. It is on these topics that more culturally specific moralities emerge as we build cognitive consistency and familiarity.

Civil Sphere Theory (CST) provides a roadmap for understanding these more culturally specific moralities, reflecting democratic civil societies and prevailing notions of justice (Alexander 2006). CST argues that there exists a structured discourse of civil society (Alexander and Smith 1993; Alexander 2006) narrated through shared civil and anticivil cultural codes. This discourse is structured by notions of sacred and profane, as they are meaningful within the broader cultural context of civil societies. Civil and anticivil cultural codes focus on three related areas: the motives of actors, the social relations they may form from their motives, and the social institutions they may create out of their relations. I argue that this discourse supplies the upper-level meaning system in my theory of cultural work, relevant within democratic civil societies and distinct cultural environments, events, situations, and referents (see figure A.1).

Returning to Cultural Work

What does this scholarship mean for my study of cultural work? In times of disaster and crisis and the collective traumas that follow with the extended settling period, it is the meanings associated with these distinct cultural codes that are threatened and cause schematic failure, as our taken-for-granted lives and the embodied autopoiesis we generated from it fall apart. We can no longer extract familiar and predictable significance from our cultural environment because that cultural environment is now shaken and uncertain. Under these conditions, our moral intuitions (e.g., MFT) help us negotiate our collective traumas and solve our unfolding problems as they arise. As we work toward solving our shared problems and reestablishing a familiar and routine cultural environment, we reformulate normative meaning systems and social motives within these newly created cultural environments. Emotional energy sets of avoidance and attraction provide the bodily energy to act in relation to these motives.

In a New Orleans settling from Hurricane Katrina, both pragmatic and normative meaning systems exist in the reasons people offered for why they started and continued to blog and in the blog content they created. They were also important in how unacquainted individuals using blogs to learn and share information on the recovery and rebuilding work created trusting social ties and voluntary relations with each other and in their willingness and ability to work together, over time, to create new organizations and organize collective actions. Yet they existed in a relationship, a structured relationship, I argue, in which the deeper moral foundations served as grounding for the creation and (re-)creation of a civil and anticivil discourse of more culturally specific codes and referents, as well as social rewards, goals, and motives.

Embodied autopoiesis always takes place within an environment composed of meaning systems, tools, practices, and technologies. In this sense, it is a cultural phenomenon and demands cultural work. Such cultural work is motivated and guided by shared problems we face and the system of rewards and goals that emerge from our engagement with those problems. Our problems may involve avoiding harm and being treated fairly by loyal others, as these are threats to our collective autopoiesis. Anticivil codes around people's motives, social relations, and institutions may serve as culturally relevant mechanisms that constitute these threats. Conversely, social rewards of belonging and self-enhancement may involve demonstrating our care, fairness, and loyalty to others, as these help us sustain collective autopoiesis. Civil codes around motives, social relations, and institutions may serve as culturally relevant mechanisms for achieving these social goals.

It is how these meanings resonate with our affective and emotional states that energize and inform the action we ultimately take. Our actions are in two basic directions: those of attraction and those of avoidance. These are homologous to Patterson's (2014) layered definition of culture, with actions of avoidance underlying the problem-solving component of culture and actions of attraction informing the normative motives of social belonging and self-enhancement. To be absent routine, predictability, and stability is to be in an uncomfortable emotional state, one of fear, anxiety, and worry associated with the disruption of cultural scaffolding and schematic failure, one that threatens embodied autopoiesis. These are feeling states that we typically wish to avoid, especially if we have little control over them. As we seek answers to these fundamentally important questions, social motives of belonging and self-enhancement emerge, resonating with newly formed or re-created normative systems unfolding within specific cultural environments. The emotional rewards we earn by demonstrating our social belonging and enhancing our sense of self in this context constitute the goal-seeking motives that attract us. These are the pride, joy, happiness, and satisfaction we feel and enjoy when we do right in the minds of ourselves and others, within particular contexts.

This is cultural work and the model of emotionally meaningful action on which it is energized and oriented.

NOTES

PREFACE

1. In the 1985 movie *Back to the Future*, Marty (played by Michael J. Fox) meets Doctor Emmett Brown (played by Christopher Lloyd) in the middle of a suburban mall parking lot late one night. Here, Doc shows Marty how he converted a DeLorean into a time machine. In explaining how it works, Doc shows Marty the central feature, what he calls the "flux capacitor," explaining that "this is what makes time travel possible."

INTRODUCTION

1. Of course, all media are social, as Lindner and Barnard (2020) note, but I am referring to the personalized, digital, networked social media we see today with Facebook, Instagram, TikTok, and Twitter, among others.
2. Occasionally there might be pockets of instability, such as during protests, but for the most part, most of life is taken as settled. Home life, work life, school life, life with family and friends, life in public—while one might be disturbed, often the others are not. A second note is that due to the ongoing COVID-19 pandemic, sociologists are beginning to seriously questions the notion of unsettlement. Indeed, the theme for the 2022 ASA conference was unsettled times.
3. When possible, I offer descriptive and background information on the bloggers. This is usually the case with those I met for interviews, when I could collect much of that information. There are times I will reference a blogger but not offer much by way of description. This is often the case when I am drawing on blog content, as I did not personally meet some of those bloggers and so did not gather such information. Further, I did not anonymize blogger names, as this was their public persona and doing so would be futile, as it would be easy to find them simply by searching the text from their blog posts that I highlight in this book.

CHAPTER 1. SETTLING TIMES

1. It would be a week before full evacuations were completed (Kates et al. 2006).
2. This is a conservative number and does not reflect the countless deaths that occurred due to the stress and health issues that arose over the settling period. With regard to financial costs, the collective damage was estimated to cost approximately $125 billion in 2005, constituting the most expensive disaster in US history. Twelve years later, much work has been completed, with other projects still under way or yet to be done.

3. To add insult to injury, the city would be hit with another hurricane, Hurricane Rita, less than a month after Katrina (in mid-September), resulting in more flooding and hindering relief efforts. Moreover, roughly a year and a half later, the entire nation would experience the "Great Recession."
4. Erikson (1976) similarly notes the significance of silence in the wake of the Buffalo Creek Flood. In the prologue to his reissued book *Everything in Its Path: Destruction of Community in the Buffalo Creek Flood*, he briefly returns to this theme while discussing how Hurricane Katrina ravaged New Orleans: "The carnage stretches out almost endlessly: more than a hundred thousand such homes, at least fifty thousand such automobiles, the whole mass being covered by a crust of gray mud, dried as hard as fired clay by the sun. It is the silence of it, the emptiness of it, that is the story" (iii).
5. See the local news station WWL's report on New Orleans East and neglect after Hurricane Katrina (WWL Staff 2019). It is important to note that this was reported in August 2019, fourteen years after the flood.
6. Other work might examine unsettled circumstances, but often from the perspective of outsiders whose lives are relatively settled (for an example of international professional journalists covering war-torn regions, see Markham 2013).

CHAPTER 2. FROM PERSONAL DISASTER AND COLLECTIVE TRAUMA

1. My use of "collective trauma" is similar to but different from that of Erikson (1976). For Erikson, collective trauma refers to "a blow to the basic tissues of social life that damages the bonds attaching people together and impairs the prevailing sense of communality" (154). This was certainly the case for those who experienced Hurricane Katrina, but they also shared in their experiences with different social institutions and agencies that were involved in the aftermath, and these shared experiences as sources of pain, frustration, anger, and such are where I locate collective trauma.
2. Often, in the wake of crisis, this rebuilding period serves as an opportunity to implement neoliberal policies and practices that would have been too difficult to implement without the massive disruption. In New Orleans, these policies came in the form of newly created public-private partnerships (Hoffman and Oliver-Smith 1999; Gotham and Greenberg 2014).
3. Indeed, J.-Y. Jung (2012) cites a 2011 Nomura Research Institute survey that reports that the two main goals that people had immediately after the Tohoku earthquake and tsunami in Japan were (1) to communicate with one's family and friends to check their safety, as well as to let others know about one's own safety, and (2) to obtain information about the earthquake. The same can be said for those who were affected by Hurricane Katrina and the flood.
4. This insight was based on a personal communication with my former neighbor, who was trapped in his attic as the floodwaters rose and made a final call to his brother to say good-bye. As night fell, he found a crack in the ceiling of his attic

and chiseled away at it until he was able to escape onto his roof and be rescued by helicopter a couple of days later.
5. Text messaging was common because the cellphone networks were clogged. Text messages take up only a small amount of data, requiring only a brief moment of cellular space to open up for the message to be sent and/or received.
6. This was largely before people were using Twitter and Facebook (see the blogger Ray Shea, in Jasper and Folse 2010, xiii).
7. According to the blog list kept at Rising Tide and measured by date of first post.
8. Indeed, this growth constituted the "shitload of new blogs" that Loki noted in the epigraph to this chapter, suggesting that a "shitload" is equal to about two hundred.
9. Measuring the correspondence of blogs with a physical geographic area is challenging. Most of the blogs listed on the Rising Tide blogroll were of New Orleans residents. Some were people who had ties to the city for other reasons (e.g., children going to college there). Nonetheless, this blog roll certainly reflects the networks of those who created it and only captures a slice of what I, for lack of a better word, call "a" local blogosphere. I stress "a" rather than "the" so as to emphasize that there were other bloggers who were not part of this group of bloggers.

CHAPTER 3. COLLECTIVE TRAUMA WITH BLOGS
1. For more on the use of online message forums during Hurricane Katrina, see Klinenberg 2007.
2. Sadly, NOLA Slate / Katrina Refrigerator (Sam [Bec] Jasper) passed away in mid-August 2021. A number of her old blogger friends posted touching stories about her on their social media pages. She was much liked, had a good heart, and will be missed by many.

CHAPTER 4. COMMUNICATING TRAUMA
1. Consider this post alongside NOLA Slate's statement at the beginning of chapter 2, on abandonment and not feeling a part of the United States anymore.

CHAPTER 5. THE CREATION OF A COLLECTIVE DISCOURSE
1. While this discourse is situated in the context of long-term disaster recovery in New Orleans, many characteristics of it are common to other forms of formal and informal moral communication, such as the news, rumor, and storytelling, both today and throughout much of recorded history (Stephens 1988; Lule 2001).
2. Indeed, the only status that may matter is that of human, a term that has been socially defined differently and with different implications for senses of moral worthiness.
3. The number of archetypes do not equal the number of moral foundations because one character may engage in several actions associated with moral foundations. For example, a trickster's actions may be harmful, cheating people, and a sign of betrayal all at the same time.

206 | NOTES

4. Compassion accounted for 243 emotional expressions. This involves both sympathy (n = 147) and empathy (n = 96). The frequency and copresence of both anger and compassion are important for understanding the development of social ties and ultimately mobilizations, as anger is an activating emotion and compassion is a social bonding emotion. Together these provide the motivations to act collaboratively. I engage this aspect of action and cultural work in chapter 6.
5. Tipitinas is a storied local music venue, a "must see" for anyone visiting the city who wants to see live music.

CHAPTER 6. BLOGGING AND COLLECTIVE ACTIONS

1. To see a list of speakers, panels, pictures, and other material since 2006, see the Rising Tide home page: http://risingtidenola.com.
2. It was April 2006 when Oyster first contacted Scout Prime.
3. This was in the spirit of the Wonder Twins from the DC comics and later television cartoon series *Super Friends*.
4. In a blog post also from mid-July 2006, Loki defines a "boggle" as "a collective noun used to describe a group or gathering of bloggers, usually accompanied by libation, conversation, and strange paranormal events."
5. "A blog reborn: The 'heritage' that gave rise to The Lens" May 2, 2012: Gadbois, Karen. 2012. "A blog reborn: The 'heritage' that gave rise to The Lens." The Lens. May 02. www.thelensnola.org
6. Nagin was released from federal prison in spring 2020 due to COVID-19 concerns.
7. Dambala also published investigative news on other stories, some of which also had significant outcomes. For example, his work on former senator David Vitter and his affair with a local sex worker is largely believed to have led to Vitter's eventual resignation. Dambala would have thousands of hits on his website per day, with the FBI and other law enforcement officials contacting him periodically as they investigated city officials.
8. The discussion around District Attorney Eddie Jordan, as with Mayor Ray Nagin's "Chocolate City" comment, highlighted one of the areas where Black and white city residents (and to some degree Black and white bloggers) tended to differ in their perspective.
9. This incident, like many others, also has roots in Hurricane Katrina. New Orleans is a city of neighborhoods and strong identities tied to those neighborhoods. With the city's school system in disarray, students were sent to schools across the city. This introduced tensions, with some turning violent. The conflict between Shaver's stepson and other students at his new school arose from this context (see Sakakeeny 2013).

CHAPTER 7. AS THE CITY SETTLES

1. Upon beginning this project, I expected many of those with whom I spoke to have lots to say about the city's flood protection. I was surprised to find that this was

not the case. I came to discover that there was a lot of fatigue around that topic and that it was very complicated.
2. After the untimely passing of the blogger Ashley Morris in 2008, organizers of the Rising Tide conference decided to create an award in his honor. Later, David Simon, creator of *The Wire* and *Treme*, based the character Chreighton Bernette (played by John Goodman) on Ashley Morris, except Chreighton Bernette chooses YouTube as an outlet for his famous "Fuck you you fucking fucks" (FYYFF) rant rather than his blog (www.youtube.com/watch?v=1PcVDSz7-MM).
3. Like Cliff of *Cliff's Crib*, Dambala won Rising Tide's annual Ashley Morris Award a few years earlier. His award went down in local memory because Cedric Richmond and some of his "friends" showed up at the conference, looking to "talk" with Dambala. Dambala had not yet "come out" and was still blogging anonymously. Conference organizers noticed Richmond and his friends and warned Dambala. Upon his being presented with the Ashley Morris Award, another blogger volunteered to go onstage and accept it. This was an internal comedic story that many bloggers shared for years but also one that indicated their significance and, for some, their risk.
4. It is also telling that this mostly white blogosphere has been largely silent on the current movement for Black lives and the racism and police violence from which it emerged. This was of one of the "blind spots" that bloggers of color sought to bring to light as part of their collective writing.
5. Indeed, this was the case for the few bloggers of color who were part of this blogosphere. One additional reason for their writing was to illuminate the city's Black population and its experiences with the flood and aftermath, as many of the white bloggers in my sample, while liberal, nonetheless remained largely ignorant of these realities.

CONCLUSION

1. Indeed, the sense that residents were "not OK" may also be seen in Puerto Rico after Hurricane Maria hit the island in 2017 and national attention quickly drifted elsewhere.
2. After all, how can we reconcile the popularity and influence of Marxism with the "evils" toward which it has been put to use (e.g., Stalinism and Maoism, for example).

METHODOLOGICAL AND THEORETICAL APPENDIX

1. I was not impressive. Thanks to Eban of *NOitsjustme* for his encouraging and supportive gestures while sitting in the audience and watching me bomb.
2. Action is commonly understood as meaningful movement. Meaning is necessary for action but not movement. For example, a twitch or impulse is an example of movement but not necessarily of action.
3. The basic notion that people seek pleasure and avoid pain dates back to the Greek philosopher Democritus of Abdera (460–370 BCE). More recently, it is seen in

the writings of Jeremy Bentham, William James, and Sigmund Freud. Indeed, there is a strong literature in psychology (renewed in the 1990s) on approach-avoidance motivations (Elliot 2008). But much of this scholarship is not well integrated or articulated in sociology. Sociology's strength here lies in its ability to take the basic notion of approach and avoidance and link it to broader social trends, including social relationships, organizations, and institutions, and to how work that manipulates situations and settings in a laboratory might apply or be of use in understanding collective trends outside the lab. It is here that this appendix differs from and builds on the psychological scholarship.

REFERENCES

Abend, Gabriel. 2013. "What the Science of Morality Doesn't Say about Morality." *Philosophy of the Social Sciences* 43 (2): 157–200.
Abramson, Corey M. 2012. "From 'Either-Or' to 'When and How?': A Context-Dependent Model of Culture in Action." *Journal for the Theory of Social Behavior* 42 (2): 155–180.
Adler, Patricia, and Peter Adler. 1983. "Shifts and Oscillations in Deviant Careers: The Case of Upper-Level Drug Dealers and Smugglers." *Social Problems* 31 (2): 195–207.
Agnew, Robert. 1992. "Foundation for a General Theory of Crime and Delinquency." *Criminology* 30:47–87.
Al-Ani, Ban, Gloria Mark, and Bryan Semaan. 2010. "Blogging through Conflict: Sojourners in the Age of Social Media." *Proceedings of the 3rd ACM International Conference on Intercultural Collaboration, ICIC '10*, 29–38.
Albas, Cheryl A., and Daniel C. Albas. 2003. "Motives." In *Handbook of Symbolic Interactionism*, edited by Larry T. Reynold and Nancy J. Herman-Kinney, 349–366. Lanham, MD: AltaMira.
Alexander, Jeffrey C. 2003. *The Meanings of Social Life: A Cultural Sociology*. New York: Oxford University Press.
———. 2004. "Toward a Theory of Cultural Trauma." In *Cultural Trauma and Collective Identity*, edited by Jeffrey C. Alexander, Ron Eyerman, Bernhard Giesen, Neil J. Smelser, and Piotr Sztompka, 1–30. Berkeley: University of California Press.
———. 2006. *The Civil Sphere*. New York: Oxford University Press.
———. 2007. "The Meaningful Construction of Inequality and the Struggles against It: A 'Strong Program' Approach to How Social Boundaries Change." *Cultural Sociology* 1 (1): 23–30.
———. 2013. *Performative Revolution in Egypt: An Essay in Cultural Power*. London: Bloomsbury Academic.
Alexander, Jeffrey C., and Phillip Smith. 1993. "The Discourse of American Civil Society: A New Proposal for Cultural Studies." *Theory and Society* 22 (2): 151–207.
Altheide, David L., and Christopher J. Schneider. 2013. *Qualitative Media Analysis*. 2nd ed. Los Angeles: Sage.
Armstrong, Elizabeth A., and Mary Bernstein. 2008. "Culture, Power, and Institutions: A Multi-institutional Politics Approach to Social Movements." *Sociological Theory* 26 (1): 74–99.
Ball-Rokeach, Sandra J. 1985. "The Origins of Individual Media-System Dependency: A Sociological Framework." *Communication Research* 12 (4): 485–510.

———. 1998. "A Theory of Media Power and a Theory of Media Use: Different Stories, Questions, and Ways of Thinking." *Mass Communication and Society* 1 (1–2): 5–40.
Ball-Rokeach, Sandra J., and Joo-Young Jung. 2009. "The Evolution of Media System dependency theory." In *Sage Handbook of Media Processes and Effects*, edited by Robin L. Nabi and Mary Beth Oliver, 531–544. Thousand Oaks, CA: Sage.
Bankston, Carl L., III. 2017. Foreword to *Weathering Katrina: Culture and Recovery among Vietnamese Americans*, by Mark J. Vanlandingham, xv–xx. New York: Russell Sage Foundation.
Barry, John M. 1998. *Rising Tide: The Great Mississippi Flood of 1927 and How It Changed America*. New York: Simon and Schuster.
Barthes, Roland. 1972. *Mythologies*. New York: Hill and Wang.
Bennett, Lance W., and Alexandra Segerberg. 2013. "The Logic of Connective Action." *Information, Communication & Society* 15 (5): 739–768.
Berlant, Lauren. 2011. *Cruel Optimism*. Durham, NC: Duke University Press.
Bourdieu, Pierre. 2008. *Outline of a Theory of Practice*. Cambridge: Cambridge University Press.
Boyns, David, and Sarah Luery. 2015. "Negative Emotional Energy: A Theory of the 'Dark-Side' of Interaction Ritual Chains." *Social Sciences* 4 (1): 148–170.
Bucher, Taina, and Anne Helmond. 2017. "The Affordances of Social Media Platforms." In *The Sage Handbook of Social Media*, edited by Jean Burgess, Thomas Poell, and Alice Marwick, 233–253. Thousand Oaks, CA: Sage.
Buerger, Christian, and Douglas Harris. 2015. "How Can Decentralized Systems Solve System-Level Problems? An Analysis of Market-Driven New Orleans School Reforms." *American Behavioral Scientist* 59 (10): 1246–1262.
Bullard, Robert D., and Beverly Wright. 2009. *Race, Place, and Environmental Justice after Hurricane Katrina: Struggles to Reclaim, Rebuild, and Revitalize New Orleans and the Gulf Coast*. Boulder, CO: Westview.
Campanella, Richard. 2008. *Bienville's Dilemma: A Historical Geography of New Orleans*. Lafayette: Center for Louisiana Studies, University of Louisiana at Lafayette.
Campbell, Colin. 1996. "On the Concept of Motive in Sociology." *Sociology* 30 (1): 101–114.
———. 1999. "Action as Will-Power." *Sociological Review* 47 (1): 48–61.
———. 2009. "Distinguishing the Power of Agency from Agentic Power: A Note on Weber and the 'Black Box' of Personal Agency." *Sociological Theory* 27 (4): 407–418.
Campbell, Joseph. 1949. *The Hero with a Thousand Faces*. New York: Pantheon Books.
Carey, James W. 1989. *Communication as Culture*. New York: Routledge.
Cavalcante, Andre. 2018. "Affect, Emotion, and Media Audiences: The Case of Resilient Reception." *Media, Culture & Society* 40 (8): 1186–1201.
Cerulo, Karen A., ed. 2002. *Culture in Mind: Towards a Sociology of Culture and Cognition*. New York: Routledge.
———. 2010. "Mining the Intersections of Cognitive Sociology and Neuroscience." *Poetics* 38 (2): 115–132.

Chamlee-Wright, Emily, and Virgil Henry Storr. 2009. "'There's No Place like New Orleans': Sense of Place and Community Recovery in the Ninth Ward after Hurricane Katrina." *Journal of Urban Affairs* 31 (5): 615–634.

Chanin, Jesse S. 2021. "The Rise and Fall of the United Teacher's Union of New Orleans." PhD diss., Tulane University.

Chung, Deborah S., and Sujin Kim. 2008. "Blogging Activity among Cancer Patients and Their Companions: Uses, Gratifications, and Predictors of Outcomes." *Journal of the American Society for Information Science and Technology* 59 (2): 297–306.

Clark, Candace. 1997. *Misery and Company: Sympathy in Everyday Life*. Chicago: University of Chicago Press.

Collins, Randall. 2004. *Interaction Ritual Chains*. Princeton, NJ: Princeton University Press.

Cottle, Simon. 2004. *The Racist Murder of Stephen Lawrence: Media Performance and Public Transformation*. Westport, CT: Praeger.

Curato, Nicole. 2017. "Beyond the Spectacle: Slow-Moving Disasters in Post-Haiyan Philippines." *Critical Asian Studies* 50 (1): 58–66.

David, Clarissa C., Jonathan Corpus Ong, and Erika Fille T. Legara. 2016. "Tweeting Supertyphoon Haiyan: Evolving Functions of Twitter during and after a Disaster Event." *PLOS One* 11 (3).

DiMaggio, Paul. 1997. "Culture and Cognition." *Annual Review of Sociology* 23:263–287.

Earl, Jennifer, and Katrina Kimport. 2011. *Digitally Enabled Social Change: Activism in the Internet Age*. Cambridge, MA: MIT Press.

Edelmann, Achim. 2018. "Culturally Meaningful Networks: On the Transition from Military to Civilian Life in the United Kingdom." *Theory and Society* 47 (3): 327–380.

Elliot, Andrew J. 2008. "Introduction and Overview: Approach and Avoidance Motivation." In *Handbook of Approach and Avoidance Motivation*, edited by Andrew J. Elliot, 3–14. New York: Psychological Press.

Emirbayer, Mustafa, and Ann Mische. 1998. "What Is Agency?" *American Journal of Sociology* 103 (4): 962–1023.

Erikson, Kai. 1976. *Everything in Its Path: Destruction of Community in the Buffalo Creek Flood*. New York: Simon and Schuster.

Espeland, Wendy N., and Mitchell L. Stevens. 1998. "Commensuration as a Social Process." *Annual Review of Sociology* 24:313–343.

Esposito, Linda. 2016. "The Surprising Emotion Behind Anxiety." *Psychology Today*, July 25, 2016. www.psychologytoday.com

Eyerman, Ron. 2008. *The Assassination of Theo Van Gogh: From Social Drama to Cultural Trauma*. Durham, NC: Duke University Press.

———. 2015. *Is This America? Katrina as Cultural Trauma*. Austin: University of Texas Press.

Fine, Gary Alan. 2004. "Adolescence as a Cultural Toolkit: High School Debate and the Repertoires of Childhood and Adulthood." *Sociological Quarterly* 45:1–20.

———. 2013. "Sticky Cultures: Memory Publics and Communal Pasts in Competitive Chess." *Cultural Sociology* 7 (4): 395–414.
Frailing, Kelly, and Dee Wood Harper Jr. 2015. "Through the Lens of Katrina: Long-Term Disaster Recovery in the United States." *American Behavioral Scientist* 59 (10): 1207–1213.
Freese, Jeremy, Jui-Chung Allen Li, and Lisa D. Wade. 2003. "The Potential Relevances of Biology to Social Inquiry." *Annual Review of Sociology* 29:233–256.
Fussell, Elizabeth. 2015. "The Long-Term Recovery of New Orleans' Population after Hurricane Katrina." *American Behavioral Scientist* 59 (10): 1231–1245.
Gadbois, Karen. 2007. "Dead House Walking." *The Lens*, July 22, 2007. www.thelensnola.org.
Geertz, Clifford. 1973. *The Interpretation of Cultures*. New York: Basic Books.
Gibson, J. J. 1979. *The Ecological Approach to Visual Perception*. Boston: Houghton Mifflin.
Giddens, Anthony. 1984. *The Constitution of Society: Outline of a Theory of Structuration*. Chicago: University of Chicago Press.
———. 1991. *Modernity and Self-Identity: Self and Society in the Late Modern Age*. Stanford, CA: Stanford University Press.
Goffman, Erving. 1963. *Stigma: Notes on the Management of a Spoiled Identity*. New York: Simon and Schuster.
Goodwin, Jeff, and James M. Jasper. 2006. "Emotions in Social Movements." In *Handbook of the Sociology of Emotions*, Handbooks of Sociology and Social Research, edited by Jan E. Stets and Jonathan H. Turner, 611–635. New York: Springer.
Goodwin, Jeff, James M. Jasper, and Francesca Polletta. 2004. "Emotional Dimensions of Social Movements." In *The Blackwell Companion to Social Movements*, edited by David A. Snow, Sarah A. Soule, and Hanspeter Kriesi, 413–432. Malden, MA: Blackwell.
Gotham, Kevin Fox. 2007a. *Authentic New Orleans: Tourism, Culture and Race in the Big Easy*. New York: New York University Press.
———. 2007b. "Critical Theory and Katrina: Disaster, Spectacle and Immanent Critique." *City* 11 (1): 81–99.
———. 2015. "Limitations, Legacies, and Lessons: Post-Katrina Rebuilding in Retrospect and Prospect." *American Behavioral Scientist* 59 (10): 1314–1326.
Gotham, Kevin Fox, and Mariam Greenberg. 2014. *Crisis Cities: Disaster and Redevelopment in New York and New Orleans*. New York: Oxford University Press.
Griswold, Wendy. 2014. *Cultures and Societies in a Changing World*. 4th ed. London: Sage.
Gubrium, Jaber F., and James A. Holstein. 2000. "The Self in a World of Going Concerns." *Symbolic Interaction* 23 (2): 95–115.
Hadfield, J. A. 1955. *Psychology an Morals: An Analysis of Character*. London: Methuen.
Haidt, Jonathan. 2012. *The Righteous Mind: Why Good People Are Divided by Politics and Religion*. New York: Vintage Books.

Haidt, Jonathan, and Jesse Graham. 2007. "Planet of the Durkheimians, Where Community, Authority, and Sacredness Are Foundations of Morality." In *Social and Psychological Bases of Ideology and System Justification*, edited by J. T. Jost, A. C. Kay, and H. Thorisdottir, 371–401. New York: Oxford University Press.

Hajj, Nadya. 2021. *Networked Refugees: Palestinian Reciprocity and Remittances in the Digital Age*. Berkeley: University of California Press.

Hay, Robert Bruce. 1998. "Sense of Place in a Developmental Context." *Journal of Environmental Psychology* 18:5–29.

Hitlin, Steven, and Monica Kirkpatrick Johnson. 2015. "Reconceptualizing Agency within the Life Course: The Power of Looking Ahead." *American Journal of Sociology* 120 (5): 1429–1472.

Hochschild, Arlie. 1983. *The Managed Heart: Commercialization of Human Feeling*. Berkeley: University of California Press.

Hoffman, Susanne M. 1999. "The Worst of Times, the Best of Times: Toward a Model of Cultural Response to Disaster." In *The Angry Earth: Disaster in Anthropological Perspective*, edited by Anthony Oliver-Smith and Susanna M. Hoffman, 134–155. New York: Routledge.

Hoffman, Susanne M., and Anthony Oliver-Smith. 1999. "Anthropology and the Angry Earth: An Overview." In *The Angry Earth: Disaster in Anthropological Perspective*, edited by Anthony Oliver-Smith and Susanna M. Hoffman, 1–16. New York: Routledge.

Houston, J. Brian, Joshua Hawthorn, Mildred F. Perreault, Eun Hae Park, Marlo Goldstein Hode, Michael R. Halliwell, Sarah E. Turner McGowen, Rachel Davis, Shivani Vaid, Jonathan A. McElderry, and Stanford A. Griffith. 2014. "Social Media and Disasters: A Functional Framework for Social Media Use in Disaster Planning, Response, and Research." *Disasters* 39 (1): 1–22.

Houston, J. Brian, Betty Pfefferbaum, and Cathy Ellen Rosenholtz. 2012. "Disaster News: Framing and Frame Changing in Coverage of Major U.S. Natural Disasters, 2000–2010." *Journalism & Mass Communication Quarterly* 89 (4): 606–623.

Hutchby, Ian. 2001. "Technologies, Texts and Affordances." *Sociology* 35 (2): 441–456.

Jasper, James M. 2011. "Emotions and Social Movements: Twenty Years of Theory and Research." *Annual Review of Sociology* 37:285–303.

———. 2018. *The Emotions of Protest*. Chicago: University of Chicago Press.

Jasper, Sam, and Mark Folse, eds. 2010. *A Howling in the Wires: An Anthology of Writing from Postdiluvian New Orleans*. New Orleans: Gallatin and Toulouse.

Joyce, Cynthia. 2015. *Please Forward: How Blogging Reconnected New Orleans after Katrina*. New Orleans: University of New Orleans Press.

Jung, Carl. 1969. *The Archetypes and the Collective Unconsciousness*. Princeton, NJ: Princeton University Press.

Jung, Joo-Young. 2012. "Social Media Use and Goals after the Great East Japan Earthquake." *First Monday* 17 (8).

Kane, Anne. 1991. "Cultural Analysis in Historical Sociology: The Analytic and Concrete Forms of the Autonomy of Culture." *Sociological Theory* 9 (1): 53–69.

Kates, Robert W., Craig E. Colten, Shirley B. Laska, and Stephen P. Leatherman. 2006. "Reconstruction of New Orleans after Hurricane Katrina: A Research Perspective." *PNAS* 103 (40): 14653–14660.

Kemper, Theodore D. 1991. "Predicting Emotions from Social Relations." *Social Psychology Quarterly* 54 (4): 330–342.

Khazraee, Emad, and Alison N. Novak. 2018. "Digitally Mediated Protest: Social Media Affordances for Collective Identity Construction." *Social Media + Society*, January–March 2018, 1–18.

Kjellberg, Sara. 2010. "I Am a Blogging Researcher: Motivations for Blogging in a Scholarly Context." *First Monday* 15 (8). https://firstmonday.org.

Klinenberg, Eric. 2007. *Fighting for Air: The Battle to Control America's Media*. New York: Metropolitan Books.

Kroll-Smith, Steve, Vern Baxter, and Pam Jenkins. 2015. *Left to Chance: Hurricane Katrina and the Story of Two New Orleans Neighborhoods*. Austin: University of Texas Press.

Lamont, Michèle. 2012. "Toward a Comparative Sociology of Valuation and Evaluation." *Annual Review of Sociology* 38:201–221.

Lazarus, Richard S., and Susan Folkman. 1984. *Stress, Appraisal, and Coping*. New York: Springer.

Lee, Spike, dir. 2006. *When the Levees Broke: A Requiem in Four Acts*. 40 Acres and a Mule Filmworks, New York.

Lindner, Andrew M., and Stephen R. Barnard. 2020. *All Media Are Social: Sociological Perspectives on Mass Media*. New York: Routledge.

Lizardo, Omar. 2017. "Improving Cultural Analysis: Considering Personal Culture in its Declarative and Nondeclarative Modes." *American Sociological Review* 82 (1): 88–115.

Lizardo, Omar, and Michael Strand. 2010. "Skills, Toolkits, Contexts and Institutions: Clarifying the Relationship between Different Approaches to Cognition in Cultural Sociology." *Poetics* 38:204–227.

Lo, Ming-Cheng M., and Yun Fan. 2022. "How Narratives of Disaster Impact Survivors' Emotionality: The Case of Typhoon Morakot." *Poetics* 93 (Part A). https://doi.org/10.1016/j.poetic.2021.101579.

Luft, Rachel D. 2009. "Beyond Disaster Exceptionalism: Social Movement Developments in New Orleans after Hurricane Katrina." *American Quarterly* 61 (3): 499–527.

Lule, Jack. 2001. *Daily News, Eternal Stories: The Mythological Role of Journalism*. New York: Guilford.

Lupton, Deborah. 1999. *Risk*. 2nd ed. New York: Routledge.

Macias, Wendy, Karen Hilyard, and Vicki Freimuth. 2009. "Blog Functions as Risk and Crisis Communication during Hurricane Katrina." *Journal of Computer-Mediated Communication* 15:1–31.

MacKinnon, Neil J. 1994. *Symbolic Interactionism as Affect Control*. Albany: State University of New York Press.

Markham, Tim. 2013. *The Politics of War Reporting: Authority, Authenticity and Morality*. Manchester, UK: Manchester University Press.

Massanari, Adrienne, and Philip N. Howard. 2011. "Information Technologies and Omnivorous News Diets over Three U.S. Presidential Elections." *Journal of Information Technology & Politics* 8 (2): 177–198.

Massey, Douglas S. 2002. "A Brief History of Human Society: The Origin and Role of Emotion in Social Life." *American Sociological Review* 67 (1): 1–29.

Massumi, Brian. 2002. *Parables for the Virtual: Movement, Affect, Sensation*. Durham, NC: Duke University Press.

Mast, Jason L. 2020. "Representationalism and Cognitive Culturalism: Riders on Elephants on Turtles All the Way Down." *American Journal of Cultural Sociology* 8:90–123.

Mayer, Vicki, 2017. *Almost Hollywood, Nearly New Orleans: The Lure of the Local Film Economy*. Berkeley: University of California Press.

McFarlane, Alexander C., and Fran H. Norris. 2006. "Definitions and Concepts in Disaster Research." In *Methods for Disaster Mental Health Research*, edited by Fran H. Norris, Sandro Galea, Matthew J. Friedman, and Patricia J. Watson, 3–19. New York: Guilford.

Mills, C. Wright. 1940. "Situated Actions and Vocabularies of Motive." *American Sociological Review* 5 (6): 904–913.

Mische, Ann. 2009. "Projects and Possibilities: Researching Futures in Action." *Sociological Forum* 24 (3): 694–704.

Monnot, Katy Davidson. 2015. "Rising Tide Conference." GoFundMe, July 30, 2015. www.gofundme.com.

Nagy, Peter, and Gina Neff. 2015. "Imagined Affordance: Reconstructing a Keyword for Communication Theory." *Social Media + Society*, July–December 2015, 1–9.

New York Times. 2005. "Barbara Bush Calls Evacuees Better Off." September 7, 2005. www.nytimes.com.

Nicolini, Davide, and Pedro Monteiro. 2017. "The Practice Approach: For a Praxeology of Organisational and Management Studies." In *The Sage Handbook of Process Organization Studies*, edited by A. Langley and H. Tsoukas, 110–126. London: Sage.

Nigg, Joanne M., John Barnshaw, and Manuel R. Torres. 2006. "Hurricane Katrina and the Flooding of New Orleans: Emergent Issues in Sheltering and Temporary Housing." *Annals of the American Academy of Political and Social Science* 604 (1): 113–128.

Norman, Donald A. 2002. *The Design of Everyday Things*. New York: Basic Books.

Norris, Pippa, and Ronald Inglehart. 2019. *Cultural Backlash: Trump, Brexit, and Authoritarian Populism*. New York: Cambridge University Press.

Norton, Matthew. 2020. "Cultural Sociology Meets the Cognitive Wild: Advantages of the Distributed Cognition Framework for Analyzing the Intersection of Culture and Cognition." *American Journal of Cultural Sociology* 8:45–62.

Olick, Jeffrey, K. 2010. "What Is 'the Relative Autonomy of Culture'?" In *Handbook of Cultural Sociology*, edited by John R. Hall, Laura Grindstaff, and Ming-Cheng Lo, 97–108. New York: Routledge.

Ortiz, David G., and Stephen F. Ostertag. 2014. "Katrina Bloggers and the Development of Collective Civic Action: The Web as a Virtual Mobilizing Structure." *Sociological Perspectives* 57 (1): 52–78.

Ostertag, Stephen F. 2009. "Establishing News Confidence: A Qualitative Study of How People Use the News Media to Know the News-World." *Media, Culture & Society* 32 (4): 597–614.

———. 2016. "Expressions of Right and Wrong: The Emergence of a Cultural Structure of Journalism." In *The Crisis of Journalism Reconsidered: Democratic Culture, Professional Codes, Digital Future*, edited by Jeffrey C. Alexander, Elizabeth Butler Breese, and María Luengo, 264–281. New York: Cambridge University Press.

———. 2021a. "Building Trust through Social Media in Times of Crisis: Cultural Persuasion, Citizen News, and the Cultural Affordances of Blogs." *Global Perspectives* 2 (1): 24961. https://doi.org/10.1525/gp.2021.24961.

———. 2021b. "A Cultural Sociology of Social Media: Social Drama, Cultural Affordances and Blogging in the Wake of Hurricane Katrina." *Cultural Sociology* 15 (1): 113–133.

Ostertag, Stephen F., and Lucas Díaz. 2017. "A Critical Strong Program: Cultural Power and Racialized Civil Exclusion." *American Journal of Cultural Sociology* 5:34–76.

Ostertag, Stephen F., and David G. Ortiz. 2013. "The Battle over Meaning: Digitally Mediated Processes of Cultural Trauma and Repair in the Wake of Hurricane Katrina." *American Journal of Cultural Sociology* 1 (2): 186–220.

———. 2015. "'Katrina Bloggers Activate!': The Long-Term Effects of Digital Media on Civic Participation." *Sociological Inquiry* 85 (1): 28–54.

———. 2017. "Can Social Media Use Produce Enduring Social Ties? Affordances and the Case of Katrina Bloggers." *Qualitative Sociology* 40 (1): 59–82.

Ostertag, Stephen F., and Gaye Tuchman. 2012. "When Innovation Meets Legacy: Citizen Journalists, Ink Reporters and Television News." *Information, Communication & Society* 15 (6): 909–931.

Papacharissi, Zizi. 2015. *Affective Publics: Sentiment, Technology, and Politics*. New York: Oxford University Press.

———. 2016. "Affective Publics and the Structures of Storytelling: Sentiment, Events and Mediality." *Information, Communication & Society* 19 (3): 307–324.

Parsons, Talcott. 1937. *The Structure of Social Action*. New York: Free Press.

Patterson, Orlando. 2014. "Making Sense of Culture." *Annual Review of Sociology* 40:1–30.

———. 2015. "The Social and Cultural Matrix of Black Youth." In *The Cultural Matrix: Understanding Black Youth*, edited by Orlando Patterson and Ethan Fosse, 45–135. Cambridge, MA: Harvard University Press.

Peterson, Gretchen. 2006. "Cultural Theory and Emotions." In *Handbook of the Sociology of Emotions*, Handbooks of Sociology and Social Research, edited by Jan E. Stets and Jonathan H. Turner, 114–134. New York: Springer.

Picou, J. Steven, and Brent K. Marshall. 2007. "Social Impacts of Hurricane Katrina on Displaced K–12 Students and Educational Institutions in Coastal Alabama Counties: Some Preliminary Observations." *Sociological Spectrum* 27:767–780.

Pignetti, Daisy. 2010. "Writing to (Re)New Orleans: The Post–Hurricane Katrina Blogosphere and Its Ability to Inspire Recovery." PhD diss., University of South Florida.

Polletta, Francesca. 1998. "Contenting Stories: Narrative in Social Movements." *Qualitative Sociology* 21 (4): 419–446.

Polletta, Francesca, and Jessica Callahan. 2019. "Deep Stories, Nostalgia Narratives, and Fake News: Storytelling in the Trump Era." *American Journal of Cultural Sociology* 5 (3): 392–408.

Powell, Lawrence N. 2012. *The Accidental City: Improvising New Orleans*. Cambridge, MA: Harvard University Press.

Raine, Lee. 2005. "The State of Blogging." Pew Research Center for Internet & Technology, January 2, 2005. www.pewinternet.org.

Reed, Isaac Ariail. 2015. "Deep Culture in Action: Resignification, Synecdoche, and Metanarrative in the Moral Panic of the Salem Witch Trials." *Theory and Society* 44 (1): 65–94.

Rising Tide. 2015. "A Conference on the Future of New Orleans." Rising Tide X Schedule, August 29, 2015. www.risingtidenola.com

Robinson, Sue. 2009. "'If You Had Been with Us': Mainstream Press and Citizen Journalists Jockey for Authority over the Collective Memory of Hurricane Katrina." *new media & society* 11 (5): 795–814.

Sakakeeny, Matt. 2013. *Roll with It: Brass Bands in the Streets of New Orleans*. Durham, NC: Duke University Press.

Schatzki, Theodore R. 1996. *Social Practices: A Wittgensteinian Approach to Human Activity and the Social*. Cambridge: Cambridge University Press.

Scheff, Thomas, J. 1990. *Microsociology: Discourse, Emotion, and Social Structure*. Chicago: University of Chicago Press.

Schmitt, Christopher S., and Candace Clark. 2006. "Sympathy." In *Handbook of the Sociology of Emotions*, Handbooks of Sociology and Social Research, edited by Jan E. Stets and Jonathan H. Turner, 467–492. New York: Springer.

Schrock, Andrew Richard. 2015. "Communicative Affordances of Mobile Media: Portability, Availability, Locatability, and Multimediality." *International Journal of Communication* 9:1229–1246.

Schudson, Michael. 1989. "How Culture Works: Perspectives from Media Studies on the Efficacy of Symbols." *Theory and Society* 18:153–180.

Scott, Marvin B., and Stanford M. Lyman. 1968. "Accounts." *American Sociological Review* 33 (1): 46–62.

Shibutani, Tamotsu. 1966. *Improvised News: A Sociological Study of Rumor*. Indianapolis: Bobbs-Merrill.

Shklovski, Irina, Moira Burke, Sara Kiesler, and Robert Kraut. 2010. "Technology Adoption and Use in the Aftermath of Hurricane Katrina in New Orleans." *American Behavioral Scientist* 53 (8): 1228–1246.

Simko, Christina, and Jeffrey K. Olick. 2020. "What We Talk about When We Talk about Culture: A Multi-facet Approach." *American Journal of Cultural Sociology*, January 25, 202. https://doi.org/10.1057/s41290-019-00094-7.

Small, Mario, David J. Harding, and Michèle Lamont. 2010. "Reconsidering Culture and Poverty." *Annals of the American Academy of Political and Social Science* 629 (1): 6–27.

Smelser, Neil. 2004. "Psychological Trauma and Cultural Trauma." In *Cultural Trauma and Collective Identity*, edited by Jeffrey C. Alexander, Ron Eyerman, Bernhard Giesen, Neil J. Smelser, and Piotr Sztompka, 31–59. Berkeley: University of California Press.

Spence, Patric R., Kennety A. Lachlan, and Jennifer M. Burke. 2007. "Adjusting to Uncertainty: Coping Strategies among the Displaced after Hurricane Katrina." *Sociological Spectrum* 27 (6): 653–678.

Spillman, Lyn. 1995. "Culture, Social Structure and Discursive Fields." *Current Perspectives in Social Theory* 15:129–154.

Stephens, Mitchell. 1988. *A History of News: From the Drum to the Satellite*. New York: Viking.

Summers-Effler, Erika. 2004. "A Theory of the Self, Emotion, and Culture." *Advances in Group Processes* 21:273–308.

Swidler, Ann. 1986. "Culture in Action: Symbols and Strategies." *American Sociological Review* 51 (April): 273–286.

———. 2001a. *Talk of Love: How Culture Matters*. Chicago: University of Chicago Press.

———. 2001b. "What Anchors Cultural Practices." In *The Practice Turn in Contemporary Theory*, edited by Theodore R. Schatzki, Karin Knorr Cetina, and Eike von Savigny, 74–92. London: Routledge.

Sykes, Gresham M., and David Matza. 1957. "Techniques of Neutralization: A Theory of Delinquency." *American Sociological Review* 22 (6): 664–670.

Sztompka, Piotr. 1999. *Trust: A Sociological Theory*. Cambridge: Cambridge University Press.

Tavory, Iddo, and Nina Eliasoph. 2014. "Coordinating Futures: Toward a Theory of Anticipation." *American Journal of Sociology* 118 (4): 908–942.

The Lens. 2017. "The Lens 2017 Annual Report." www.thelensnola.org

Thelwall, Mike, and David Stuart. 2007. "RUOK? Blogging Communication Technologies During Crises." *Journal of Computer-Mediated Communication* 12:523–548.

Thomas, Lynnell. 2014. *Desire and Disaster in New Orleans: Tourism, Race, and Historical Memory*. Durham, NC: Duke University Press.

Tierney, Kathleen. 2015. "Resilience and the Neoliberal Project: Discourses, Critiques, Practices—and Katrina." *American Behavioral Scientist* 59 (10): 1327–1342.

Turiel, Elliot. 1983. *The Development of Social Knowledge: Morality and Convention*. Cambridge: Cambridge University Press.

Turner, Jonathan H., and Jan E. Stets. 2005. *The Sociology of Emotions*. Cambridge: Cambridge University Press.

———. 2006. "Sociological Theories of Human Emotions." *Annual Review of Sociology* 32:25–52.

Turner, Victor. 1980. "Social Dramas and Stories about Them." *Critical Inquiry* 7 (1): 141–168.

Vaisey, Stephen. 2009. "Motivation and Justification: A Dual-Process Model of Culture in Action." *American Journal of Sociology* 114 (6): 1675–1715.

Vaisey, Stephen, and Omar Lizardo. 2010. "Can Cultural Worldviews Influence Network Composition?" *Social Forces* 88 (4): 1595–1618.

Vanlandingham, Mark, J. 2017. *Weathering Katrina: Culture and Recovery among Vietnamese Americans*. New York: Russell Sage Foundation.

van Troost, Dunya, Jacquelien van Stekelenburg, and Bert Klandermans. 2013. "Emotions of Protest." In *Emotions in Politics*, Palgrave Studies in Political Psychology Series, edited by Nicolas Demertzis, 186–203. London: Palgrave Macmillan.

Vila-Henninger, Luis Antonio. 2014. "Toward Defining the Causal Role of Consciousness: Using Models of Memory and Moral Judgment from Cognitive Neuroscience to Expand the Sociological Dual-Process Model." *Journal for the Theory of Social Behavior* 45 (2): 238–260.

Wagner-Pacifici, Robin. 1986. *The Moro Morality Play: Terrorism as Social Drama*. Chicago: University of Chicago Press.

Wahl-Jorgensen, Karin. 2020. "An Emotional Turn in Journalism Studies?" *Digital Journalism* 8 (2): 175–194.

Weber, Andreas, and Francisco J. Varela. 2002. "Life after Kant: Natural Purposes and the Autopoietic Foundations of Biological Individuality." *Phenomenology and the Cognitive Sciences* 1:97–125.

Weber, Max. (1922) 1978. "The Nature of Social Action." In *Weber: Selections in Translation*, edited by W. G. Runciman, translated by E. Matthews, 7. Cambridge: Cambridge University Press.

———. 1946. "The Social Psychology of the World Religions." In *From Max Weber*, edited by H. H. Gerth and C. Wright Mills, 267–301. New York: Oxford University Press.

Weick, Karl E. 1993. "The Collapse of Sensemaking in Organizations: The Mann Gulch Disaster." *Administrative Science Quarterly* 38:628–652.

Wellman, Barry, Anabel Quann-Haase, James Witte, and Keith Hampton. 2001. "Does the Internet Increase, Decrease, or Supplement Social Capital? Social Networks, Participation, and Community Commitment." *American Behavioral Scientist* 45 (3): 436–455.

Wilkinson, Iain. 2001. *Anxiety in a Risk Society*. New York: Routledge.

Winchester, Daniel, and Jeffrey Guhin. 2019. "Praying 'Straight from the Heart': Evangelical Sincerity and the Normative Frames of Culture in Action." *Poetics* 72:32–42.

Wright, John Paul, and Francis T. Cullen. 2012. "The Future of Biosocial Criminology: Beyond Scholars' Professional Ideology." *Journal of Contemporary Criminal Justice* 28 (3): 237–253.

WWL Staff. 2019. "What Happened to New Orleans East?" WWL TV, August 20, 2019. www.wwltv.com.

Yao, Abigail. 2009. "Enriching the Migrant Experience: Blogging Motivations, Privacy and Offline Lives of Filipino Women in Britain. *First Monday* 14 (3). https://journals.uic.edu.

Zerubavel, Eviatar. 1996. *Social Mindscapes: An Invitation to Cognitive Sociology*. Cambridge, MA: Harvard University Press.

INDEX

Abramson, Corey, 188–89, 190
affordances, 152–54, 161, 166; communicative, 153; cultural 153–54, 161, 166; imagined, 153; mechanical, 153–54, 161, 166; "perceived," 153
A Howling in the Wires: An Anthology of Writing from Postdiluvian New Orleans, 180
Alexander, Jeffrey, 184–85
American Zombie, 54, 70–71, 98, 121–22, 126, 143–44, 146
Anderson, Michael, 123
anger, 108–9, 128
archetypes, 83–84, 90–95, 104–5, 155, 165
Army Corps of Engineers, 12, 71, 86, 89, 102, 156

Bankston, Carl, 170
Barry, John M., 112
Bentham, Jeremy, 192, 207–8n3
Black Lives Matter, 174
Blanco, Kathleen, 13, 71, 102
blogosphere (New Orleans), 39–43, 63, 102, 127, 135, 140, 145–50, 165–66, 181, 205n9, 207nn4–5
blogrolls (lists), 153–54, 205n9
blogs: reading, 45–48; writing, 48–56
Bond, David, 123
Bonding theme, 109–10. *See also* Need to Act theme
Brown, Michael ("Brownie"), 13, 65, 86, 102, 109. *See also* Federal Emergency Management Agency

Bush, Barbara, 48, 53
Bush, George W., 65, 86, 89, 102, 104, 109, 156, 157

Campbell, Colin, 185
Carey, James, 82
Cerulo, Karen, 188
"Chinese drywall," 15, 70
Charity Hospital, 16
Cheney, Dick, 65
Chicory, The, 79–80
City Business (newspaper), 143
civility/anticivility, 83–90, 128, 158, 199
Civil Sphere Theory (CST), 199
Cliff's Crib, 49–50, 72, 77–79, 86, 87, 88–89, 92–93, 99–100, 141, 157, 207n3
Cohen, Ariella, 120
collective actions, 107–35. *See also* Bonding theme; Need to Act theme
collective agency, 25–26, 164, 169, 174, 190
collective cosmological series, 32, 34–39, 45, 56, 57–61, 64, 82, 97, 108, 136, 155, 164, 166, 188
collective movement, 25–26, 43, 135
communication, 27–30; cultural, 82, 161; and general information needs, 27–28; and information usage, 28; and personal information needs, 28, 38; ritual view of, 105; theory, 35–37; transmission view of, 105
Communication Infrastructure Theory (CIT), 36–37, 39
Compass, Eddie, 102–3
compassion, 108–9, 127–33, 168

221

Cooper, Anderson, 86, 118, 159
coping, 17, 21, 27, 56, 60, 63, 105; collective practice of, 9, 98, 108
"cosmology episode," 32, 37
crisis, 35–37
crisis ordinariness (Case 1), 172–73. *See also* hate and the dark side of modernity(Case 3); status and identity threats (Case 2)
cultural codes, 21, 83–95, 104, 128, 155, 165, 199;
cultural objects, 63, 155, 180
cultural power, 25
cultural referents, 83–90, 155, 165
cultural sociology, 4, 6, 166–71; cognitive, 190–91; strong program in, 187–88
cultural work, 4–6, 17–21, 23–27, 29–30, 55–62, 64, 83–84, 104, 105–6, 107–9, 126, 147–50, 164, 165, 166–76, 190–201
culture: and action, 23–27, 163–76, 182–87; causal power of, 4, 60, 64, 105, 169–71, 187–91; and cognition, 188–89; deep, 84; "sticky," 147–50; as a toolkit, 185–187

Danziger Bridge, 16
Dean, Howard, 113
Democritus of Abdera, 207–8n3
DiMaggio, Paul, 188
disasters, periods in, 17–21, 23–27, 35–37; emergency period, 18, 22, 23, 28–29; first reconstruction, 18, 23, 29, 51; restoration, 18, 22, 23, 28; second reconstruction, 18, 23, 29, 51
discourse, collective, 63–81, 82–106; first-order meaning in, 84–90, 104–5; second-order meaning, 84, 90–95, 104–5
Durkheim, Emile, 184

embodied autopoiesis, 58–62, 83–84, 164–66, 171, 174, 193–200
embodied cognition, 58, 193–94

emotional energy sets, 195–97
emotionality, 83, 95–104, 167
Erikson, Kai, 56, 204n4 (chap. 1), 204n1 (chap. 3)
Ernst Memorial Convention Center, 14
Eyerman Ron, 155

Facebook, 2, 149, 161, 203n1, 205n6
Federal Emergency Management Agency (FEMA), 13, 40, 52, 63, 65, 156
"federal flood," 12, 20, 160, 179
First Draft (national blog), 113, 147
Fox News, 86, 109, 156
Freimuth, Vicki, 35
Freud, Sigmund, 207–8n3

Geek Dinners, 115–16, 126, 155–56
Geertz, Clifford, 184
Gotham, Kevin, 3
Greenburg, Mariam, 3
GulfSails, 42, 73, 102–103, 130–131

Hadfield, J. A., 192
Hajj, Nadya, 173
Hastert, Dennis, 65, 156
hate and the dark side of modernity (Case 3), 175–76. *See also* crisis ordinariness; status and identity threats
Hill, Helen 125
Hilliard, Karen, 35
Honoré, General Russel L., 13
Humid City, 55, 148–49
humiliation, collective, 73–74
Hurricane Ida, 149–150
Hurricane Isaac, 141
Hurricane Maria, 147–148, 207n1
Hurricane Rita, 204n3

informational needs/uses, 35. *See also* social needs/uses
Inglehart, Ronald, 175
Instagram, 161, 203n1
Interaction Ritual Theory (IRT), 196–97

James, William, 207–8n3
Jordan, Eddie (District Attorney), 67, 109, 123–25, 138, 146, 156, 206n8
Jung, J.-Y., 204n3

Kates, R. W., 18
"Katrina bloggers," 83, 107, 110, 114, 152
Katrina Refrigerator, 54, 141, 205n2

Lake Pontchartrain, 12, 42, 112
Landrieu, Mitch, 138, 146
Last Magnolia, 40
Lawrence, Stephen, 155
Lens, The (journalistic organization), 111, 120–21, 143, 180–81
Liprap's Lament, 52, 131
Lizardo, Omar, 189

Macias, Wendy, 35
Maitri's VatulBlog, 47, 115
Mardi Gras, 8, 32, 57, 61, 76, 81, 116, 142
mass media, 35–36, 155
McClelland, Mac, 112
Media System Dependency (MSD) theory, 35–36
meaning systems, 197–99; dynamic emotional, 85, 89, 95, 99, 105
Meffert, Greg, 121–22, 156
Mississippi River, 12, 14
Moral Foundation Theory (MFT), 90–92, 95, 128, 133, 198
Moral Intuition Theory, 197–98
morality, 83–84, 90–95, 104, 128–33, 158
Moro, Aldo, 155
Morris, Ashley, 103, 114, 141; annual award, 141, 207nn 2, 3
MR-GO Canal, 12, 71–72

Nagin, C. Ray, 65–66, 79–80, 86, 89, 94 ,98, 104, 109, 121–22, 125, 138, 146, 156, 206n6
Need to Act theme, 109–10. *See also* Bonding theme

New Orleans Affordable Homeownership (NOAH), 119
New Orleans Police Department (NOPD), 102–3
New Orleans Saints, 14, 21, 88, 94, 158
New Orleans Times-Picayune, 87, 157–58
NOitsjustme, 61, 207n1
Nola Slate Blogger, 49, 50, 54, 56, 60, 61, 140, 141, 205n2 (chap. 3), 205n1 (chap. 4)
Norman, Donald, 152–53
Norris, Pippa, 175

Olick, Jeffrey, 167–168
Ortiz, David G., 28, 181

Papacharissi, Zizi, 154
Parsons, Talcott, 182–84, 190; action theory of, 182–84
Patterson, Orlando, 24–25, 59, 170, 191–93, 200
People Get Ready, 88, 94, 158
PEW Research Center, 40
Phillips, Elton, 124
place bloggers, 6
Please Forward: How Blogging Reconnected New Orleans after Katrina (blog post collection), 141
practice theory, 186–187

Ray in Exile, 67
Red Cross, 26
Reed, Isaac Ariel, 84
resource mobilization usage, 28
Riley, Warren, 98
Rising Tide Conference, 110–14, 126, 136, 141, 142–43, 150, 155–56, 180, 207n2
Rose, Chris, 87, 112, 157–58, 159

Schudson, Michael, 24
Schutz, Alfred, 192
settled times, 4, 21, 23–24, 34, 59, 171, 194
"settling period," 3–4, 22, 37–39, 44–45, 56, 63–64, 107–35, 163–64, 166, 190

settling times, 11–30, 34
Shavers, Dineral, 123, 125
Simko, Christina, 167–68
Simon, David, 112
social drama, 154–62, 165–66; narrating, 155–59; performing, 159–62
social needs/uses, 35. *See also* informational needs/uses
social networks, 153–54
social semiotics, 86
solidarity, 127–33
Spillman, Lyn, 189
Squandered Heritage, 40, 46–47, 51, 117–121, 126, 127, 143, 146
status and identity threats (Case 2), 173–74. *See also* crisis ordinariness; hate and the dark side of modernity
Stein, Jill, 143
"storytelling network," 104
Stuart, David, 27
Swidler, Ann, 190
symbolic interactionism, 182

Thank You Katrina, 40
Thelwall, Mike, 27
TikTok, 203n1 (Introduction),
Tims Nameless Blog, 77, 139–140
Tin Can Trailer Trash, 40
Toulouse Street, 141

trauma, 31–33, 63–81, 165; collective, 32–33, 37, 38–39, 42, 44–62, 97, 104, 133, 150, 165, 166; cultural, 44, 51, 53–56, 73–81, 132; personal, 32, 37, 56–57; social, 44, 51, 57, 65–73, 80
"transitional moments," 195
Treme (TV series), 16
Trump, Donald, 147–48, 175–76
Turner, Victor, 155
Twitter, 2, 152, 203n1, 205n6

University Medical Center, 16
unsettled times, 18–20, 23–24, 59, 171, 194–95, 197
unsettlement, 22–23, 31–35

Vaisey, Stephen, 189
Veterans Administration Medical Center, 16
Vila-Henninger, Luis Antonio, 189–90

Wall Street Journal, 118
Weber, Max, 23, 181–84, 190, 192
Weick, Karl, 32
Wet Bank Guide, 141

Your Right Hand Thief, 92
YouTube, 161

Zerubavel, Eviatar, 188
Zurick, Lee, 143

ABOUT THE AUTHOR

STEPHEN F. OSTERTAG is Associate Professor of Sociology at Tulane University. He is interested in questions about reciprocity and trust, action and performance, ritual and social inclusion/exclusion, especially in the areas of citizen news/journalism, crime, racism, and control. His current scholarship involves envisioning new ways to theorize culture and action and how these insights might inform innovative thinking about inclusion, equity, and other projects of social justice.

www.ingramcontent.com/pod-product-compliance
Lightning Source LLC
Chambersburg PA
CBHW020251030426
42336CB00010B/714